Seeing Politics

Seeing Politics

Film, Visual Method,
and International Relations

SOPHIE HARMAN

McGill-Queen's University Press
Montreal & Kingston • London • Chicago

© McGill-Queen's University Press 2019

ISBN 978-0-7735-5730-7 (cloth)
ISBN 978-0-7735-5731-4 (paper)
ISBN 978-0-7735-5787-1 (ePDF)
ISBN 978-0-7735-5788-8 (ePUB)

Legal deposit second quarter 2019
Bibliothèque nationale du Québec

Printed in Canada on acid-free paper that is 100% ancient forest free
(100% post-consumer recycled), processed chlorine free

Funded by the   Financé par le
Government   gouvernement
of Canada   du Canada

Canada

Canada Council   Conseil des arts
for the Arts   du Canada

We acknowledge the support of the Canada Council for the Arts.
Nous remercions le Conseil des arts du Canada de son soutien.

Library and Archives Canada Cataloguing in Publication

Title: Seeing politics : film, visual method, and international relations /
Sophie Harman.
Names: Harman, Sophie, author.
Description: Includes bibliographical references and index.
Identifiers: Canadiana (print) 20190074302 | Canadiana (ebook) 20190074345
  | ISBN 9780773557314 (softcover) | ISBN 9780773557307 (hardcover) | ISBN
  9780773557871 (ePDF) | ISBN 9780773557888 (ePUB)
Subjects: LCSH: Politics in motion pictures. | LCSH: International relations.
  | LCSH: World politics—Research.
Classification: LCC PN1995.9.P6 H37 2019 | DDC 791.43/6581—dc23

This book was typeset in 10.5/13 Sabon.

Contents

Tables and Figures

TABLES

FIGURES

Preface

Seeing Politics is about pushing the disciplinary boundaries of how we do research, how we communicate research, and what counts as scholarship in world politics. It is about how we see and do International Relations (IR) differently. The book was initially for people who wanted to make a film about politics and IR and to give them a sense of what it would involve from pre-production to production to post-production and consumption. It was for those who wanted to make the leap from reading visual politics to writing visual politics, to give them insight and demystify the whole process. However, I could not write this book without a direct account of my own role and position within the research process, particularly with reference to the ways in which I have navigated both the co-production with various project partners and the gatekeeping aspect to how stories are told and seen. I therefore wanted to write a book that would confront the uncomfortable aspect of co-produced research and show the politics of conducting fieldwork in a country that is not one's own. This is a politics that is discussed in informal settings but erased in any formal discussion on research methods or practices. This is a politics that is fundamental to understanding both transnational feminist practice and Africa and international relations. In my process of writing and discussing the book with colleagues, *Seeing Politics* came to be about something more than film as a compelling method in which to see hidden politics; it is about bigger questions of knowledge – how we produce it, how we consume it, and what counts as academic scholarship.

Up until 2015, I was an academic who knew nothing about film. My background is not in film production, visual politics, or visual ethnography; it is in IR, with a specific focus on global health politics. Given this lack of knowledge and expertise, why and how did I end up making a film and then writing a book about it?

I made a film out of frustration with both global health and IR. My frustration arose from an absence of seeing how global health policies affected people's lives in complex ways; how politics played a role within this; and how, for a field that is interested in the improvement of people's well-being, it does not see or ask them about their needs. Global health policies and initiatives tend to reduce people to numbers in data sets. We see tokenistic storytelling of need (to secure international funds), success stories (to maintain international funds), or carefully organized "field" visits for national and global policy experts. That is if people are considered at all. A great amount of work in global health governance and politics is interested in scientific innovation as a solution to complex health problems, institutions, and policy-makers. The majority of research takes place in the global health hubs of Washington and Geneva where policies are made, not in the small towns and villages where the policies are implemented. The only exception seems to be in public health anthropology. This means that global health governance misses the basic needs of populations, and lacks nuance as to how policies become translated in practice and, crucially, how political structures such as gender can bar people's access to health care and healthy lives. Global health has a substantial gender problem: it does not see women or gender.

Such frustrations are particularly acute in the global HIV/AIDS response. The majority of people living with HIV are women, yet their experiences and agency are instrumentalized (for care roles, advocacy, or positive-donor narratives), and the free labour they provide is assumed as given. These women are framed as security threats, passive recipients of HIV treatment, or risky numbers. Their everyday lives of managing their status, accessing treatment, raising children, maintaining employment, and navigating gender inequality goes unseen in global health policy.

My second frustration stemmed from the way in which women are seen in IR. Women living with HIV/AIDS or carrying the burden of under-resourced and weak health systems are rarely seen as relevant to the study of IR. They are only relevant when framed as a threat to international security. While interest in global health has grown within IR, such interest is framed within the usual references to state interests, institutions, norms, orders, and security. The exceptions here are feminist research that seeks to reveal the unseen or hidden ways international relations affects everyday life, and how everyday life underpins international relations; and decolonial research that seeks to confront the epistemological basis of knowing in IR. Feminists, and particularly decolonial feminists, have known and shown for decades how women, particularly women living in sub-Saharan Africa, are ignored or unseen in IR. Nevertheless, the problem persists.

After years of writing and talking about the need to see women in global health and IR and of growing frustration at the lack of progress, I decided to change my methods of getting women and gender seen. To get people to see for themselves and to allow women living with HIV/AIDS to express themselves require different, bolder, and new methods of seeing. I needed a visual method that would appeal to global audiences and get them thinking and feeling about the subject. I decided to make a film.

While I did not have previous experience in filmmaking, I did have experience working in sub-Saharan Africa. I have conducted fieldwork in Kenya, Sierra Leone, Tanzania, Uganda, and Zambia, and in 2006 I established a non-governmental organization (NGO) in Tanzania that provides free transportation for people living with HIV/AIDS in rural communities to care and treatment clinics. My existing research in Africa and my networks in Tanzania gave me access to communities affected by HIV/AIDS (to community health workers, peer educators, local politicians, doctors, and women living with HIV/AIDS) to make a film set in a real town with real people. The film, *Pili*, is a feature-length drama that not only focuses on the politics of the everyday lives of women living with HIV/AIDS but also is made in a way that allows a particular group of women to tell their own story. The story is based on the lives of eighty women from the Pwani region of Tanzania, triangulated with my existing knowledge and the skills of narrative filmmakers. The story is therefore not of one individual but of a number of women represented by the lead character, Pili.

My initial intent was to communicate the lives of women living with HIV/AIDS to as broad an audience as possible. However, over the course of making *Pili*, it became increasingly apparent to me that the project was more than just a means of communication; the process was challenging how I thought about knowledge, research, and international relations. It was in the process of film production, of trying to engage in the practice of co-production and a different way of working, and of navigating the hierarchies of film distribution that I came to think about how we produce, communicate, and consume knowledge in IR and the politics that we do not see or to which we become wilfully blind.

Seeing Politics can help us see women who are conspicuously invisible from international relations and to see the informal, formal, and hidden politics and dimensions of international relations that have an impact on their lives. It is about film as a method of seeing those who are invisible from politics, policy, and global health research, and about the ways in which we see ourselves as researchers and agents in IR. It is about how film can be a form of co-produced research that allows the invisible to be seen to a diverse range of audiences in its own representation and voice. The book is also about the politics of seeing: the transnational relationships and discomfort that stop us from seeing, and the gatekeeping practices of the state and of the global hierarchies of film governance that control the stories we see. The politics of seeing is thus not only about what the film shows us but also about how the practice of film production opens up new ways of seeing inside the black box of the state, transnational feminism, the political economy of global governance, and our own research practices.

Fundamentally, *Seeing Politics* is about how narrative feature film challenges and advances the methods and outputs of IR. Film is not just a way of communicating research or having research impact; it is also a research method that enables co-production of research and visibility, which in turn advances research practice and knowledge in IR. *Seeing Politics* is about the politics of seeing, being seen, and what stops us from seeing.

Acknowledgments

Thank you to AXA Research Fund for the Outlook Award that funded this research. The funding allowed me to take risks that made both the film and the book possible.

Thank you to Queen Mary University of London (QMUL) for innovation seed funding and for my sabbatical in 2018 that provided much-needed time to finish the book. Thanks go to colleagues at the School of Politics and International Relations for their support of this project – specifically early supporters Lee Jones and Marlon Gomes (even when I turned the school's office into that of a film production company), and readers Clive Gabay, Madeleine Davies, Lisa Tilley, Robbie Shilliam, and Kim Hutchings. Big thanks go to James Dunkerley who supported the film from the outset, helped to source funding, and provided moral support throughout, and whose advice and mentorship have been crucial to this book and my scholarship during the period in which it was written. Thank you to Kathrin Fischer for her super-efficient research assistant skills.

Thanks go to Holly Ryan for reading chapter 6 and the Bowie quotes, and Dusan Petkovic for letting me pick his visual anthropology brain. Thanks go to Carl Death for being the first person to suggest I write something about film as method, and to my fabulous academic friends Ruth Blakeley, Sara Davies, Clare Wenham, Cat Durose, and Lucy Ferguson for their encouragement when I was writing this book.

Seeing Politics is a direct response to a question posed to me at a Research in Practice seminar at the University of Sussex in 2016: "Is it IR?" Questions and provocations from research presentations and/or screenings of *Pili* at the universities of Sussex, Manchester,

Bristol, Sheffield, and Birmingham (United Kingdom), Oslo (Norway), and Griffith, Queensland, and Australian National University (Australia); the European International Studies Association conference in Barcelona in 2017; and the International Feminist Journal of Politics conference in Delhi 2017; and film festival audience question-and-answer sessions have all provoked, shaped, and refined my argument and analysis.

Thanks go to Richard Baggaley for getting my idea and recognizing what I wanted to do. He is a supportive editor and saw what this book was about before I did. Two anonymous reviewers provided insightful and hugely helpful feedback on the proposal and the full manuscript; they engaged with what I wanted to do and made it better. Many thanks also go to Roland Bleiker for not only generously reviewing the proposal and the full manuscript but also being so welcoming and encouraging as I explored a body of work that was new to me at the beginning of this project.

None of this would have been possible without the incredible talent, trust, and commitment of the cast and crew involved in *Pili* and the wider communities of Miono and Makole. They are fully listed in the credits to *Pili*. This book is my narrative and analysis of events, whereas the film is a unique and genuine co-production. I would like to thank Leanne Welham in particular. *Seeing Politics* shows the difficult aspects of making *Pili* and the frustrations of co-producing film, as a research method, from a university rather than from a production company. No average director would have managed this, and *Pili* is a testament to Leanne's talent. Things have not always been straightforward, but we could not have done it without each other or the belief and trust of the group of women in the film – Bello Rashid, Sikujua Rashid, Sesilia Floran Kilimila, Mwanaidi Omari Sefi, Siwazurio Mchuka, Mwantumu Hussein Malongine – and those who shared their stories with us.

Kieran Read's love, support, and timely "everything will be okay" reminders are the basis on which I risked making a feature film and then writing a book about it. He makes everything seem possible.

PERMISSIONS

Sections of the book have appeared in "Making the Invisible Visible in International Relations: Film, Co-produced Research, and Transnational Feminism," *European Journal of International*

Relations; and in "Film as Research Method in African Politics and International Relations: Reading and Writing Film on HIV/AIDS in Tanzania," *African Affairs* (October 2016); and are reproduced here with permission from SAGE Publications and Oxford University Press, respectively.

Seeing Politics

Seeing the Invisible

Pili told me she had a stomach ache when I met her in a small community hall down the hill from the care and treatment centre in Mbwewe for people living with HIV/AIDS and expectant mothers. She was in a lot of pain, and the local doctors had told her that she needed further care in the bigger hospital in Bagamoyo, 100 km from this small town located next to the busy A14 road where inter-city buses competed to overtake each other and pick up passengers on the journey "up country" from Dar es Salaam to Tanga. She could not afford to pay for this journey or the fees at the hospital in Bagamoyo, so instead she returned every day to visit the local doctor to see if he could do anything more for the pain. As a doctor, could I do anything to help? I explained that I was not a medical doctor but that she could travel with us to Bagamoyo and even on to Dar es Salaam later that week. She looked crestfallen and in considerable pain. I suggested that we should perhaps leave her, given her discomfort, and talk to her another time, but, no, Pili wanted to share her story. I had come to Mbwewe with the film's writer-director and the translator with whom I was working to hear the stories of women living with HIV/AIDS, and she wanted to tell hers.

Pili was thirty-eight years old in November 2015 and living as a single parent with her four children. She had moved back to Mbwewe to live with her husband's family after he and his second wife had died of AIDS in 2008. She was pregnant with twins at the time and did not know about her husband's HIV status until his death. Friends encouraged Pili to get tested. When her results came back positive, she began treatment at the Chalinze care and treatment centre 75 km from Mbwewe. The timely intervention of her friends and follow-up by Pili meant she was able to access free treatment so that her HIV status did not progress to AIDS and the virus was not transmitted to her twins. They were born HIV free. However, not everyone in the community was as supportive and understanding as her friends were. Upon learning about her status, the family member with whom she was living locked her and her children out of the home. Pili then took her children to live with her sister-in-law, who did the same. Being made homeless for the second time on account of her HIV status led Pili to attempt suicide. She swallowed rat poison and was found by her eldest child, who took her to the local police station and begged her to live. The police helped Pili to survive her suicide attempt and referred her to a local politician who said that he would cover the cost of shelter for her and her children. It was at this time that, as Pili put it, "life became normal again." Her children began to attend school regularly, and she found a support group for women living with HIV/AIDS through the new care and treatment centre that had opened in Mbwewe. She no longer had to travel far for treatment and had found a group of women with whom she could share her problems. She was also able to secure a loan from the group to start her own small business, selling tea and small snacks such as chapati and *mandazi* (Tanzanian doughnuts). She was in financial debt to the support group and in patronage debt to the politician who had helped her, but she was accepting of her HIV status. That was until her stomach pain started and she worried again about her health affecting her well-being, livelihood, and care of her children.

I did not see Pili again after that day in Mbwewe. The translator with whom I was working tried calling Pili to see if she wanted to travel to Bagamoyo and Dar es Salaam with us, but her number was unavailable. I followed up with her friends and contacts at the local care and treatment centre, but they said they had not seen her and did not know where she was. Maybe she had borrowed some money and already travelled to the bigger hospital. No one seemed to know. My final notes from meeting her read: "thinks something is wrong."

In many ways, Pili's life is a microcosm of the everyday international politics of living with HIV/AIDS; it reflects the gendered dynamics of the disease and the changes in treatment provision and reveals who is the end point or referent object of discussions over policy prioritizations, development goals, and "securitizing" diseases such as HIV/AIDS. The majority of people living with HIV in the world are women, most of whom are concentrated in sub-Saharan Africa (UNAIDS 2017, 12; UN Women 2016). There are differing explanations for why this is the case. A prominent explanation is that women are over-represented in groups of "vulnerable populations" such as commercial sex workers, and as survivors of sexual violence (UN Women 2016; The World Bank 2004). Another explanation is that, owing to concurrent or polycentric relationships in sub-Saharan Africa, (predominantly) men have multiple female partners or wives, thus increasing the number of sexual partners and increasing the risk (Epstein 2007; Gupta 2002; Hamblin and Reid 1991). An alternative explanation is that HIV/AIDS is a social disease of poverty and inequality, where your wealth and gender determine your ability to negotiate safe sex, access to care and treatment, and the educational and social capital resources to learn about prevention (Seckinelgin 2012; UNFPA et al. 2004). A lack of access to political, financial, and health-based resources curtails the ability of women to control and manage their own health. Women bear the brunt of care and informal labour roles in the HIV/AIDS response (Harman 2011a; UNFPA et al. 2004). HIV-positive women face a double social reproduction burden: the burden of traditional care roles, with the extended load of preventing the transmission of HIV; and the burden of providing care and psycho-social support for people living with HIV/AIDS. Pili is no different in this regard. As a single mother, she bears responsibility both for child-rearing and for ensuring that her children are born free from a virus that she herself contracted from her husband. Her day-to-day well-being and financial security depend on personal and informal relationships with male politicians, on her female support network, and on micro-lending schemes for women living with HIV.

The short time frame of Pili's awareness of her HIV status reflects significant changes in the access to treatment for people living with HIV/AIDS. Pili's diagnosis and her ability to access treatment to manage her HIV status and prevent transmission of the virus to her children are a direct consequence of decades of transnational advocacy around HIV treatment and of global initiatives to provide free anti-retroviral treatment for people living in poverty. Grassroots campaigns such as ACT UP! in the United States, and the Treatment Action Campaign (TAC) in South Africa, provided the foundation for global advocacy by establishing the norm that health and access to treatment is a human right and that governments have a social responsibility to ensure the health and well-being of people living with HIV/AIDS (Cameron 2005; Geffen 2010). The Global Fund to Fight AIDS, Tuberculosis and Malaria (the Global Fund) and the United States President's Emergency Plan for AIDS Relief (PEP-FAR) were the two significant game changers in treatment financing. Established in 2002, the Global Fund is a public-private financing mechanism that leverages and disperses funding for HIV/AIDS in low- and middle-income countries. In contrast, PEPFAR is a government-led initiative established by George W. Bush in 2003, which by 2017 had enacted US$75 million towards HIV/AIDS treatment and prevention around the world (PEPFAR 2017). PEPFAR's impact has been significant with regard to the numbers of people living with HIV who are able to access treatment and voluntary counselling and testing, and the plan has established a precedent for large-scale, bipartisan, government-led initiatives to have global impact and tangible outcomes. Between 2006 and 2013, funding towards HIV/AIDS rose from commitments of approximately US$10 billion to nearly US$20 billion (Garrett 2017). Without PEPFAR and the transnational advocacy that HIV treatment should be free and accessible to those who need it, Pili would not be able to access treatment to keep herself alive and would not have been able to prevent her children from being born with HIV. Her HIV story maps the impact of increased funding on the HIV response: first, treatment is only available in major towns, then new care and treatment centres are built, support groups become more visible, and micro-lending to help people living with HIV/AIDS is introduced. The status of HIV/AIDS as a somewhat exceptional health issue (see Benton 2015) means that access to treatment becomes increasingly accessible, but other health concerns such as Pili's stomach ache do not have the same level of services available. Pili would have to travel to a larger town and seek money to pay for both the diagnosis and the treatment for her stomach condition. Pili is thus not distinct from the global politics of HIV/AIDS; her case is embedded in the financial trends, policy preferences, development priorities, and shifts in global health.

As an HIV-positive woman, Pili is both a potential threat to international security and a bulwark against the spread of the virus as she prevents transmission to others such as her children and future partners; she is responsible for "securing" the world. In 2000 the United Nations Security Council Resolution 1308 recognized "that HIV/AIDS, if unchecked, may pose a risk to stability and security" because of its threat to society and international peacekeeping. Resolution 1308 marked the first time that a health issue was seen as a potential threat to international security and was in many respects a key point at which global health, and HIV/AIDS in particular, had become securitized (Youde 2012; Harman 2012a). Since the passing of Resolution 1308 there has been a thriving debate as to what is particular about the new global health security; what the process of securitization entails; whether a disease can be a threat to security, and, if it is, who or what is the referent object of threat; and what are the potential politics of discrimination that may follow (McInnes and Rushton 2013; Rushton 2011). One direct consequence of this debate is that global health security has become normalized in global health governance and international relations. This is evident in the growth of monographs (see the Global Health Section Book Prize list of the International Studies Association) and in institutional research centres that take an explicit focus on global health security. As another consequence, a number of scholars argue that it was the security frame rather than the advocacy frame that led to the exceptionalism of HIV/AIDS in both its status as a United Nations (UN) Millennium Development Goal (MDG 6) and the large amounts of funding channelled to prevention and treatment (Singer 2002). What is less evident is the consequence that such debates over HIV/AIDS and security have on people living with HIV/AIDS, people like Pili. Securing the world from the threat of infectious diseases such as HIV/AIDS depends on Pili's behaviour and ability to navigate the socio-economic complexity of disease.

Between November and December 2015 I met and heard the stories of many women like Pili from Mbwewe and Miono, a small town further inland towards the national park in Saadani. Single motherhood, HIV stigma and discrimination, support groups, periods of acute illness, the hard work of small-scale farming and informal employment, and familial and financial debt were all common themes to these women's life stories. Having worked on the international politics of HIV/AIDS in Africa for over ten years, I did not find such stories new or surprising, but they were always shocking when told by one woman after another. These stories are also not new to anyone familiar with the lives of women living with HIV/AIDS in sub-Saharan Africa (see Nguyen 2010) or rural poverty in Tanzania, or to scholars and practitioners working in international development or global gender inequality. However, the lives of women such as Pili and how they make sense of the politics of living with HIV/AIDS are unseen or invisible from the international processes of policy-making and practice and the methods and outputs of research in politics and IR. They are seen on the cover of high-level UN agency reports, in NGO fundraising campaigns, and in the annual data sets of the HIV/AIDS epidemic. Their stories are instrumentalized for funding, political will, and campaigns, but they are one-dimensional stories of success in adversity and in educational and sanitized narratives, or as morality tales of risk and redemption. The stories lack the complexity of human existence or the political choices and structures that limit and enable agency. In research on IR and global health we rarely see women such as Pili. Research methods in global health politics prioritize elites in the hubs of Washington and Geneva rather than people living with HIV/AIDS in communities such as Mbwewe. Global health is often concerned with telling people like Pili what to do – how to prevent transmission, how to access treatment, how to find the best science – rather than how to make sense of this. Scholars such as Hakan Seckinelgin (2012) and Colleen O'Manique (2005), and Emma-Louise Anderson (2015)'s work on gender, HIV, and security, have provided important interventions on debates over gender; however, the mainstream security discourse around HIV/AIDS does not see women. We know little about the lives of those women who constitute such a threat and about the ways in which the rhetoric of security can have direct impacts on the everyday stigma they face and on their own protection in the communities where they live, work, and raise their children. While IR is good at explaining the securitization of HIV/AIDS, the implications for understanding security, and the global practices of policy-making in global health (McInnes 2006; McInnes and Rushton 2006; Prins 2004), it struggles to understand the role of individual people and communities and the end point of such a security frame.

Not seeing women like Pili misses a key agent in the international system. As this section has shown, Pili is the end point of international policies; she is the referent object of health security; she is the absorber and instigator of international norms; and she has her own agency and knowledge of her health and how it intersects with structures of poverty, gender, and disease. To understand IR and how power manifests at every level of governance, we need to see and understand the lives of women such as Pili. This book focuses on what stops us from seeing Pili, on the potential for new methods of seeing, on the new research outputs for how women such as Pili see themselves, and on how invisible or hidden politics can be seen.

THE PROBLEM

The problem of not seeing women such as Pili is a problem of the types of methods we use and the research outputs we produce in IR. Since the "third debate" in IR and extensive feminist research and advocacy, the ontological and epistemological biases within the discipline have shifted to recognize the everyday and lives of women such as Pili as relevant and important in understanding power in the international arena. Drawing from one of the central feminist positions – that the personal is political – feminist IR scholars have revealed how international power relations shape and are shaped by personal relationships, the domestic realm, the banal, and the hidden or unseen spaces in more traditional forms of international relations, for example in the rural HIV clinic rather than in the UN Security Council. This research has documented the ways in which the everyday lives of women embody and underpin the structures and practices of international relations in a range of ways: from war and conflict (Sjoberg 2013, 2014) to peacebuilding (Shepherd 2017) to global production chains (Elias and Ferguson 2010) to post-conflict reconstruction and state building (McLeod 2015), and to the combat of climate change and Zika (Davies and Bennett 2016). Their stories and experiences matter in revealing the role of reproduction and social reproduction in peace and war and in the global political economy and how gender manifests and is reproduced in conflict, governance, political-economic systems, and foreign policy. Though diverse, the components of this body of work shares a common normative commitment to improving the lives of women and to exploring the hidden aspects of power that go unseen, by asking the straightforward question of a feminist researcher, "Where are the women?," as a means of highlighting the "margins, silences and bottom rungs" (Enloe 1996, 187). Feminist ethics emphasize a relational ontology in that what exists cannot be separated from context or politics (Hutchings 2000). In so doing, feminist IR has fundamentally challenged and changed the mainstream or "accepted" ontological practices of the discipline as to what constitutes a suitable object or subject inquiry for the field of IR by highlighting the relevance and importance of the everyday and women like Pili.

While feminist IR has made significant advances in seeing women such as Pili within the discipline, problems of seeing still persist. Women such as Pili are now recognized but not necessarily accepted; feminists still have to justify the subject of inquiry and the methods and to navigate the disciplinary question, "Is it IR?" The third debate questioned the positivist bias of IR – depicted here using Smith's definition of "positivism-as-methodology," a commitment to quantitative and behaviouralist method (S. Smith 1996) – and the tools and agents of the discipline. A key part of the third debate has been the growth of the amorphous *critical theory*, a term that broadly speaking includes post-modernism, post-structuralism, post-colonialism or de-colonialism, and feminism and the wide debates within them (S. Smith 1996). Such growth has meant that questions that seemed to be marginal within IR before the third debate are now common to international conferences, journals, and teaching of the discipline. For some, this has pushed the discipline forward; for others, it has hollowed out the fundamental basis of IR to the point of identity crisis (Dunne, Hansen, and Wight 2013). As a consequence, seeing women such as Pili or the use of new methods is easily dismissed as not IR or as sociology, anthropology, or international development, and feminist scholars have to consistently reassert the relevance of their subject of inquiry and methods of working.

A further problem of seeing is the position of women such as Pili and the value of their knowledge in the research process. Postcolonial and decolonial feminists (hereafter referred to as decolonial feminists) question how women such as Pili are reified, used, and positioned as the "other" by researchers. The decolonial critique is concerned with the process and outcomes of visibility, and who can speak and who is heard (Dingli 2015; Parpart 2010; Tickner 1997). Research that involves women such as Pili needs to be cognizant of power relations not only within the academy and their own biases or white lenses but also between the feminists who conduct research (predominantly in high- and middle-income countries) and the subject of much feminist IR (predominantly in low-income countries). Decolonial feminists have highlighted the importance of engaging women in a way that does not universalize or homogenize experience (Blackwell, Briggs, and Chiu 2015), thereby reinforcing hierarchies of women from the north as the speakers and women from the south as those being spoken of. Methods of seeing need to recognize such power relationships and the social and historical context in which research takes place. As Mohanty argues, there is a need to move beyond the understanding that third-world women "cannot represent themselves, they must be represented" (2003, 42). For scholars like Ling, such decolonial practice "calls for building communities trans-subjectively: that is, between you and me, not you *for* me" (Ling 2007, 144).

It is not enough to just see women such as Pili; methods of seeing need to allow such women to see and represent themselves, and to value their knowledge and co-contribution to the research process. Women such as Pili understand the structures that limit their choices, their access to treatment, and the security in their communities and everyday surroundings. While they may not have the knowledge of an HIV epidemiologist or public health economist, or know where the money for their anti-retroviral treatment comes from and the politics of why it is free, they do understand the politics of stigma, how access is limited, and how these international priorities operate in their own context. They know how gender is performed, how they can or cannot access decision-making, and how they are seen as a threat in their own families and communities. This knowledge and experience is not just relevant to anthropological studies of disease; it is fundamental to the way in which international relations works in practice. Their knowledge is either ignored or appropriated without reciprocity or recognition, or it is reified. Decolonial feminism is replete with red flags or warnings as to how knowledge is co-opted, coerced, misrepresented, or pursued in an unequal manner with significant issues of reciprocity (Agathangelou and Turcotte 2010; Harcourt, Ling, et al. 2015; Mohanty 2003). A feminist approach to method advocates, on the one hand, a blurring between the researcher and the researched and, on the other, a need to recognize the difference and positionality of the researcher vis-à-vis the researched. The problem of seeing women such as Pili thus becomes not only how to see them but also knowing whether the invisible want to be visible, how the invisible can represent themselves, and what the politics are of doing so.

The final problem with seeing is that the field of global health is years behind IR with regard to feminist and decolonial challenges to the ontology and epistemology of research. Global health maintains a positivist bias drawn from biomedical science and public-health-research practices. Women such as Pili are conspicuously invisible in global health politics. Women and gender are conspicuous in every aspect of global health, from the voluntary care worker in a village in Zambia to the minister for health and social welfare in Tanzania. Gender cuts across how men and women become sick, how they access treatment, and how they make sense of illness; it informs different life-expectancy outcomes and drives certain diseases (Barry, Talib, et al. 2017; Talib, Burke, and Barry 2017). However what makes women and gender conspicuously invisible in global health is the sidelining of gender as an analytical category, located only in discussions on "women's health" such as maternal health, and forgotten or overlooked in times of pandemic response and preparedness (Davies and Bennett 2016; Harman 2016). Global health has not critically engaged at any length the ways in which its policies reproduce gender norms and differing roles and responsibilities for women and men (Dhatt, Kickbusch, and Thompson 2017).

The problem with seeing women like Pili is thus not whether they should be seen but how to see them and get them seen. If we are serious about the needs to see women and how their experiences relate to the international, to decolonize sources of knowledge and not speak for the subaltern, and to innovate our use of methods and our seeing of invisible power relations, we need new methods of research and new ways of understanding. We need new ways in which women such as Pili can represent themselves and collaborate as co-producers of knowledge rather than as subjects of enquiry. We need to provide new dimensions in which to understand both the informal and complex everyday politics of living with HIV/AIDS and the performance of security and risk. As Guillaume argues in his review of Hobson and Seabrooke's collection on the everyday, our problem in exploring the everyday is "how to methodologically approach everyday tactics – like humor, svejkism, or silence – via ethnographic or discourse analysis methods within the field of international studies?" (2011, 461). For those who are quick to securitize disease, we need to see the referent object of security, the consequences of security frames, and the risks these pose to the lives of millions of women. To use an old feminist saying, we need deeds, not words. Questions of who is missing and who speaks remain fundamental to feminist and postcolonial IR; however, to advance our answers to these questions, we need new methods of seeing and being seen. The ambition and scope of research in IR has grown, and feminist and decolonial scholars have made significant advances in who and what knowledge count, but the methods by which we find, produce, and exhibit new knowledge are stagnant. This book is about how the lives of women such as Pili can be seen through the use of a new method and output in IR: a co-produced feature film.

WHAT THE BOOK IS ABOUT

The method of seeing and being seen that this book explores is the use of narrative feature film. Interest in the use of film as method has grown in politics and IR as part of a wider interest in visual, aesthetic, and "trans-disciplinary" methods (Shapiro 2013). Scholars such as Bleiker (2009a, 2009b) and Shapiro (2013) have advocated the use of aesthetics to draw on the full register of knowledge and research methods and to make sense of the world. As chapter 1 discusses in further detail, this has produced fruitful discussion and analysis of what aesthetics reveal about the sublime; emotional engagements with international politics; and visual representations of war, security, and disease. The "aesthetic turn" (Bleiker 2009a) of the early 2000s within IR has been significant in the growth of reading aesthetics and the visual; however, what is less evident is the use by scholars of visual methods to write the international. The use of film as method is rare in IR. Films have been read through different theoretical lenses, and a handful of scholars have produced short documentary films (Callahan 2015; Der Derian 2009, 2010; Weber 2010). For example, Cynthia Weber's pioneering work in this area has explored nationality, security, and identity politics through the short-film form. The use of film as method is thriving in the established sub-disciplines of visual anthropology, sociology, and geography. However, even within these disciplines, the form tends to be documentary as visual ethnography rather than narrative.

Film in IR stands as a teaching device, as something to read politics in, and, in some instances, as a format in which to disseminate research. In a handful of cases documentary film is used as method and output of research. Narrative feature films are completely absent as methods of IR research and are under-developed within the visual social sciences. This is a curious gap given the growing interest in visual methods, the dominance of the visual in both academic and everyday life, and a curiosity towards seeing unknown or hidden structures of power. It is even more curious given that academics are now meant to generate research impact and engage public audiences. As chapter 2 argues, film has the potential to be a source of co-produced feminist method and to attract large and diverse audiences. This potential may be problematic in how it is realized or redundant in the insights it produces; however, it is odd that the form and potential have not been fully explored or have been left to other disciplines through a dismissal of film as being visual ethnography, or in some cases considered not IR.

  Seeing Politics seeks to fill this gap and explore the potential of film as a method and scholarly output for seeing politics. It does so by critically engaging with the politics of seeing, being seen, and what stops us from seeing, through the production of the narrative feature film *Pili*. *Pili* marks the first time that a narrative feature film has been used as a method and output in the discipline of IR. Co-produced, it is set in rural Tanzania over four days. The lead character is not one woman, such as the real Pili introduced at the start of this book, but a "Pili" derived from the stories of over eighty women living in the Pwani region of Tanzania. The film is set in real locations, such as functioning HIV/AIDS care and treatment centres, and only features one trained actor; the rest of the cast are drawn from the community in which the film is set and from the eighty women on whose stories the film is based. Sixty-five per cent of the cast are self-declared as being HIV positive. *Pili* was shot over five weeks in Tanzania with a mixed Tanzanian and British cast and premiered at the Dinard British Film Festival, where it won two awards in competition with other independent feature films in 2017. In 2018 *Pili* secured global sales and a UK distribution deal. I produced the film from inception to distribution.

  Seeing Politics shows how film as a method and output of research can help us see women like Pili and the informal, formal, and hidden politics and dimensions of international relations that have an impact on their lives. It is about film as a method of seeing those who are invisible from politics, policy, and global health research and of seeing ourselves as researchers and agents in IR. It is about the ways in which film can be a form of co-produced research that allows the invisible to be seen to a diverse range of audiences in their own representation and voice. The book is also about the politics of seeing: the transnational relationships and discomfort that stop us from seeing, and the gatekeeping practices of the state and global hierarchies of film governance that control the stories we see. The politics of seeing is thus about not only what the film shows us but also how the practice of film production opens up new ways of seeing inside the black box of the state, transnational feminism, and the political economy of global film governance. In so doing, it reveals the difficult, messy, and at times unpleasant everyday realities of transnational partnership and international relations – from state corruption and detention to the compromise of individual health and well-being for immediate gain. The book draws on calls made by authors such as Doty (2004) and Dauphinee (2013a, 2013b) to see ourselves in the way we research, write, and see politics. Fundamentally, *Seeing Politics* is about how narrative feature film challenges and advances the methods and outputs of IR. Film is not just a way of communicating research or having research impact; it is a research method that enables co-production of research and visibility, which in turn advances research practice and knowledge in IR.

The book makes four central arguments. First, film, and most notably narrative feature film, is an important and significant method of research *and* scholarly output in the discipline of IR. It is a format in which invisible power relations can be seen and in which agents can explore, see, and express their own agency. Co-produced film as method and output provides a new and important way of delivering on the feminist project to make the invisible and hidden relations of power visible. Second, film demonstrates the importance of showing rather than explaining politics. Film can show the shifting dynamics of informal politics and the relationship between structure and agency in ways the written word cannot. International relations is a fluid and changing space with multiple dimensions; such dimensions should not be confined to written explanation. Film depicts the rhythms and temporality of the everyday and the hidden dimensions of politics that cannot be captured by the written word. Third, the process of film production itself offers new insight into how transnational relations and state-based and global gatekeeping constrain and problematize what we see and how knowledge is produced. It is through the practice of engaging in different forms of international relations that we can see old and new expressions of formal and informal politics. Finally, exploring new methods such as narrative feature film confronts the disciplinary boundaries as to what constitutes method, output, and audience – boundaries that can curtail knowledge and stop us from seeing.

STRUCTURE

The first part of the book focuses on the questions of why and how one makes a film as a method of seeing politics. Chapter 1 considers the question, "Why use film as a method of research?" To answer, it explores the relationship between film and HIV/AIDS, film as a source of African agency and feminist method, and "the aesthetic turn" in IR. In so doing, the chapter argues that, while scholars have advanced the use of aesthetics and film in understanding IR, few scholars have engaged in the writing of IR through aesthetic forms such as film. The chapter maintains that film is an overlooked method of exploring IR and of seeing politics through the practice of co-production, visual methods, and outputs.

Chapter 2 provides the empirical case material on using film as method by focusing on the way in which the feature film *Pili* was produced. This chapter is not a methodological how-to but a reflection on the informal and formal networks and partnerships required to make a film and conduct co-produced research. It explores the ethical dilemmas of the project, the recruitment of the cast and crew, the co-production of the film's story, and the different stages of production. The intent of the chapter is to demystify the practice of film production as a method in IR, to show what makes the film distinct, and to reflect on the politics and international relations inherent in the processes of seeing and being seen.

The second part of the book focuses on the politics of what stops us from seeing and being seen. It does so by looking at the local, state, and global barriers to seeing. Chapter 3 focuses on the unseen politics and tensions involved in transnational feminist research praxis. This chapter is interested in the new ways of seeing that co-production enables and in the limits, politics, and messiness of transnational collaboration that can also act as a barrier to seeing. It argues that a feminist praxis that acknowledges genealogies, difference, and positionality is fundamental to seeing informal politics and the politics involved in research processes. The chapter demonstrates that, through reflexivity and open confrontation of the messiness of such relations, feminist methods towards change can be advanced, and new forms of collaboration and decolonized knowledge production as a new way of seeing can be made possible.

Chapter 4 considers the gatekeeping practices of the state in controlling what and how we see. It demonstrates that the co-production of film and knowledge requires particular informal and formal engagements within the wider political economy of the state. The chapter shows how the production of *Pili* involved informal dynamics of patronage, crime, and petty corruption. The process of making a film unpacks the black box of the state to reveal new ways of understanding the cyclical nature of gatekeeping politics and the way it is embedded within Tanzanian society. The chapter develops this understanding to include the reinforcement of gatekeeping by, first, inequality in access to financial and political capital and, second, temporality and the prioritization of short-term and immediate need. Here, seeing politics is not just about how film shows the lives of women such as Pili, but about how the practice of film production helps us see the informal politics of state behaviour and its gatekeeping of the stories we tell.

Chapter 5 shifts the analytical focus to that of the global and the roles of consumption and the political economy of film in aesthetics and visual politics. It considers the ways in which the political economy of film governance disciplines film audiences and makers around the world with respect to what can be seen. The chapter critically looks at the practice wherein securing an audience, distribution, and an exhibition of a film requires engagement with the commercial structures and various agents within the film industry. These structures include legitimate forms of recognition, such as international film festivals and critic reviews, and the commercialization of the art through the establishment of a company and commercial licensing to enable distribution. Underpinning the chapter is a conundrum: to make the invisible lives of women like Pili visible through film requires an engagement in the political structures that govern what can be seen. The structures that reproduce hierarchies in the film industry keep women such as Pili from being seen. In situating the compromises made by the project in the wider political economy of global film governance, the chapter highlights the politics of what we see and the commercial and consumption aspects of visual methods.

Chapter 6 draws together the main contributions and arguments of the book with reference to seeing, being seen, and what stops us from seeing. In so doing, the conclusion makes the case for wider use and recognition of film as method *and* output in politics and IR research and for new methods to reflect changes in these disciplines and the world around us. The conclusion calls for new methods of seeing the formal and informal ways in which politics works, for the importance of seeing ourselves in the research process, and for pushing the parameters of what constitutes research, politics, and IR.

Members of the cast and crew are referred to by their full name in the first instance and then their first name throughout. I refer to myself in the first person or as *mzungu Sofia* (white Sophie) when discussing the way in which I was predominantly referred to by the Tanzanians in the project. The use of first names and the first person reflects the close relationship between cast and crew in the process and the importance of recognizing positionality in research. Four names are changed in the main book owing to issues discussed in greater detail in chapter 4. Unlike all other names that appear in the book, these four people were not consulted, on account of their involvement in trying to disrupt the project for material gain or political position; I have therefore made them anonymous. Finally, the different groups of women from Miono, Mbwewe, and Bagamoyo who were consulted for the story of *Pili* are referred to as "the women," and the main cast members who were drawn from Miono and Makole are referred to as "the cast" specifically, even though they also contributed to the story. Both labels do not encompass the full diversity of women involved or their contribution to the project; "the women" or "the cast" is used as writing shorthand. The main roles and contributions of these women are unpacked in detail in chapter 2.

The first chapter begins with the question "Why film?" and explores the reason that film was selected as a method of seeing politics; the gaps in what we know about film as method and output; and the ways in which film can help us understand and explain politics and IR. This chapter situates the use of film in IR within contemporary debates over visual method, feminist method, and visual anthropology. It develops some of the main themes with particular reference to seeing and being seen.

Why Film?

Film is not a common method in the field of international relations (IR). Short and documentary films are accepted methods of research in the fields of visual anthropology, sociology, and geography, but the narrative feature film is less so. The lack of film as method at the most basic level is due to cost: film production is expensive and requires specific skills, time, and external funding. The lack of film as method can also be explained as one of epistemological constraint. Film tends to be seen in IR as a form of communicating research or research impact rather than as a method of investigating transnational practices or state gatekeeping. Narrative features, especially those based on the lives of women from low-income countries, are seen as stories rather than as scholarly outputs based on academic rigour. The intent of this book is to demonstrate how film can be used as a method in IR, and thereby to challenge some of the epistemological constraints to the methods we use, the knowledge we value in the discipline, and the ways we see politics. This chapter sets out four key arguments on the use of film as method in IR, drawn from a diverse range of literature: (1) it challenges the aesthetic and historic narratives of HIV/AIDS; (2) it is a feminist method and tool of African agency that can give space for the subaltern to speak and be seen; (3) it can affect and have impact; and (4) it reaches a global audience. To make these four key arguments the chapter draws on existing literature and debate on aesthetics and visual methods in IR, on co-production and decolonial feminist method, on African agency, and on visual ethnography. While diverse, these different bodies of literature share a common theme of methods as tools of possibility or rupture. Through co-production, film has the potential both to allow the represented to represent themselves, and to challenge sources of knowledge and epistemology in IR. Moreover, film has an impact on the full "affective register" (Callahan 2015, 909) of global audiences in ways that transcend the written word.

VISUAL HIV/AIDS

If there is a disease that has been well represented in film, it is HIV/AIDS. Ebola is commonly the unnamed virus in outbreak or plague films, but it is HIV/AIDS that occupies centre stage in most dramatic and documentary films with health as the main part of the plot. Feature-length dramas such as *Philadelphia, Dallas Buyers Club,* and *120 Beats Per Minute* and documentaries such as *How to Survive a Plague* and *Fire in the Blood* have documented the human experience of disease and the resilience, desperation, and solidarity among the HIV/AIDS community in the early years of combating the epidemic. These films show that treatment for people living with HIV/AIDS and acceptance by local, national, and international communities were not always a definite but were and continue to be fought for. They provide an insight into the humanity of the disease and the inhumanity of stigma, denial, and, in some instances, the homophobia of governments. They explore the idea that rights are not given to you; you take them. Films that depict the direct action and advocacy campaigns of groups such as ACT UP! in the United States, and the Treatment Action Campaign (TAC) in South Africa, are important in telling the history of HIV/AIDS and the legacy of how such activism framed and enacted ideas of the right to health that continue to shape modern forms of campaigning (see for example Gays against Guns). The telling of such history through film contributes to the notion that HIV/AIDS is somehow an exceptional disease in the mind of the public and of global health governance (Benton 2015; Lisk 2010;). HIV/AIDS has special status as a disease to which we could all be vulnerable, as something that captures the imagination through fear or empathy, and therefore as a complex social disease that requires more than health-based interventions.

Film has three functions in the HIV/AIDS response. First, it can be instrumentalized as a form of education and behaviour-change communication. This draws on the legacy of drama in the international HIV/AIDS response in depicting ways in which individuals can protect themselves from transmission and in educating audiences about understanding as a means to combat stigma. Such drama can take the form of community theatre, television shows such as *The Normal Heart* and *Shuga,* or characters such as HIV-positive "Kami" in South Africa's *Sesame Street.* Second, and perhaps most pertinently, film can affect or have an impact on the viewer. Film can communicate ideas and instil feeling and emotion in audiences in ways that the written word cannot. This explains in part why film and film clubs are common parts of teaching in higher education. I commit two weeks to HIV/AIDS out of the twelve weeks of a post-graduate class on the Global Politics of Health, and the one teaching resource that has had the deepest resonance with students has been the documentary film *We Were Here.* The film elicits an emotional reaction (tears, sadness, humility) but also enriches an understanding of a time before many students were born, when HIV/AIDS was not normalized as something that could be lived with but was an unknown virus that could kill you and your loved ones. Third, film narrates a lived history of HIV/AIDS. The narrative of HIV/AIDS told in film is primarily that of the early period of the disease: when denial and stigma were paramount, the virus was labelled a "gay disease" or gay-related immunodeficiency syndrome (GRID), and the campaign was to find out what caused AIDS and how to treat it. These films and this history are vital for understanding the governance of HIV/AIDS and how activism and scientists combined to advance treatment and give access to people living with HIV. However, they present a specific historical narrative and aesthetic of HIV/AIDS, of the skinny male living in North America or Europe. This aesthetic was of a time and should be widely seen and acknowledged as such.

The current aesthetic of HIV/AIDS is different from that seen in existing feature films on HIV/AIDS; it is varied and it is female. As the introduction highlighted, the majority of people living with HIV/AIDS are women in sub-Saharan Africa (UNAIDS 2016). HIV/AIDS is increasingly gendered. Women make up the majority of people living with the disease; women are responsible for the prevention of mother-to-child transmission; women act as carers for family and community members who are living with disease and as peer educators where they live; and grandmothers care for orphans and vulnerable children when their own children die of AIDS. It was women who were at the forefront of making the South African government acknowledge that HIV caused AIDS and that treatment should be available for all pregnant mothers as a constitutional right

(Treatment Action Campaign 2010). With the exception of a handful of films such as *Fire in the Blood* and *Not Without Us,* women living with HIV/AIDS in sub-Saharan Africa, especially poor women, are not represented in feature-length film. They are missing from the historical film narrative and aesthetic of HIV/AIDS.

That women are missing from film and the aesthetic of HIV/AIDS is perhaps not surprising when you consider the political economy of the disease and film. As the introduction discussed, women living with HIV/AIDS predominantly reside in southern and eastern Africa. There are two predominant ways of explaining the high prevalence rate among women in this part of Africa: the first is the behavioural paradigm that highlights the role of polygamous relationships, the value ascribed to large families, and women's rights as wives; the second, more complex and convincing explanation is that cycles of poverty and inequality cause high rates of HIV/AIDS prevalence (Harman 2010, 3). Poverty can restrict access to health care (treatment, prevention, care) and education (prevention and treatment) and can make individuals more susceptible to risky behaviour (transactional sex, problems negotiating safe sex, commercial sex work) (Harman 2010, 2011b). Given the poverty explanation, film is perhaps not the priority for women living with HIV/AIDS. Even if film were a concern or priority, as chapter 5 unravels in detail, few women living with HIV/AIDS have access to the financial and technical resources to produce a feature-length film or to the partnership networks that enable such production. Even fewer have relationships to the international film festivals and distribution companies that would garner an audience for a film. Film industries such as Nollywood in Nigeria and Swahiliwood or "Bongo film" in Tanzania are thriving; however, they also depend on patronage networks of contacts and investors and on the gatekeeping practices of the state that limit which stories are told. As in Hollywood, the majority of producers in Nollywood are male. Stories are told by the people who have the money to tell them and the networks to screen them.

The absence or invisibility in film of women living with HIV/AIDS has potential consequences for how we understand both the contemporary everyday realities of living with the disease and the ideas communicated by the dominant film aesthetic of the skinny white male. Film representations suggest that people living with HIV/AIDS are predominantly men living in Europe, North America, or South Africa, rather than women living in sub-Saharan Africa. The focus

Fig. 1 Cast member Mwantumu Hussein Malongine, production assistant Ansity Noel, and producer Sophie Harman meeting people in the Miono care and treatment centre, 2015. Care and treatment centres like these are the focal point of in-country prevention and treatment initiatives across sub-Saharan Africa.

on the fight to access affordable treatment for people living with HIV has now shifted from campaigns targeting pharmaceutical pricing and government provision to the everyday structural barriers that limit access, such as treatment centre waiting times, infrastructure, and gender. People still die of AIDS; however, the rate of death is no longer the main depiction in films about the disease. Historical narratives and stories about the fight against HIV/AIDS focus on the "big men" of institutional leaders such as Peter Piot and Jonathan Mann and of campaigners and advocates such as Zachie Ahmat (Cameron 2005; Geffen 2010; Piot 2012). Women living with HIV are invisible in film or only present in one dimensional photography. As Bleiker and Kay argue (2007), photographic representations of people living with HIV/AIDS position them in a naturalist, pluralist, and/or humanist frame. Combined, these aesthetic representations create a historical narrative of HIV/AIDS that is missing the voices of those whom the disease effects and affects the most. It also ignores the contemporary issues for people living with HIV/AIDS.

The first reason to make a film is therefore to provide a different aesthetic on HIV/AIDS that represents the contemporary everyday realities of women living with the disease in a specific part of sub-Saharan Africa. The story is not universal to all women living with HIV/AIDS on the continent, but it engages the lives of a group of women and the risks and mundanity of these lives. A film that focuses on women living in sub-Saharan Africa provides a different aesthetic for HIV/AIDS and contributes to the wider historical narrative around the disease.

FILM AS FEMINIST METHOD AND AFRICAN AGENCY

The absence of women in aesthetic representations of HIV/AIDS in film points to two fundamental questions that guide feminist, postcolonial, and decolonial research in IR: Where are the women? Can the subaltern speak? This section argues that film is a feminist method. Film allows the subjects of research to represent themselves. It is a moving image that allows women to be multi-dimensional problematic characters and to express themselves in their own language and movement. Film as method thus has the capacity for co-production of research and of self-representation. This allows new forms of exploration as to the possibilities of disrupting or embedding asymmetries of power within knowledge production in IR. Film both encapsulates the transformative potential of feminist method – representation, storytelling, and giving visibility to the hidden voices – and has the potential to challenge stereotypes and the coded, gendered, and racialized narratives of women in film and international relations. The second reason to make a film is therefore to provide a method of co-production of knowledge that confronts distinctions between the knower and the known and allows the invisible to represent and speak for themselves. In so doing, film is a feminist method of research and source and a site of African agency.

Film Is Feminist

Feminist research in IR is a diverse field underpinned by a unifying commitment: research is for the transformation of the lives of women, and the methods used derive knowledge from and speak to these everyday lives and experiences (Fonow and Cook 2005; Harding and Norberg 2005; Tickner 2005). Method in IR should tell us not only about the macro-economy or state security agendas but also about the everyday realities of lived experience from around the world and the ways in which people resist, assume, or adapt to such macro processes (Desai 2009; Tickner 1997). The types of methods used by feminist researchers are diverse, drawing on qualitative and quantitative, positivist and post-positivist approaches to research questions. For many feminists working in IR, positivist methods and an emphasis on the objective should not be to the exclusion of diverse, mixed methods, which can capture the diversity and breadth of individual and groups of women's experiences in international relations (Elias and Kuttner 2001). The research process is a political exercise of power, and thus such power should be recognized through reflexivity and positionality on the part of the researcher and through an awareness that objectivity is an impossible ideal because of the ontological biases brought by all researchers to the research process (Harding and Norberg 2005). Feminist research methods give space for both the political and the subjective because they act as socially engaged, transformative tools *and* they challenge hierarchies of knowledge.

Commitment to socially engaged methods and the investigation of hidden structures of power has led feminists to experiment with co-produced research. Co-produced research or "participatory action research" (PAR) is recognized by some scholars as a research methodology and by others as an "orientation to inquiry" (Grant, Nelson, and Mitchell 2008; Reason and Bradbury 2008). The key components of a PAR methodology or inquiry are collaboration; iterative processes of research, learning, and action; and recognition of many ways of knowing (Grant, Nelson, and Mitchell 2008; Reason and Bradbury 2008). Co-production or PAR is seen as a remedial intervention, particularly in newly independent states, to recognize both the sources of knowledge that were either appropriated or ignored under colonial rule and the lack of reciprocity in the relationship between the researcher and the researched. The intent of such intervention is to give voice, effect change, blur the boundaries of the researcher, and crucially address power imbalances (Gaventa and Cornwall 2008; Grant, Nelson, and Mitchell 2008). As Durose, Beebeejaun, et al. (2012) argue, participatory and co-produced research methods traverse "dialogical" engagements between the researcher and the researched to move towards transformative research. In this respect, PAR is a political project that emphasizes transformation through action-based research.

Co-produced research, while sharing similar aspects to PAR, is also an epistemological position that values knowledge derived from lived experience and the position of such knowledge in democratizing the research process. It is the epistemological position of co-produced research that aligns it to feminist method. However, as Reid and Frisby (2008, 94) argue, research using PAR or co-production methods has failed to fully account for gender relations or has tended to homogenize women and their experiences; in addition, feminist theory has become distanced from the practical realities of marginalized women. As a result, PAR and co-produced knowledge have been dismissed by aspects of feminist theory, which in turn has generated some frustration among feminists who are interested in co-production or participatory research. To address these tensions, Reid and Frisby advocate for feminist participatory action research that acknowledges and builds on such tensions and ambiguities. The potential of co-produced or PAR research for feminists is to actualize the transformative intent that underpins feminist research; to address the problematic encounters as to who is represented, who speaks, and who is heard; and to promote global solidarity in and democratization of knowledge.

While co-produced research is common in politics, sociology, geography, and development studies (Durose, Beebeejaun, et al. 2012), it is less prevalent in IR. This can be explained in part by the type of research methods, training, and practice in the discipline and the epistemological challenges as to what constitutes knowledge and where it is created or derived. Co-produced research is, for some, a blunt instrument in addressing the representation question and leads to research that can exacerbate inequalities. This point is strongly argued by Cooke and Kothari (2001) who suggest that participatory methods can both romanticize local knowledge (the epistemological critique) and exacerbate inequalities (the decolonial critique) rather than address them. The two critiques suggested by Cooke and Kothari's work – the epistemological critique and the decolonial feminist critique – highlight the problematic encounters of such research and the disciplinary boundaries of research methods in the discipline.

The substantive critique of co-produced research concerns the epistemological question as to whether lived experience constitutes knowledge. The epistemological critique comes from both positivist claims to knowledge and the problematizing of the everyday and experience within feminist theory. The positivist critique of co-produced research is that knowledge based on lived experience is subjective, lacks rigour because of issues with verification and replication, and is more aligned to storytelling than scholarly inquiry. Knowledge derived from experience is thus empirically weak. As the introduction highlighted, feminist IR theorists have responded to the positivist critique at length and used it as an opportunity to advocate further for subjective non-positivist methods of research (Elias and Kuttner 2001; Enloe 2004; Harcourt, Ling, et al., 2015; Tickner 1997). The other epistemological critique, which is perhaps more relevant here, lies within feminist theory and the wider debate on standpoint feminism. This debate focuses on the issues of essentialism and foundationalism within a feminist epistemology that recognizes lived experience and the everyday as a site of knowledge (Weldon 2006). Such an epistemology is essentialist in that one set of experiences or standpoint does not represent a shared understanding of a particular group from a similar position or standpoint (J.W. Scott 1991), and it is based on implicit foundationalism in the way in which such knowledge can be adjudicated for political purposes (Sylvester 1994). As Joan Scott (1991) argues in her seminal work on experience and visibility, knowledge derived from experience or the standpoint of the everyday can essentialize experience and mask its discursive character. Knowledge, including that derived from experience, is constructed and does not necessarily break silence or invisibility, but it reproduces the structures of power that silence or make invisible. For Scott, experience is not the basis for knowledge but the basis of what is to be explained; experience should be historicized and recognized as discursive, contested, and political. The tension therefore exists not only in what counts as knowledge but also in how knowledge derived from experience is used, contested, and valued; and how, and to what end, knowledge is made visible.

Compounding debate over epistemological essentialism and foundationalism is the importance of recognizing the structures in which visibility or invisibility is reproduced *and* consumed. For Dingli, there is a need for "a radical re-imagining of silence in IR" that recognizes the pluralism in the world and, thus, "silence as spirituality, docility, suffering and active collusion with existing norms" (2015, 732). Instead of accepting the "liberal feminist" and postcolonial notion of silence as being something oppressive or violent, the author suggests that silence is accepted as a permanent feature of IR that is brought about by both a willingness to be silent and a willingness to listen. The structures of silence and the politics of who hears reflect a wider debate in feminist theory as to who constructs knowledge and how such knowledge can silence.

The decolonial critique of co-produced research is concerned with the process and outcomes of visibility, with who can speak, and with who is seen or heard (Dingli 2015; Parpart 2010). Here I use the term *decolonial* rather than *postcolonial* to reflect some of the early feminist work in this area by scholars such as Chandra Talpade Mohanty who have informed my thinking. This is not to dismiss the term *postcolonial* or the relevance it has to feminist scholars working in IR that I also draw on here. Instead, as McLaren argues, "decoloniality or a decolonizing approach challenges mainstream, hegemonic, dominant theories of knowledge, language, power, and politics. It differs from post-colonialism because it unsettles the concept of colonialism in the first place; whereas post-colonialism is the 'after' of colonization, de-coloniality is the liberation from colonial structures, including values, methods, and knowledges ... Decolonization offers the possibility of new, creative, and innovative approaches to contemporary problems" (2017, 8).

The main emphasis of the decolonial critique is that feminists need to be cognizant of (1) power relations within the academy, and their own biases or Western lenses that reinforce such power relations; and (2) the relationship between feminists who conduct research (predominantly in high-income countries) and the subject of much feminist IR (predominantly in low-income countries). Both relations should be recognized and used as a basis for action through the disruption of "geopolitical foreclosures that pit us against one another in the various power struggles of global politics" (Agathangelou and Turcotte 2010, 55). Mohanty encapsulated this critique in her seminal essay "Under Western Eyes: Feminist Scholarship and Colonial Discourses" (2003), in which she drew attention to the problematic ways in which feminists situated the "other" within their research and research practices. Mohanty has called for feminism without borders in which feminists democratize, rather than colonize, by paying attention to not only women's lives that are differently placed but also how different women see themselves, their knowledge of themselves and their context, and their agency. For Mohanty (2003, 42), there is a need to move beyond the understanding of third-world women that "they cannot represent themselves, they must be represented" (Chowdhury 2006); that is, third-world women must be able to see and show themselves, and feminist scholars should see how these woman see both themselves and their knowledge.

The decolonial critique is principally one of epistemology and the relationship between the knower and the known. The first problem here is how the knower positions the known in the research: by speaking for them, by homogenizing their lives, and by robbing them of agency and knowledge. The second problem is the distinction between the knower and the known. The final problem is how these distinctions lead to what Tilley (2017) depicts as a politics of extraction and piratic methods in which knowledge is taken from the known and added value through academic processes. The relationship between the knower and the known can overlook the source of knowledge, lack reciprocity within this, assume that the known cannot be a knower or represent themselves, and rests on an epistemological hierarchy of what it is to know.

The issue of representation is important here, particularly the representation of blackness and black female bodies. Much debate over the reading of film has been about the relationship between the gaze of the filmmaker (director, producer) and the bodies, life, and representation of the subject of film. Through readings of films like *Out of Africa* and *Birth of a Nation*, scholars such as E.A. Kaplan (1997) and Smith have demonstrated that the male gaze and patriarchy are also imbued with the imperial gaze that has "established codes of narrative film practice and circulated as truth a range of black stereotypes for record-breaking audiences" (V. Smith 1997, 1). While speaking more directly to films depicting the African-American experience, the work of scholars such as Smith and hooks demonstrates the ways in which film codes positive and negative stereotypes and black-white binaries and can also reinforce white, patriarchal hierarchies (hooks 1992; V. Smith 1997). For such scholars the work of feminist film critique is not only to illuminate the racial codes and their relationship to wider systems of hierarchy and oppression but also to challenge these codes and biases in filmmaking. Hence, when using film as a method of seeing politics, it is important to question the ways in which such visibility is done, the codes and stereotypes that such film narratives can write, and who is conducting the research or producing the film. This requires feminist researchers to recognize their own position of power in the design and conduct of research and the trap of universalisms therein (Chowdhury 2002; Mohanty 2003, 34).

To address the decolonial critique, feminist research needs to engage women in a way that does not universalize or homogenize experience (Blackwell, Briggs, and Chiu 2015) and does not reinforce hierarchies of women from the north as the speakers and women from the south as those who are spoken of. For scholars such as Ling, such decolonial practice "calls for building communities trans-subjectively: that is, between you and me, not you *for* me" (Ling 2007, 144). Shohat similarly argues that a new way of thinking would be through "multicultural feminism" that decolonizes issues of representation by asking "for a transnational imaginary that places in synergistic relations diverse narratives offering prospects of critical community affiliations" (1998, 52). Alternative methods of addressing feminist concerns of representation, voice, and agency have emphasized black feminist praxis "that articulates the way in which invisibility, otherness, and stigma are produced and re-produced on black women's bodies" (Hammonds 1997, 182), as well as feminist democracy based on de-colonialism and anti-colonialism (Alexander and Mohanty 1997). In actuality, such practice takes time and physical and mental labour (Polhaus 2017, 47). As Alcoff (2017, 24) argues, decolonizing feminism does not include adding on another form of difference but is a completely different way of thinking about methods. The utility of feminist method is to inform researchers of such concerns in order to make them recognize their own positionality and subjectivities and act upon these in ways that rewrite gendered and racialized narratives of women in the world.

Common to these alternatives is the need to decolonize thinking and practices around research. What is crucial to these debates is the recognition that, whatever form or term is ascribed to forms of transnational feminist solidarity or co-production, such relationships are never easy. As Desai (2007) argues, these are "messy relationships" underpinned by multiple differences in class, gender, race, genealogy, sexuality, wealth, and knowledge that can in some instances enhance inequalities among women. However, crucially for Desai, "this does not preclude other possibilities, as is evident in the work of feminists around the world" (797). The answer is to not ignore entrenched power inequalities, or what Carty and Mohanty call the "discomforting truths in feminism," but "engage in a praxis of counter vigilance that will create solidarity among feminists across these divides" (Carty and Mohanty 2015, 88). Such praxis requires recognition of the genealogies of difference, of the difference of the effects of solidarity practices, and of histories; a shared sense of struggle "against all forms of patriarchal power and control, violence and exploitation as they are manifested in neoliberalism, militarism, religious fundamentalisms across north-south divides and state borders" (Baksh and Harcourt 2015, 9); and critical reflection (Carty and Mohanty 2015). It is through recognition, solidarity, and reflection, and not through the exacerbation of division and the closing down of collective solidarity, that one creates knowledge and disrupts those hierarchies that divide feminists. Feminist praxis that seeks to engage with forms of transnational solidarity and to decolonize such solidarity practices and wider international relations should therefore engage in what Desai calls a "dual politics of possibilities" that recognizes what is possible within existing politics, our role and positionality within this, and a vision for what can be possible (2007, 801).

Given that co-produced research is contested as a form of knowledge and that the practice of co-produced research is seen to reproduce the hierarchies and inequalities that the feminist project seeks to dismantle, it is perhaps unsurprising that co-produced research is not common in IR. This is an oversight. Co-produced research offers new methods and sources of knowledge and a potential means of decolonizing IR. The critique of co-produced research serves to strengthen its use as a way of thinking and practising research. The epistemological critique highlights the importance of triangulation and the *co-* element of *co-production* in the research process. Experience and the everyday must be subjected to the same forms of knowledge triangulation that are common to established qualitative research processes. This is not to add value to extracted knowledge, as Tilley (2017) would argue, but to combine and test different sources of knowledge in order to refute and strengthen the ways in which such knowledge can be used to understand and see politics. The everyday is thus one aspect of knowledge in the *co*-produced process that is combined and tested with other sources of knowledge. Experience and the everyday stories of a rural woman living in the coastal region of Tanzania have the same validity as the data from an interview with a senior politician in the region and as such should be subjected to the same form of reflection, scrutiny, and triangulation.

The decolonial critique is important in bringing to the fore the red flags and messy underpinnings of such work – white gaze, women from the north representing or speaking of the everyday experiences of women from the south, and reproduced hierarchies – and in being attentive to difference and genealogies. However, rather than providing evidence to suggest that the messiness of co-production should prevent such work, critical reflection and thinking on the messiness informs different ways of thinking and doing feminist research and transnational feminist method. The intent here is not to shy away from Carty and Mohanty's (2015, 88) "discomforting truths of feminism" but, as Desai (2007) suggests, to see how practical engagements and situating oneself in the present can lead to possibilities in the future. As Reid and Frisby conclude in their work on feminist co-produced research, their greatest finding was "the importance of living in places of discomfort, taking action and not becoming paralyzed while grappling with important questions" (2008, 102). Rather than ignoring inherent tensions and hierarchies in the research process, feminists have used such concerns as a basis on which to think about new methods of research that enable and prioritize transnational solidarity, decolonial representation, and inclusive forms of knowledge. Such tensions have not closed down the lines of inquiry for being too problematic or difficult but have opened up research design to new methods and ways of thinking about research in IR. Finally, it is through involving new sources of knowledge and drawing on different epistemological positions that the discipline of IR can advance. Epistemological boundaries and lack of new research methods narrow the field rather than expand the knowledge and understanding of the international.

Instead of closing down opportunities for co-production, this book argues that film has the potential to act as feminist method. Film as method has been used by feminists in a range of ways in which to read security and explore masculinities and militarism in popular media and public discourse (Cohan and Hark 1993; Dalby 2008). Feminists have read films in ways ranging from militarism and masculinity, through films such as *Coriolanus, Charlie Wilson's War, Fahrenheit 9/11* (Baker 2016; Lidinsky 2005; Rasmusson 2005); to military peace movements (Tidy 2015); to coloniality in pornographic film (Britt 2015); to citizenship and identity (Weber 2010). Such readings draw on the wider work of feminist film critique and debate over representation; female bodies within film, with particular reference to black female bodies; and social realist and avant-garde film (Chamarette 2015; Doane 2004). The writing of film to challenge and offer new narratives of women in the world has been less common in feminist method in IR. A small number of scholars have produced individual and series of short films or participated in documentaries (Callahan 2015; Der Derian 2009, 2010; Germano 2014). One feminist scholar who has brought the writing of film in from the methodological margins is Weber with her work on the politics of security and identity in the United States. Weber has used film both in her reading of gender and the grammar of IR and as a means of exploring alternative grammars. Weber's "I Am an American" project (2010) is a series of short films, shot and edited by Weber to document different experiences of citizenship and hidden America in the aftermath of 9/11. Deeply personal and affecting, the films are stories and portraits of the everyday person that contrast with elite constructions of moral grammars on citizenship and war. This work has been groundbreaking within IR in its use of film as method and in the audience that such a medium attracts beyond the academy.

The potential of representation, co-produced knowledge, and visibility of the everyday and the unseen structures of power makes film a potentially revealing form of feminist method. Film has engaged feminist inquiry through a variety of readings, and scholars such as Weber have harnessed film as a method of research production and dissemination. Feminist debate over method suggests a variety of cautions to be considered in the engagement of any method, particularly new methods of co-production and film. Such cautions are vital to the potential of film as feminist method. Film production presents a new way of seeing politics and of being seen. As with all methods of research, it entails unseen difficulties and problematic encounters; however, it is through inhabiting and exploring such challenges that new methods can be developed and the feminist project advanced.

Film as African Agency

Film is a source and site of agency in postcolonial Africa. For some, thinking about film or aesthetic representations of Africa means images of malnourished or ill African children as depicted in fundraising films of international non-governmental organizations or images of civil war, famine, and genocide. Representations of Africa in film, particularly films made for more Western markets, have encountered problematic stereotypes of a Conrad-esque "dark continent" that homogenizes the experiences of a pluralist continent to Africa as a country that is violent and full of disease, with corrupt dictators; Achebe acutely puts it as "the dehumanization of Africa and Africans which this age-long attitude has fostered and continues to foster in the world" (1977, 5). Africa-based films that have attained global audiences depict the region as "the dark continent" full of "tribal" conflict (*Black Hawk Down*), ruthless dictators (*Last King of Scotland*), inner-city violence (*Tsotsi*), genocide (*Hotel Rwanda*), government corruption and collusion with capitalist interests (*The Constant Gardener*), and resource plunder (*Blood Diamond*). A number of these films are loosely based on real events and raise important political and social questions that appeal to both Western film critics and audiences.[1] Even films that focus on the musical heritage of countries such as Mali and Nigeria, for example *Finding Fela!* and *They Will Have to Kill Us First*, use the politics of conflict and division as defining parts of the films' narrative. These films and images become the international narrative of the continent in the world to the exclusion of its other stories.

Mbembe's argument that Africa serves as a metaphor through which the West, specifically Britain, can make sense of its own identity can similarly be applied to filmmaking (Gallagher 2009; Mbembe 2001; Nothias 2014). Lewis, Rodgers, and Woolcock argue that most films about development are not about the subject matter or the main characters but about Westerners trying to understand their own role in the development process (2014). Hence film set in Africa for international audiences not only subscribes to Afro-pessimistic stereotypes but moreover tells us something about how the international relates to this continent. Films on Africa often obscure the colonial history underpinning the Afro-pessimistic narrative of conflict and corruption. Instead, films on Africa for Western audiences help build the narrative of Western states providing support and solutions to African "problems," which shapes the identity of such states (Harrison 2010, 392 and 408).

Such international narratives are not the single story of the continent and are in many respects based on lazy stereotypes and narratives shaped by the international acting upon Africa. To examine film through the lens of African agency – how Africa acts on the international rather than how the international acts on Africa – requires looking beyond such international narratives and stereotypes to consider the broad work on African cinema and film as a source of reimagining the continent in different ways. Drawing on Brown and Harman's use of the term, *African agency* is an intellectual intent "to take African politics, actions, preferences, strategies and purposes seriously, to get beyond the tired tropes of an Africa that is victimised, chaotic, violent and poor" (2013a, 1–2). Engagement with knowledge on African cinema demonstrates that film has been a key source of the way in which Africa imagines and represents itself in the international. Film is a common medium through which the politics, society, and everyday lives and experiences of people living in sub-Saharan Africa are taught and understood around the world. Film as a source and site of African agency is evident in how, through the thriving Nollywood, Swahiliwood, and Bongo film industries, it has been used to raise consciousness and challenge colonial representations of the continent, the rise of middle-class aspiration, and pockets of wealth.

As scholars of African cinema such as Diawara, Gugler, and Pfaff have noted, film was historically a space in which African states and filmmakers were able to confront and reshape representations of the continent in the international, to tell stories, and to reimagine the future of their countries (Diawara 1992; Gugler 2003; Pfaff 2004a). The advent of the moving picture at the turn of the twentieth century coincided with the consolidation of European colonial rule over much of Africa. The early history of film in the continent is therefore intertwined with the colonial legacy of producing "improving" and educational films for African audiences that were made by colonial film units, while at the same time restricting access to European films (Diawara 1992). Film in the continent was therefore based on the international narrative – in this case, of the European colonizers – of film as something that acts upon Africans to improve their behaviour and educate them. Post-independence, such narratives were challenged when film became used as a form of national identity and creativity and as an outlet for people to tell their own stories. This was particularly the case in West Africa where state leaders in Ghana and Nigeria, and French investment in ex-colonies, stimulated a rise in African auteur cinema (Diawara 1992). At the time, film and culture were seen as important aspects of independent state building and identity and therefore something to be fostered.

A driving force behind film as a source and site of African agency is the Fédération Panafricaine des Cinéastes (FEPACI; Pan African

Federation of Filmmakers), a pan-African movement set up to create African films produced in and by Africans, national associations of filmmakers, and perhaps the most famous international film festival on the continent, the Festival Panafricain du Cinéma de Ouagoudougou (FESPACO; Pan-African Film and Television Festival of Ouagoudougou) (Diawara 1992). FEPACI and the 1975 Algiers Charter on African film established the foundations on which to shift the origins of African cinema from a tool of colonial powers' "civilizing" and "educational" missions to that of postcolonial statehood (Cham 2004; Diawara 1992; Gugler 2003). The charter consolidated this growing movement to recognize that film had an essential role in education and consciousness-raising on the continent (Pfaff 2004b; Thackway 2003). The combination of state-leader commitment to culture in the reimagining of the postcolonial state, finance from the French government, and FEPACI's agency led to a golden period of auteur African cinema in the 1970s and 1980s. As Diawara outlines, this golden period can be defined by three styles of cinema: colonial confrontation, a return to the source, and social realism (1992). While the first two genres played directly to the project of nationhood and independence in postcolonial state formation, the third genre of social realism drew on the African oral traditions of storytelling and Italian neo-realist filmmaking (Diawara 1992; Gugler 2003).

Auteur African cinema remains a contemporary source of storytelling and agency in international film festivals. However, mirroring film audiences around the world, it is not auteur cinema that draws the big audiences, but films full of drama, comedy, and action. The main source of film as African agency is expressed no longer just through auteur cinema but also through Nollywood and the growing copy industries of Bongo films in East Africa. Nollywood in West Africa and the Bongo industry in East Africa are in many respects the result of the technological revolution of the late 1990s, when the growth and affordability of digital software and cameras made film production cheaper and consequently more accessible. Previously, movies had been shot and edited on physical film, using expensive specialist cameras and editing suites; now, anyone with a smart phone could make a film. According to the UN, in 2013 Nollywood generated an estimated US$590 million in revenue, and, according to the International Monetary Fund (IMF), the industry accounted for 1.42 per cent of Nigeria's gross domestic product (Moudio 2013; Omanufeme 2016). These industries are a source of agency in not only representation but also job and wealth creation. The popularity of Nollywood and Bongo films shows the growing talent and demand for African films made by Africans in Africa, which are, as Ogola argues, "a primary catalyst in an emergent continent-wide popular discourse in what it might perhaps mean to be African" (2015, 36). It is such discourse that stimulates debate within the African film world between "auteur" and Nollywood filmmakers.

One consequence of the notion that thanks to technology anyone can make a film is that many people do so, with diminishing returns on quality. Criticism of Nollywood suggests both an element of snobbery about the low-value production quality and a concern about the type of modern Africa represented by such films. As Krings and Okome argue, the critique here is directed at the emphasis that Nollywood and Bongo films put on problematic forms of modernity based on conspicuous consumption, and the reinforcement of international stereotypes through a focus on witchcraft and religious deliverance (2013). As such, some critics see Nollywood and Bongo films as a setback to African consciousness. This debate demonstrates the flourishing nature of film as African agency because it shows that African actors are defining themselves through a range of forms and complexities of identity that do not speak to single narratives of "Africa as country" and Africans as a homogeneous category. Through auteur cinema and popular film, African actors have expressed, shaped, debated, and represented the complexity of African society, politics, and economics and have confronted international narratives of the continent through worldwide distribution.

As chapter 5 explores in greater detail, the agency of film, like much African agency, exists in tight corners constrained by a dependence on international financing and the vagaries of international film distribution. The degree to which film has been a tool of decolonization has been mixed. After independence a number of West African governments such as those of Ghana, Nigeria, and Burkina Faso did invest in the production of film. Kwame Nkrumah, for example, "built the most sophisticated infrastructure of film production in Africa" (Diawara 1992, 6). However, this was the exception rather than the rule; most governments prioritized other aspects of state building, and, as larger demands for public-sector reform and welfare needs grew, investment in the arts became less of a priority. Until the 1990s and the rapid development of Nollywood, the majority of African films were financed, co-produced, and edited by European, Lebanese, and North American donors (Diawara 1992; Thackway 2003). Although Nollywood and Bongo films are popular on the continent and find audiences in parts of the African diaspora, they have not crossed over into global audiences or secured big theatrical releases and international film festival presence. A handful of African films, such as *Tsotsi* and *Beasts of No Nation*, have had critical acclaim and attained worldwide distribution and audiences; however such films tend to be co-productions between African and European or North American production companies. Therefore, while film is a source of African agency, such agency is constrained by the international politics of film distribution and financing that support the international narratives of the continent as violent and poor. It is therefore imperative when using film as method to consider the hierarchies and structure inherent to film production and consumption that both promote and restrict this agency, as chapter 5 considers in detail.

Film as a source of African and feminist agency therefore offers a second explanation as to the utility of film as a method for exploring international relations. Similar to the argument of feminist methodology that seeks to question where the women are and to explore how their everyday experiences contribute to our understanding of the international, a focus on African agency questions how film is used to enact, subvert, and create representations and narratives of Africa in the international. Film has a history of social consciousness and the building of postcolonial narratives that seek to decolonize stories of Africa. Film has the potential to tell different stories of Africa in the international that confront the ways in which the discipline of IR, at best, frames and, more often, ignores the continent. Moreover, film draws on the legacy of the storytelling of history and culture across Africa and offers a form of representing such stories on a bigger platform. In the case of Nollywood and Bongo, film offers a medium in which to explore the changing nature of Africa in the international, and contemporary African societies, economies, and politics. It is through stories that people can explore identity, history, and heritage, and it is through storytelling via film that such stories can reach wider, global audiences.

AFFECT: AESTHETICS AND IR

The combination of moving image and sound organized around a narrative structure produces emotional reaction, resonance, and affect within audiences. This in turn encourages audiences to think through their emotional response to film and their connection with the characters and images they see. The combination provokes a reflection on the images and issues encountered in the film. The film personalizes these issues, producing images and scenes that cannot be unseen. For example, researchers can write about transactional sex being a driver of HIV and about the difficulty women face when negotiating safe sex, and readers can have a good grasp or understanding of the issues. However, watching a scene in which a woman plays out these negotiations – her physical withdrawal, her gaze, the discomfort of the character and the audience, and the will of the audience for her not to be in that position – both develops an understanding of the issue and has an emotional impact or affect on the viewer. The combination of the visual, sound, and story has a profound affect on audiences that written research cannot reach. It is the relationship between aesthetics and affect that constitutes a critical argument for the use of film as method in IR.

According to scholars such as Bleiker, IR has undergone an "aesthetic turn" since 2000 (Bleiker 2009a, 2009b; Shapiro 2013). The aesthetic turn in IR represents a movement beyond the theoretical and methodological boundaries of the discipline to include new tools of addressing issues within global politics. The general notion is that IR has progressed our understanding of peace and security, yet violence, inequality, and confrontation rather than co-operation still exist. If we are to advance our depth of knowledge or make sense of world politics, we must draw on all methods available, not overlooking how we can use artistic methods and read aesthetics. Contrary to theorists such as Wendt (1999), Bleiker argues that art can help to explain issues of international relations such as war, poverty, inequality, and economics (2009b, 2). For Bleiker, aesthetic politics recognizes the gap between the represented and representation and is about challenging how we think and represent politics beyond "mimesis" (8). Bleiker's use of "mimesis" speaks directly to classical debates between Plato and Aristotle on the role of art and aesthetics and the distinctions between politics and poetics. While acknowledging the limitations of art offered by Plato, many scholars who address the role of art and aesthetics in IR draw on Aristotle's work to acknowledge the role of mimesis as inevitable to art and artistic interpretation; however, such interpretation can still produce new forms of thinking about humanity. Aesthetics can be used as a means of interpreting, provoking, and understanding the emotion, impact, feeling, and uncertainty of international relations. It is from such interpretation and provocation that ruptures in thinking can occur, and new knowledge of world politics can emanate.

Echoing feminist-standpoint method, advocates of the use of aesthetics argue that we cannot separate ourselves from our relationship to events or facts and that research is always imbued with personal and societal power structures (Bleiker 2009b, 522). The aesthetic turn is therefore a turn away from positivist forms of knowledge about the world that understand the world in a linear "as is" manner, to a more interpretivist way of thinking about world problems and different methods of understanding, such as poetry, art, and film (Bleiker 2009a, 172). Aesthetics and art help us go beyond the fixed and representational to provoke, assemble, and, for authors such as Barabantseva and Lawrence (2015), engage new vulnerabilities. It is about using a range of sources and methods and the "full register of human intelligence and creativity" to address complex world problems (Bleiker 2006, 77). As such, "aesthetics is an important and necessary addition to our interpretive repertoire. It helps us understand why the emergence, meaning and significance of a political event can be appreciated only once we scrutinize the representational practices that have constituted the very nature of this event" (Bleiker 2009b, 519). A core part of the recent aesthetic turn in IR has therefore been about the use of pluralist methods to understand the world. Advocates of the use of art and aesthetics emphasize the need for collaborative (rather than interdisciplinary) research (Danchev 2012; Danchev and Lisle 2009, 777). As Bleiker (2015) and Shapiro (2013) argue, a pluralist method or an "assemblage" of methods is not about using many different new methods independently of each other but about drawing on a range of traditional, non-traditional, and "seemingly incompatible" methods in combination.

The use of aesthetics and art as method can be seen as part of a wider debate in the discipline over representation, ideal ontologies, interpretivist ideas of performance, and "the dirt" (Aradau and Huysmans 2014, 607) of doing research in IR. Scholars such as Aradau and Huysmans (2014) have argued that, when seen as devices, methods can be disruptive acts: when you conceive of methods as political and performative rather than representational, they can rupture world orders. Hence, underpinning this aesthetic turn is a commitment to use aesthetics and an *assemblage* of new, critical research methods and ideas to address complex world problems (Aradau and Huysmans 2014; Bleiker 2006, 2015). For Shapiro, such assemblage recognizes the utility of visual method and "trans-disciplinary method" as a critical encounter to rupture or discombobulate the ways in which space, security, and people in the world are seen and understood (Amoore and Hall 2010; Ingram 2011; Jabri 2006; Lisle 2007; Shapiro 2009, 2013).

Discussion on the relationship between art, politics, and rupture points to the work of Rancière. For Rancière, fundamental to seeing politics is the blurring of the boundaries between the domestic, the economic, and the social. Aesthetics blur boundaries "between the logic of facts and the logic of fictions and the new mode of rationality that characterizes the science of history" (Rancière 2004, 37) and can therefore be a political space that precludes and promotes particular modes of being. Aesthetics, for Rancière, is thus a mode of thought or thinking about art that, when read in conjunction with the "distribution of the sensible," divides what is visible and audio within a particular "aesthetico-political regime" (2004). He sees politics and art as being "contingent notions," subject to the constraints of modernity and possibilities of making and doing (2004). In other words, it is through the distribution of the sensible that boundaries as to what is seen and heard and what is not seen or heard are constructed as practices, and consequently the politics of possibility can be understood. Scholars interested in the relationship between art, aesthetics, and IR have developed Rancière's ideas on the aesthetico-political regime in different ways. For example, Holly Ryan draws on Rancière to explore the political role of street art in Latin America and to show "what art can do" in presenting new ideas or modes of political rationalities (2017).

Shapiro's work on aesthetics draws on both Foucault's emphasis on assemblages of knowledge and resistance to institutionalized spaces of what we think we know and Rancière's ideas of making the new subjects and objects visible in order to disrupt who can speak on what. Shapiro argues that aesthetics and art are important for what they reconfigure, disrupt, and reveal (2013, 30–31).

Aesthetic politics is deliberately provocative and ambiguous, as well as offering alternatives, for people to interpret and make sense of the world in which we live. Through art and aesthetics we can begin to think about spaces, imaginaries, and frames of knowledge. Shapiro's work has drawn on musical composition such as Duke Ellington's *Black, Brown and Beige*, both drama and documentary film, and television (Shapiro 2009, 2013). However, it is film, or "Cinematic Politics," that, for Shapiro, offers the greatest potential to disturb and provoke critiques of violence (2009, 40–41 and 47). Through such reading, Shapiro has argued that "a turn to the arts – rather than to the psychological framework of social sciences – yields a different kind of political apprehension of security, framing it within a different political ontology and a different spatial imaginary" (2013, 11).

Central to such aesthetic ruptures and differential spatial imaginaries is something that is often overlooked or dismissed in more positivist forms of IR: emotion. The visual – be it television footage of 9/11, pictures of people in full personal-protective-equipment suits working in Ebola treatment units, or short films of migrants in trafficker boats in the Mediterranean Sea – creates and expresses emotional reactions in ways that the written word cannot. The visual can capture or convey feeling and emotion when words are missing; it can also produce different emotional responses when words are found wanting. As such, the visual matters in IR because it can create affect; as Callahan argues, aesthetics are a fundamental part of IR's "affective register" (2015, 893 and 909).

Much of the discussion on affect and aesthetics in IR engages with Kantian notions of the sublime. The rupture or discombobulation affect of an aesthetic politics has its origins in Kantian understandings of the sublime in which a powerful aesthetic can confront the limits and fears of humanity and comprehension (Bleiker 2006, 80; 2009b, 513–28; Shapiro 2009, 99–110; 2013, 30). The sublime can be both pleasurable and terrorizing. The sublime presents the unforeseen or unknowable that evokes something or promotes some reaction. While use of the sublime in IR tends to refer to large-scale and sometimes violent events such as the classic eruption of a volcano or airplanes flying into twin towers, aesthetic sources can produce less violent confrontations with disruptive affect (Bleiker 2009a, 68 and 77). Aesthetics are therefore important to our understanding of IR owing to the affect – affirming, disruptive, and discombobulating

– and the assemblage of critical method that deepens knowledge, understanding, and representation.

The role of affect and emotion as a basis for thinking about international relations is a relatively new phenomenon. As a discipline, IR has tended to frame emotion as irrational and therefore of only limited use to understanding complex security questions and policy decisions (Hutchison 2016). However, path-breaking work of scholars such as (but not limited to) Hutchison (2016), Crawford (2000), Fierke (2012), T. Hall and Ross (2015), and Mercer (2010) has challenged this easy dismissal by critically showing how emotions and affect can be a basis on which to theorize international politics (see also Bleiker and Hutchison 2008). Such scholars have advanced the work on the politics of emotions by authors like Nussbaum (2003) and Ahmed (2004) to critically engage with emotion and trauma, war, peace, identity, international alliances, and security dilemmas. Similar to the work on aesthetics, scholarship on emotions and affect in IR has been fundamental to thinking in new and different ways about how world politics is shaped and challenged. Emotions have affective agency and, as a consequence, are directly relevant to thinking about the potential rupture and imaginaries of aesthetic politics and the potential of film as method in IR.

The place of affect, emotion, trauma, and the sublime in the aesthetic turn is commonly understood in the context of 9/11. The events of 11 September 2001, and the War on Terror provoked a variety of engagements with art; the visual in understanding IR and security; and the Kantian sublime (Danchev 2012). These engagements have focused the use of aesthetics in the War on Terror as a tool of patriotic nationalism and policing borders; they have shown how war and security can read through aesthetics and how aesthetics can be used as a form of resistance. Aesthetics have been fundamental to the ways in which governments, individuals, and scholars have made sense of 9/11. For Debrix, the US government pursued its post-9/11 interests through the aesthetics of violence and the emotional affect and trauma of the sublime image of two airplanes crashing into the twin towers (2006). Visual representations of the sublime helped shape and justify support for the Iraq war and provoke counteractions or responses to such representations (Debrix 2006, 771–2). Debrix reads Kant's understanding of the sublime as the effect or response – discomfort, bewilderment, shock – not as the end in itself, but as a means to an unrealized end: "The spectator of the sublime image is placed in an expectant emotional state whereby she or he must desperately wait for a subsequent explanation or justification in order to surmount the initial traumatic and unbearable scene" (Debrix 2006, 770). Hence for Debrix the sublime act – 9/11 – and the aesthetic and visual representations of the act produce the emotional state in the populace in which following acts of violence or war can be justified. For other scholars such as Devetak, storytelling is intrinsic to humanity, emotion, and meaning and thus is fundamental to how we make sense of events such as 9/11 and their impact on the world (Devetak 2009). Drawing on an Aristotelian reading of *White Noise*, he suggests that it is through stories that we construct political narratives of events and ourselves. Lisle's work has similarly considered how art and spaces of art such as museums have been used as a form of discipline, regulation, and patriotism in how the United States wrote its security and nationality after 9/11 (Lisle 2007, 233–50). For scholars such as Bleiker, these representations and uses of aesthetics have generated stereotypes of "crisis imagery." Bleiker uses poetry, architecture, media representations of refugees, and music as a basis on which to understand post-9/11 world politics (2006, 80 and 85; 2009a; Bleiker, Campbell, and Hutchison 2014). Such readings have pointed to the problematic metaphors that can arise from the visual methods of representation that often play on stereotypes of "crisis imagery," from gendered stereotypes of mothers and children to orientalist depictions of people living with HIV/AIDS (Bleiker, Campbell, and Hutchison 2014; Bleiker and Kay 2007, 159).

Political geographers have been at the forefront of reading 9/11 through art and aesthetics, particularly with regard to surveillance and borders. Amoore has explored how the use of image in the War on Terror produced a form of "watchful politics" in which visuals create boundaries between the observer and the observed and between the I or us and the "other," and how art has been used to confront or resist both real and imagined borders (2007, 218; Amoore and Hall 2010). For Amoore, the visual is very much a part of how states write their own security and how artistic interventions can confront, resist, or rework rituals associated with such writing of security (2007, 218; Amoore and Hall 2010). Such visuality extends to those at the forefront of the War on Terror who make sense of their role and position through soldier photography and what Kennedy depicts as "miliblogging" (2009). Amoore's work points to a further theme in the role of aesthetics for understanding security post-9/11: the visual and the aesthetic as political acts in themselves. Drawing on Rancière's work, Ingram argues that it is through artistic acts that contestation over aesthetics and politics takes place, "reflecting, contesting and reframing the 'new normal'" (2011, 221). Engaging with artistic acts such as Jeremy Deller's *Baghdad* at the Imperial War Museum and Wafaa Bilal's *Dog or Iraqi*, Ingram demonstrates that art can both be about and enact certain kinds of geopolitics.

Bounded within debates on 9/11 and aesthetics is the wider question of how we speak or enact security. Perhaps most pertinent here is the work of Hansen on the visual in speaking security through a reading of the Muhammad cartoon crisis in Denmark. Hansen argues that visuals and visual securitization need to be understood in their own right rather than subjected to their textual basis or discourse, because visuals "do not enter security discourse seamlessly but rely upon processes of radicalization and homogenization to become fully fledged securitizations" (2011, 69). It is the immediacy of the visual, how it interacts with texts and discourses or the "circulability" and the "ambiguity" of interpretation, that makes the visual speak security differently than text does (2011).

Developing more of a critical approach to the politics of art, Jabri suggests that, while art can have political affect, it is important for art to recognize its own boundaries of the subject and the politics of the conditions in which art, or artistic acts, takes place. She argues that acts of awe, terror, and affect should not be read through the medium of the sublime, which suggests a "passive subjectivity," but through Foucault's understanding of a Cartesian moment in which the uncertainty of the subject is brought to the fore (Jabri 2006). The sublime is open to discourse and interpretation and is often depicted as having unchallenged affect or power, whereas depictions of art or artistic acts as Cartesian moment situate the body and the subject and their agency more directly in understandings of aesthetics and IR.

This short overview of a rich and diverse debate showcases the ways in which art and aesthetics have been used to read security, representation, identity, and nationalism in post-9/11 IR. It demonstrates the prominence of aesthetics in making sense of IR. The use of aesthetics and art is therefore not at the margins of the discipline but a central part of the methods that we use to further our understanding and explanations of the world.

What is less common in the use of aesthetics as method is the writing of aesthetics and art. Only a handful of scholars have engaged in writing IR through visual methods such as film and photography. For those scholars, like Callahan, it is less about debates on representation and aesthetics but more about "what visual images can 'do' that is different from the written word," and valuing creativity through "new sites and senses of international politics" (Callahan 2015, 893 and 901). For example, Callahan's short film *Toilet Adventures* about people's engagement with lavatories in China engages with the everyday, orientalism, and the relationship between emotions (fear, disgust, apprehension) and the different kind of knowledge produced by such emotion.

James Der Derian both reads and writes film in IR. He explores the intersection between academics, filmmakers, and the "other" subject of the film, which in his work predominantly refers to civilian defence experts and the role and function of mimesis and the military-industrial complex (Der Derian 2010, 2015). In his earlier work, Der Derian explores MIME-NET – the military-industrial-media-entertainment network – to argue that the War on Terror was a war of mimesis. For Der Derian, mimetic war refers to the blurred boundaries of war imitation, representation, and familiarity that take place through MIME-NET. This blurring of boundaries gives space for the familiarity that sanctions violence (Der Derian 2009). Der Derian developed his work on media, mimesis, and war through his provocative documentary *Project Z* (2015), a film that draws on a range of visual skills in storytelling not only to explore militarism and violence in the contemporary world but also to confront the audience with a different view of the world. What is notable about *Project Z* is the ambition of the project within IR as an extended documentary film. It thus provokes the audience into thinking and seeing the world differently and is pivotal in advancing how the audience sees the role of film in IR.

As the earlier discussion on feminist method in this chapter suggests, another scholar to fully engage the register of reading *and* writing IR through visual methods is Cynthia Weber and her seminal project *I Am an American*. Like many writings on aesthetics and IR in the post-9/11 context, much of Weber's earlier work has drawn on the Kantian sublime, with a particular focus on the second part of the sublime: from rupture to order (Weber 2006a, 2006b). In so doing, she considers how fear is both politically mobilized and mobilizing through campaigns such as "We Are Not Afraid" in the United Kingdom and how artistic acts such as film create interpretive codes and a moral grammar of war (2006b). Weber reads the grammar of films such as *Black Hawk Down, Pearl Harbor*, and *In the Bedroom* to demonstrate the ways in which films can depict a grammar of war, and how such grammar can be gendered (2006b). Moreover, drawing on feminist debates, she argues that such films are based on heteronormative and gendered romantic notions of the family that construct particular grammars of morality. The family therefore becomes central to the wider narrative of identity, statehood, and morality and thus to the relationship between film and wider questions of security. As Weber argues, by reconsidering "film and family, it [moral grammars of war] suggests, one may also reconsider the official stories of US foreign policy and the morality tales that provide them with their specific grammars of war" (2006b, 8). Reading particular moral grammars of war through film is in part the impetus for Weber's writing of an alternative grammar of identity and post-9/11 politics through her project *I Am an American* – a series of short films, shot and edited by Weber to document different experiences of citizenship and hidden America in the aftermath of 9/11 (2010). "My project does not forget those who died on 11 September. But it does insist that US Americans also remember those living, often 'intolerably different' US citizens who bear the consequences of the US foreign and domestic policies of the War on Terror because they live in the shadow of the promise of what it means to be an American" (Weber 2010, 200).

The work of scholars such as Weber, Callahan, and Der Derian demonstrates the ways in which we can write international relations and see politics through aesthetic and artistic mediums like film. These scholars have shown that the use of film as method in IR is a possibility and can produce fruitful outputs, impacts, and knowledge. However, the use of film as method is not common in the discipline, and in many ways film is seen as a means of communicating existing research rather than as a standalone research output. Aesthetics and visual methods such as film have a complex relationship within the discipline of IR. The position of aesthetics in IR has followed a similar debate to that of aesthetics and politics in the 1930s, 1960s, and 1970s, between Bertolt Brecht and Georg Lukács and between Theodor Adorno and Walter Benjamin (Adorno, Benjamin, et al. 1977). Those debates focused on the social and political roles of art in capitalist societies, the role of art for art's sake, and culture and debates over social realism and art having social purpose. While the authors may agree that art has a role in understanding the world and politics, it can depend on the type of art (social realist or the surrealist avant-garde), the co-optation of art by political interests, and how the political is addressed; that is, do you use comedy to mock an authoritarian ruler, or use social realist drama or documentary to demonstrate the social consequences of authoritarianism? In IR such a debate manifests itself between those who advocate for aesthetics as part of a wider need for pluralist method in understanding the complexities of the contemporary world and those who dismiss aesthetics and art as existing for art's sake, or who see some methodological insight but little utility in the way aesthetics contribute to theorizing world order.

This book acknowledges both the critique of art existing for art's sake and the utility of aesthetics as a basis on which to theorize world order. I align with Bleiker's and Shapiro's argument that international relations are complex and need our full range of methods to address them. People understand the world through images, and at times of protracted crises – migrant crises, pandemic outbreaks, beheadings, racist attacks – images can provoke response and in some instances change. Social media outlets like Facebook, Instagram, and Snapchat are predominantly visual platforms for sharing information, presenting narratives, exploring identities, and discussing politics and international relations. Such visual platforms bombard the users with images of world events and issues of current affairs in a way that can desensitize them to violent acts, poverty, poor health, and humanitarian crises, mislead them with images out of context, and mobilize them into action.

Visual images have become both a language of how societies engage in and understand international relations and their own politics and a way of creating affect and impact. Visual images can have negative and positive impacts and, like words, can misrepresent, be dismissed, or be taken out of context. However, the visual has as much impact as the written or spoken word. To ignore the role of the visual and aesthetics therefore overlooks a substantive part of how everyday people and politicians make sense of the world and how the visual affects audiences. Aesthetics are bounded within contemporary practices of international relations as the world communicates and understands itself visually. Thus film as a form of aesthetic, visual method is important in IR, engaging in the visual ways in which people understand the world and using a full range of the visual and sound to cause affect in the audience. Aesthetics and visual images can provoke or challenge how individuals and collectives see politics and reimagine political possibilities or the boundaries that stop them from seeing.

AUDIENCE AND THE NARRATIVE FEATURE FILM

The final reason to use film as method, and a narrative feature film in particular, is audience. To make invisible women visible and to see politics necessitates audience and consumption of that visibility. Greater use of both reading and writing of film within the wider social sciences has been in part a reaction to changing technologies and to the use of image and aesthetics in teaching, research, and everyday social interaction. Accessible and personalized technologies have facilitated the use of images in the way that people communicate and make sense of themselves and the world around them. Film as a particular form of visual aesthetic appeals to global, academic, and non-academic audiences. Thus, film is a method of seeking a widespread, global audience for academic research. However, film is not just a method of communicating research to audiences; as chapter 5 explores in greater detail, a key to understanding knowledge in IR is not only its production but also its consumption. Film production is therefore a method in the co-production of knowledge that challenges how we see IR, and also a method by which to explore audience and the ways in which knowledge is produced *and* consumed. This section provides the final explanation and argument for film production as method in IR by exploring existing debate as to its utility in visual anthropology and the value of the narrative feature film.

Film is an accepted method of research in the disciplines of visual anthropology, sociology, and geography. However, what is less accepted or common is the use of a narrative feature film such as *Pili*, rather than a documentary film, as method. The visual sub-fields of those disciplines have articulated the different uses of film as method – from the popular "reading" of film to the "writing" (production) of film. The embeddedness of such methods is evident in academic journals, postgraduate degree programs, and the specialized awards for visual method.[2] Since 2000, other disciplines in social science have come to recognize the utility of film. For example, according to Jacobs, geography integrates aspects of visual method (e.g., cartography), yet has only developed a more critical engagement with film as method in the last fifteen years (2015).

Visual Anthropology developed from the early use of film as an educational tool linked to colonial rule in the 1920s and 1930s, to a technical research tool, to an established research method of ethnography. Ethnographers such as pioneer Margaret Mead not only advanced the use of visual method in ethnography through their own films but advocated for the potential of film as a device from which to develop theory (Mead 2003). In the 1960s, Visual Anthropology developed the work of early pioneers to suggest that film was not just a technological tool but a method of research through the practice of observational cinema. The main tenet of observation cinema as articulated by Young is that the researcher cedes control of the film: there is no director, no hierarchy, no pre-written script; the camera just observes what happens in front of it. The strength of film in comparison to notes and the written form "is that the final film CAN represent the original event or situation directly" (Colin Young 2003, 101).

In echoes of the decolonial critique of transnational feminism and co-produced research, observational cinema was criticized in part because of the unacknowledged power relations between the researcher (behind the camera) and the subject of the research (in front of the camera). Critics accused advocates of observational cinema of naive empiricism, false detachment, and lack of reflexivity on the part of the researcher (Grimshaw and Ravetz 2009; MacDougall 2003). In contrast, participatory cinema acknowledges and addresses the existence of both the camera and the researcher in the filming process: it reveals rather than conceals (MacDougall 2003). Participatory cinema emphasizes exchange and sharing of information throughout the production process. The debate over observational and participatory cinema within Visual Anthropology is important here for several reasons. First, the use of film requires recognition and reflection on the blurred relationship between the researcher and the researched, and the way in which "apparently established knowledge and forms are *experienced* requires a sensitivity to the strategic, contingent relational ways in which what is given is addressed via processes of knowledge-in-the-making" (Grimshaw and Ravetz 2004, 550). Second, Visual Anthropology has acknowledged and explored its colonial origins and taken such recognition as the starting point for thinking about ways to confront colonial ethnography and about the methods by which the subjects can represent themselves. Third, participatory cinema in many respects can be seen as a method of co-produced knowledge in its emphasis on exchange, shared knowledge, and cycles of critique and feedback. As Pink suggests, ethnography "may entail reflexive, collaborative, or participatory methods" to create and represent knowledge (2007, 22). Finally, film is recognized as an established method of research that has come to be recognized by the broader fields of anthropology, sociology, and geography (Pink 2007).

The production of a narrative film, rather than a documentary film, addresses the dual concerns of research ethics and audience. As a form of academic research, film as method has an ethical responsibility to all participants and co-producers of the project. As a narrative feature, *Pili* allows critical distance for the women who act in the film and provides the space for them to express themselves through characters rather than directly through their own lives. Even though the story of the film is based on their lives, in dramatizing the story the actors do not have to bear public responsibility or exposure for some of the more difficult choices made by the characters. This allowed the women to be open and free in their conversations about the main story of the film. In addition, the presentation of *Pili* as a story is vital in protecting the women and their children from any negative reactions to the issues raised in the film. As the previous section explored, film and storytelling have a noted lineage in the politics of Africa. Such storytelling has been common in communicating methods of prevention and treatment for HIV/AIDS and in addressing complex social issues such as stigma and denial surrounding the disease. I have witnessed first-hand community theatre productions in Kenya and Tanzania that use dance, music, and stories to explore HIV/AIDS and to engage audiences about their own lives. It is through drama and by inhabiting characters that people can explore their own fears, concerns, prejudices, and pride in ways that communicate, educate, and lead to self-reflection. Storytelling via drama is therefore in keeping with this tradition in East Africa of exploring sensitive and political issues through performance and acting.

To use film as method is to also appeal to as wide and as global audience as possible. Drama captures larger, more diverse, and global audiences, particularly those who may not ordinarily be interested in a woman living with HIV/AIDS in Tanzania. For socially

engaged films about issues of international development in Europe
and North America, the audience target is often framed around
"Claire," a woman in her mid-thirties, working full time, living in
north London, with two children under the age of five, who reads
the *Guardian* newspaper online and the *MailOnline* as her guilty
secret.[3] Claire will hopefully want to watch a film such as *Pili*; however, to attract as wide an audience as possible, the film would have
to have wider appeal through a story of relatable humanity. While
Pili may be based in the extreme poverty of Tanzania, most audiences can relate to the struggle for a better life for themselves and
their children. Drama allows the telling of a specific story with universal themes. It provides an accessible and informative entry point
for audiences to understand the everyday risk of poverty and disease
without them thinking that they are being lectured to or educated in
some way. As the next chapter demonstrates, themes of social reproduction, micro-lending, patriarchy, socio-economic risk, health-
system strengthening, and infrastructure spending are interwoven in
the story, but it is up to the audiences to engage such themes as they
choose. A documentary on the everyday risk of HIV/AIDS would
potentially limit the audiences to Claire and demographics of people interested in the politics of HIV/AIDS and global health (policy-
makers, students, and academics), fans of social realist cinema in
Europe and North America, and people interested in Swahili-speaking
film in East Africa. A social realist drama has the potential to capture
these target audiences, African audiences, and universal film viewers.

Capturing audience through affect and emotional resonance,
exploring sensitive issues through storytelling, and addressing the
ethical dynamics of research are not new issues to IR; they are central factors in the debate on the use of narrative within the discipline.
This debate applies not only to the role of narrative in engaging
with humanity through film production that can so often be written
out of academic work on IR (Doty 2004), but also to the ways in
which we see ourselves in the production of knowledge (Brigg and
Bleiker 2010). As Dauphinee (2013a, 2013b) argues, despite critical debate on how knowledge is produced and accessed, little has
changed in how "mainstream scholarship is developed and dissem-
inated." Narrative feature film is an important method in capturing
who speaks and who sees IR; however, it also provides an important
insight into the relational aspect of knowledge production and consumption and the role of the researcher within this.

CONCLUSION

The purpose of this chapter has been to provide a substantive argument for the use of film as method in IR and to situate this argument within broader debates on feminist and decolonial method, co-produced research, and aesthetics. The use of film as method enables (1) an alternative aesthetic narrative of HIV/AIDS; (2) a feminist method and a tool of African agency that provides space for the co-production of knowledge and for the represented to represent themselves and be seen; (3) the impact and resonance of aesthetic and visual forms of storytelling; (4) and the importance of audience. The chapter has argued that film is a feminist method and a form of African agency that deploys impact and affect through audiovisual narrative.

Drawing on debates about the potential of visual methods and the aesthetic turn in IR, the chapter argued that we need visual methods such as film to expand our use of methods for making sense of complex issues and reflecting the growing use of visual images in contemporary international societies. We live in a visual world, and therefore method in IR should reflect and explore the ways in which visual methods and aesthetics can be read and written to explore, understand, and deepen our understanding of international relations. Film in particular has the ability to create affect in audiences through the personalization of stories or issues and through the impact of a continuous sequence of visual images. This sequence of images follows a narrative that engages audiences in different ways from those of academic writing: the striking aspect of the visual and the narrative combined has the potential for greater impact on the audience and allows wider accessibility to the way in which politics is seen. Films are not easier or more difficult to produce than other academic work, but they invite new skills in visually translating complex ideas about politics or stories to audiences unfamiliar with academic debates. Film is not new to IR. As this chapter has shown, a range of scholars have adopted short films and documentaries as part of their method and scholarly output. Film has been a site and source of postcolonial African agency. In Africa, film has always been a way in which to express and contest international relations and write or re-write narratives on identity, history, and political society.

Across the different debates on aesthetics and affect, decolonial feminism, and African agency is an emphasis on possibility and rupture. Feminist reflection on co-produced method and transnational politics emphasizes both the difficulty and problems of doing such research and the ways in which such difficulty can become a space for possibility and change. Focus on the role of aesthetics and IR similarly emphasizes the possibility of using and combining different methods for change or rupture. Drawing on Rancière, aesthetics provokes us to think about what is being hidden and the politics of possibility as to what could be seen, as a means of disruption. Film as a source and site of African agency is used to explore identity, nationality, and the politics of the continent and to challenge or rupture the way in which Africa is seen in the world. The common thread to the four arguments in support of film as method in IR is thus one of seeing the politics of the possible and disrupting the boundaries that stop us from seeing.

The literature reviewed in this chapter points to the potential of film as method. The justification for film as method should be read with caution: taken together, the literature suggests that film has different, transformative, and important potential that is all encompassing. This is, of course, a stretch for any method. It is therefore important to recognize and explore the potential and limitations of a new method such as film. The first wave of the aesthetic turn highlighted the importance and possibilities of visual methods. The new wave of the aesthetic turn is therefore to explore and test such potential by making art – by producing a feature film.

Film is a method of understanding and producing knowledge on the everyday politics of HIV/AIDS *and* a stand-alone output that has an impact on audiences. As this chapter has argued, film is a method of writing stories (particularly those that are invisible in the discipline) and disrupting thought in international relations. The next chapter explores the ways in which to use film as a method of seeing politics. It focuses in detail on the co-production aspects of the project, not the technical aspects of filmmaking. It explores the pre-production (story, casting, locations), production (shoot), and post-production (edit, sound edit) of the film. The intent of the chapter is to consider how the themes and issues explored here – hierarchies of knowledge in co-production, aesthetic impact, feminist method, and African agency – are addressed and revealed in practice.

Film as a Method of Seeing

There are two ways that an academic researcher can make a film: you can pay a production company to do it for you, or you can produce it yourself. The former requires less direct involvement in the production aspect of the film, thus allowing the researcher more space and time to concentrate on the academic content of the story. It is also relatively straightforward and less time consuming for the researcher because the significant aspects of film production (legal contracts, copyright, music clearances) and the everyday minutiae (ensuring that lunch is on time, resolving disputes with landlords, and dealing with the different temperaments of cast and crew) are the responsibility of the production company. Paying a production company is more expensive than the cost of a researcher producing the film and, crucially, stops the researcher from gaining first-hand experience and seeing the international politics involved in film production. Both the significant aspects and the minutiae of film production are important to the use of film as method in IR because of what the process reveals about the politics and practicalities of co-produced research. *Pili* was made not by or with a professional film producer or production company but by me through my university. Running a film production out of a university meant that my school office became a production support team – issuing contracts, checking rights agreements, processing payments, looking into specialist insurance, and paying for kit. This was a big risk given that I had not made a film before and had no training whatsoever in film production, but it allowed me to witness, observe, and see the politics of making the invisible visible.

This chapter focuses on *how* film can be used as method. It outlines the making of *Pili* and, in so doing, begins to confront the
messy discomfort involved in such a transnational project. The chapter is loosely structured around the three phases of film production:
pre-production, production, and post-production. The first section
considers the role of the crew in the filmmaking and co-production
process. The second section explores both the development of the
story for *Pili* with the communities in which the film is based and
the wider politics of trust, authenticity, and reciprocity that shaped
this process. At the same time, the section provides the main basis
for understanding the method through which co-production can
give space for the unseen to speak for themselves and how this can
be triangulated with existing academic knowledge and specialized
filmmaking skill. Finally, the chapter outlines the production and
post-production process in order to demystify the practice of film
production and the importance of co-production throughout the different stages of the process.

PRE-PRODUCTION: CREW

How one sees and who sees are shaped by the political economy
of where one is born and where one lives. As outlined in chapter 1,
to explore film as a form of African agency it was my intention to
work with a full Tanzanian cast and crew. This did not happen. As
this section demonstrates, crew selection and recruitment is the first
instance of the ways in which money and knowledge hierarchies
shape and constrain co-production and film as a method of seeing.

The first constraint to co-production with a full Tanzanian crew
was material. Money is needed to make a film. My total budget to
produce the film was £75,000, which came from a research project on the everyday risk of HIV/AIDS that was funded by an AXA
Insurance Research Fund Outlook Award. Producers whom I consulted all thought that £75,000 was too small to produce a feature-length drama. "Low budget" is identified by the film database
IMDB as describing films made for US$1 million or less, but most
films classified as such tend to be made for between US$500,000
and US$5 million, with notable famous exceptions such as *The Blair
Witch Project* (US$60,000).[1] Diawara argues that it is best to hire
African filmmakers to make an African film because of their understanding of African audiences, the political economy of film, and the

need to support the African film industry; in addition, it is cheaper to use filmmakers from Africa than those from outside of the continent (1992). I agree with his first three points but not with his final point. At the outset of the project I explored working with a number of different Tanzanian production companies and Tanzanian crew members. However, I was not able to afford them. Of the production companies I consulted, a Tanzanian above-the-line crew would have cost three to four times the price of the travel and fees of a British crew; and the equipment would have been cost ten times the rate for equipment rental in the United Kingdom.

The price difference between Tanzanian and British crews reflects the film production industries in the two countries. The Tanzanian film industry is less diverse and significantly smaller, meaning that the cost of projects is standardized and relatively high because the sector is dependent on commercial work. In the United Kingdom the industry is much larger and diverse, meaning that the labour market is more flexible to non-commercial projects. Tanzanian production companies are predominantly engaged in commercial work for international telecommunications and food and drinks brands or with international development partners such as the United States Agency for International Development (USAID). Such contracts allow them to develop their business, but it also means that working for less on a low-budget, independent film such as *Pili* would be an unaffordable economic risk. The risk would not even be speculative, because any profit made from the film would go back to the women in the film. Therefore the same commercial rates apply. The important exception to this picture is the quickly made, low-production-value, and extremely popular Bongo industry in Tanzania (Krings and Okome 2013). While potentially more affordable, Bongo crews have less access to the type of equipment needed to make an internationally competitive film and less experience in using it. Bongo crews can be trained to use different kit; however, my project did not have the funds or time to train them. Substantively, the crew also determines access to and rental of the kit, which means that to work with a Bongo crew limits access to affordable quality kit. Thus Tanzanian production companies with experience of auteur cinema equipment and film production were too expensive to work with, and Tanzanian filmmakers in the Bongo industry lacked the experience and contacts needed to realize the ambition of the film.

British filmmakers similarly engage in commercial projects but can afford to balance these against more independent and artistic projects to develop their professional profiles. The breadth of the film industry and the strength of film training in the United Kingdom meant it was possible to secure talented and experienced filmmakers who were relatively young in the field to work on the project within budget. Feature films are the gold standard of filmmaking portfolios and give stature within the film industry; the opportunity for professionally young filmmakers to lead on them is rare. *Pili* provided an opportunity for filmmakers to work on a feature and be given a high degree of freedom over creativity and leadership in their roles.

PRODUCTION CREW

The crew for the main production of *Pili* was made up of five people from the United Kingdom (producer, director, sound recordist, director of photography, camera assistant) and four people from Tanzania (three translator–production assistants and one driver). For a feature film this is an extremely small crew, and therefore a number of the crew engaged in work beyond their standard roles and responsibilities. For example, as producer I would not normally hold the board, take notes for the director, and prepare props for scenes, and the full crew would not normally attend a meeting with local politicians. The cast and crew ate together and stayed in the same area and as a result could not avoid the minor and major issues that necessitated collective responses to ensure that the film was made. Film crews are hierarchical and follow a strict chain of command:

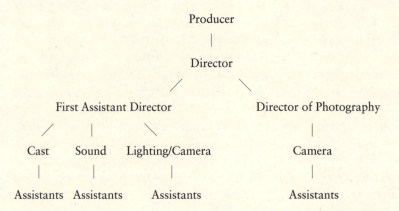

The hierarchy of a film set serves two functions. The first is order: everyone works in teams and knows their roles and responsibilities, and therefore the machine works smoothly. The second is the recognition and protection of jobs and expertise in the professional industries and the assignment of a particular wage and standing for such expertise and talent. The crew hierarchy centres upon the director: the director has to drive the film artistically and maintain communication between the production team and the cast (Goodell 1998, 223–5). The assistant directors, or director, are primarily responsible for helping the director to do this by organizing the cast and crew and ensuring that everything is set up for a shoot. Such assistant directors delegate their work to second and third assistant directors who in turn have a group of runners to support their work. Camera and sound teams are usually made up of teams of people working different cameras in support of the director of photography, and different sound recordists cover dialogue on individual microphones and boom microphones and record background soundtracks. The hierarchy of film production influences the selection of key roles. For example once a director has been hired by the producer, the director then has significant input into whom they want to work with as the director of photography and assistant director. The director of photography can then work with the production team to suggest the camera crew required.

The practice of film production begins by identifying a filmmaker with whom to work. Once I had decided that I could not afford a Tanzanian production company, I decided to work with a British filmmaker, Leanne Welham. You can find a filmmaker through word of mouth, online forums, film agents and networks, and film schools and by watching the credits of films you like, particularly those of new filmmakers at film festivals. I found my filmmaker via the Radisson Blu Hotel in Freetown, Sierra Leone. At Easter 2015 the Radisson Blu Hotel in Freetown was an ideal example of Smirl's depiction of spaces of humanitarian aid (Smirl 2015). There the informal decisions around the global response to the 2014–15 outbreak of Ebola were being made. I was in Freetown as part of a research project funded by the Marie Bashir Institute at the University of Sydney. Happy hour at the Radisson Blu bar saw a mix of people catching up on their emails and having team meetings about what they had done that day and for whom they needed to buy a drink to barter information. Like me, many of these people had arrived in Sierra Leone after the worst of the epidemic. Interspersed with the newly arrived international community combatting Ebola were middle-class Freetown families who were enjoying the pool at the weekend and aid workers who lived in the city and came to the hotel to use the good Wi-Fi. Both of these Freetown groups had seen the city through the worst of the Ebola crisis and were becoming tired of the new delegations of international agents who were fresh off the airplane to fight Ebola and researchers like me who wanted to pick apart what went wrong. One of these people was Jo Dunlop, an Australian NGO worker who wrote a blog on Sierra Leone style, *Freetown Fashpack* (Dunlop 2016). She told me about a film she was making with a talented British filmmaker and that she was looking for funds to finish the project. It was through my interest in Dunlop and post-Ebola Sierra Leone that I met Leanne. Leanne had extensive experience of working in Africa, and she was committed to Africans' telling of their own stories in their own language and style; she was unfazed at working in different environments with low budgets and had begun to make a name for herself with her short films. *Pili* would be her first feature film.

Three things changed after Leanne was signed on to the project. The first was the film, which rapidly shifted from being a documentary to being a docu-drama to being an all-out narrative feature. It was Leanne who first suggested we make a drama. Her suggestion made a lot of sense to me given my ethical concerns around the project, my experience with drama in the HIV/AIDS response, and the need for audience. The second thing to change was the producer: it became apparent that I would be the producer of the film. I had initially thought that this would be a joint enterprise in which I would contribute and have space to observe, but it soon became clear that this was not the case and that all production issues would be my responsibility. The final change was to the crew: all the above-the-line crew members – producer, director, director of photography – would be British, and all the below-the-line crew members would be Tanzanian. After signing Leanne on to the project, I visited Tanzania in November 2015 to see if there was still a possibility of collaboration with Tanzanian filmmakers as cinematographers, camera assistants, or sound recordists. However, at every stage cost was a barrier.

Once the decision had been made to work with British filmmakers, crew recruitment was relatively straightforward. I reviewed a number of suggestions and recommendations in keeping with university procurement guidelines and then had to engage in fee negotiations with agents. Agents have two interests: to obtain good work and the most money possible for their clients. Leanne recommended Craig Dean Devine as director of photography. Craig had studied at the National Film and Television School (NFTS) and at the time of production was establishing his career. *Pili* would be his second feature film. He was primarily responsible for planning with Leanne how each scene would be shot, the angle and lens of the camera, and the framing of each scene. However, in practice Craig was also responsible for the lighting, the logging and backing up of the daily rushes ("dailies"), and the editing of the stills and screen shots used for the promotion of the film.

Craig in turn recommended Gary Long as his first camera assistant. Gary provided the main support for the back-up and logging roles but was also responsible for the care of the equipment, the slate (the board), and responding to Craig's needs – for example, ensuring that the correct lens was on the camera, building the camera, and helping to frame a shot. Gary had not trained at film school but had worked his way up through the film hierarchy by working on film sets since he was sixteen years old in order to become a first camera assistant. As a consequence, he was perhaps the most experienced of the whole crew in how a film set worked in practice, as well as being the most networked crew member in the film industry. He followed the film-set hierarchy, only followed instructions from Craig, and worked within the remit of what he thought was expected of his role. Gary's position in the film industry was pivotal to sourcing high-quality kit at a low rate. In contrast to Tanzanian production companies that were able to hire out kit for commercial rates, Gary was able to leverage his work in commercial productions to get a deal on the kit for *Pili*. Camera assistants are the people who decide what kit is needed, liaise with rental companies, and ensure the safe inventory and return of the equipment. Such practical decision-making gives them power within the industry because they choose the rental companies with which to work; for example, if an international sports brand has a big budget to shoot a commercial, camera assistants have pivotal influence on which company will be awarded the contract to hire out the equipment. The high budgets of these commercials benefit the rental companies but can also inflate the costs of equipment hire, as is the case in Tanzania. Through Gary's established relationships with equipment-hire companies and the power to bring in money through commercial enterprises, he was able to negotiate a substantial discount on the rental of kit for *Pili*; a rental company would reduce the cost for *Pili*, knowing that it would recover any losses by obtaining continued contracts for commercial work with Gary.

The final UK crew member was Tom Osborn, who had been a fellow student of Craig at the NFTS. Tom managed all the sound requirements – cast microphones, boom operation, sound notes, sound storage, and additional background-sound recording. In addition to taking on all the roles of a sound unit, Tom became an indispensable handyman on set, seemingly prepared with every foreseen and unforeseen spare part needed. The sound recordist role is in many respects the most difficult. Everyone with whom I discussed the production process stressed the importance of sound because it is not something that can be easily fixed in post-production (Artis 2008). When sound is done well, no one notices; when sound is done badly, it can ruin a film. Tom navigated without complaint the myriad of challenges he faced as a sound recordist: a cast member whispering, wind, chickens, babies screaming, bars playing loud music over dialogue, and shooting day for night.

The Tanzanian crew did not have a background in film production but worked in the NGO sector. I had known the production assistant and driver "Ally"[2] for eight years through his work with a local NGO in Bagamoyo. Ally recommended a co-worker, "Rose," as an additional assistant.[3] The project-specific nature of NGO financing meant that Ally and Rose were between projects and therefore had time to work on the film. Rose was coming back from maternity leave, and Ally told me he had just finished a large project for one donor and was awaiting future funding. The final production assistant, Ansity Noel, was recommended by another NGO worker; she was a trained lawyer between internships at a law firm and the United Nations in Dar es Salaam. The production driver, "Michael,"[4] was recommended to me by a politician in the local community where *Pili* was shot. He worked odd jobs in the community and had been looking for driving work for some time. The NGO sector may have been an unlikely source for film assistants: however, in Tanzania NGO workers tend to be well educated with a proficient use of English and Swahili and well networked to assist with the local production needs.

Fig. 2 Sophie Harman and Ansity Noel entering the Miono care and treatment centre to meet with doctors and key workers, 2015. Ansity was a pivotal member of the crew throughout the production and remains the main contact between Sophie and the women in the film.

During the majority of the production process there were only two assistants at one time. The primary role of the assistants was translation. However, increasingly as the production went on, they were vital in assisting me in explaining and assessing informed consent; recruiting extras; liaising with the owners of specific locations; arranging all meals; booking accommodation for the cast members when they were staying away from home; helping to identify local carpenters, security guards, and farmers; and engaging in a whole range of miscellaneous activity. Ansity and Rose particularly excelled in these roles and, despite having no film experience, rapidly adapted to the key requirements and established a good working relationship with the female cast members. The latter role was and remains the most important. I was worried about the class dynamics between the Tanzanian cast and crew as most of the cast were working class, living at the extreme of poverty, and translators such as Rose and Ansity were evidently richer, middle-class women from

Dar es Salaam; this was evident in how they dressed, their education, and their hairstyles. In practice this did not matter so much; the women in the cast were open with Ansity and warmed to Rose, and, if anything, it was the cast who ordered and looked down on the crew, insisting on food to a certain specification – one actor would not eat a *chips mayai* (chips omelette) with less than four eggs; another would only eat chips in the evening. As a Swahili and English speaker, Ansity remains my direct contact to the women in the film. All the women in the film have my contact details and were made aware they could use them at any time.

Michael was a driver and fixer combined; he knew everyone in the community from the local politicians to the bus drivers. He worked closely with the production assistants to help source large and small props and confirm locations. In one instance, Michael entertained a bar of drinkers for three hours with stories so that we could shoot a scene across the road without the disruption of loud music. Michael drove an old Toyota Noah. The Noah changed depending on the week: as I was paying him a total fee for his labour and care rental, he tried to make more money by saving on the cost and quality of the car rental. Noah number one functioned adequately except for the faulty air conditioning; Noah number two had no air conditioning or seat belts. When I complained that we needed seat belts otherwise he would not be paid, we were introduced to Noah number three. Noah number three was an homage to the Tanzanian football team Young Africans, or Yanga, and was therefore covered in conspicuous bright yellow and green colours. Michael was very popular with the cast and crew because of his resourcefulness, his play acting with the crew, and his commitment to the project and the people in his community. Michael was the only crew member to be with Leanne and me throughout pre-production and the main production.

Crew members were paid differently depending on their level of expertise, role, and responsibility on the project. This difference was based on skilled labour and time spent on the project, and there was no distinction between British and Tanzanian crew members. The UK crew members had their accommodation costs paid for during the production, whereas some of the Tanzanian crew did and some did not, depending on the contract agreed at the outset of the project. As chapter 4 explores in further detail, this difference generated problems. During the production process, the fees and expenses of some Tanzanian members of the crew were in constant and everyday negotiation, with requests for advances, extra money, extra meal expenses, and non-agreed per diems and with contestation over the changing cost of petrol.

The labels and normative hierarchies of film crews shaped how the crew members and I were seen in the co-production process. I was uncomfortable in the position of producer – because of the mundanity and unpleasantness of everyday dispute settlement, the hierarchy in being seen as the boss of the project, and the role of being reduced to the person who pays for things – rather than a co-producer. I initially saw such hierarchies as running contrary to the aims and intent of the project and as being somewhat daft given the size of the crew and how we worked: the crew members were highly skilled in their respective jobs; however, the production itself was low budget, unpolished, and make-do. Nevertheless, the perceived hierarchy among the crew also created a more transparent and clear acknowledgment of how seeing works and how knowledge is produced and reinforces itself in the world. It is not a reflection of the project's intent but of the means and structures of seeing. The challenge thus became not how to create a film set devoid of hierarchy, which would be impossible because hierarchy would always be latent, informal, and hidden even if it were denied, but how to progress and create co-produced knowledge *within* a hierarchical system and *without* exacerbating inequalities that stop women such as Pili from seeing and being seen.

PRE-PRODUCTION: THE STORY AND THE CAST

It is one thing to want to make a film to see women and their everyday experiences of HIV/AIDS; it is another for those women to want to be seen and for their involvement to be based on a reciprocal and productive relationship. Engaging women to be involved in the film was a three-stage process: the first stage was to identify who would be involved in the co-production, to introduce the project, and to listen to stories; the second stage was to sketch out the overarching story of the film and refine and test it with the women; the third stage was to co-identify who could act and wanted to act and to build some of the characters around their personalities. As this section will explore, informed consent and the potential for withdrawal were discussed at each of these stages. The three stages established the foundation for the co-produced element of the project and were the formal aspects of the ways in which the diverse knowledges combined to make the story of the film.

As outlined in the introduction, the book uses the collective term *the women* to refer to the groups of women from Mbwewe, Miono, and Bagamoyo who were involved in the co-production of the story and the casting processes. The *cast* refers to the specific group of women involved in the main production of the film.

Stage 1: Introductions, Trust, and Finding the Story

Co-production requires an established relationship with the people one is working with, reciprocal benefits to both parties, and a shared understanding of what the project is about. Prior to my first introductory meeting in November 2015, I had not met the majority of the women involved in the project. My introduction to these women and the success of the co-production of *Pili* depended on the networks and existing relationships that I had established over ten years in the Pwani region of Tanzania through my work with the NGO Trans Tanz. This work gave me both the formal introductions that were necessary to address the bureaucratic requirements of the Tanzanian state and the informal networks that would be pivotal in establishing trust with both the women working on the film and the communities in which the film was based.

I established Trans Tanz alongside a group of friends in 2006 as a direct consequence of my doctoral fieldwork on the relationship between the World Bank and civil society organizations in the HIV/AIDS response in Kenya, Uganda, and Tanzania. Over the course of my fieldwork in 2005–06 I began to witness how, despite an increase in the financing of treatment and care, many people living with HIV/AIDS were unable to access treatment. The health centres and clinics where people living with HIV/AIDS would receive voluntary testing and counselling, CD4 tests, and anti-retroviral drugs were at considerable distances from where they lived. People did not have accessible modes of transportation to get there or could not afford to travel. On some days the clinics would have long queues or depleted stocks. For the majority of people living in rural parts of East Africa, accessing treatment was costly and time consuming. In my encounters with communities living between 10 km and 50 km from care and treatment centres, few people living with the disease were taking the anti-retrovirals that would keep them healthy and alive. People were dying in their homes, with support from family and neighbours.

Working in IR rather than public health at this time, I knew little about health-system strengthening and its wider debates and politics. Instead of reading more about this issue or reflecting on my own position as a British researcher working in East Africa, I discussed the problem with friends and doctors in Tanzania and the United Kingdom and decided to establish a charitable organization that would raise funds in the United Kingdom to pay for a bus to transport people living with HIV/AIDS in rural Tanzania to clinics for treatment and support. Trans Tanz was registered in both countries in the summer of 2006 and started full operations in early 2007 (Trans Tanz n.d.). We set up operations in Pwani under guidance from the Tanzanian government. Pwani was selected by the government because it is not far from Dar es Salaam – which made central government oversight easier – and the region was the home of the then president Jakaya Kikwete (2005–15). When Trans Tanz first began operations, there was only one care and treatment centre in the whole region, in Bagamoyo; ten years later, the pace and funds allocated to the HIV/AIDS response have resulted in the opening of new centres in Chalinze, Miono, Mbwewe, and Kwarumbo. Since 2007, Trans Tanz has formally supported 150 people a month in their access to anti-retroviral treatment; in 2018 this number increased to 350. In so doing, it has supported the prevention of mother-to-child transmission and helped people to live longer. Trans Tanz was initially intended to be a stand-alone project that, while informed by my research, would be distinct from my research and academic work. However, it has continued to shape my thinking on global health and the impact of global policy-making on everyday lives.

In the initial stages of research design (i.e., pre-production), the trustees and project manager were consulted on the proposed involvement of Trans Tanz. The organization would be used as a basis for me to introduce my plans to the communities in Pwani and to the local health workers in the region. The trustees reviewed and approved my risk assessment (outlining the potential risk to participants in the film and risks to the operations of the organization and to the service users) with the caveat that, if the film uncovered something controversial about the organization, I would inform them first so that they could both address the issue and prepare a formal response. In addition, I would uphold the potential for any participants to withdraw from the project if they so desired, in line with my preliminary ethics application, and would reinforce the understanding that their non-participation or withdrawal from the film would have no impact on their ability to use Trans Tanz's services.

Trans Tanz allowed me to introduce myself to the new district medical officer of the Pwani region and to doctors working in the care and treatment centres in Miono and Mbwewe on the basis of my ten-year history of working in the region. Such history and who you know and with whom you have worked is fundamental to establishing trust in Tanzania. Hence, while I may have been new to some of the health professionals, my knowledge of the region, the health system, and the experiences of people living with HIV/AIDS and my record of sustained engagement through Trans Tanz provided an initial entry-level of trust. The doctors in the care and treatment centres knew the work of the organization and therefore had a degree of understanding that I would do as I said I would. The district medical officers (the person in this role changed twice over the one year in which we made *Pili*) were not necessarily familiar with the work of Trans Tanz but were too embarrassed or polite to say so, and they nodded assent to the idea that I had been working in the region for a long time and therefore could be trusted. My relationship to Trans Tanz was the foundation on which those working in the health sector would support the project; it gave me a formal introduction (through letters and registration of the organization in Tanzania) and showed that I had informal networks and a ten-year history of work in the area, and was therefore committed, and that the film would potentially have monetary benefits for the community should it succeed.

My entry point to the community in Miono was the employees of Trans Tanz and affiliated volunteers. The Tanzanian project manager, Zephania, and the driver of the Trans Tanz bus, "Julius,"[5] were supportive of the project and keen to assist. They were informed at the outset of the project that their assistance or lack thereof would have no impact or effect on their employment by Trans Tanz. Zephania had worked as a project manager for six years, and Julius had been the driver for nine years. Zephania lived in Dar es Salaam and visited the project once a month to talk to the people using the bus, meet with the doctors, and ensure that Julius was paid and that everything was running as planned. In contrast, Julius lived and worked in the communities in which Trans Tanz operated. He knew everyone and had built relationships with local politicians not only for his work with Trans Tanz but also for his volunteering of time and money to help those in need. It was through Julius that I was able to meet the women who would inform the story of *Pili* and to gain their trust. I already knew some of the local peer educators who worked with the care and treatment centres to support people newly diagnosed with HIV, educated the community to promote understanding of HIV/AIDS and reduce stigma, and generally volunteered to help out where the doctors needed them. However, it was through Julius's networks and contacts that Leanne and I were introduced to the women involved in co-producing the film.

Director Leanne and I met over eighty women from Pwani who had responded to Julius's call for interest. During a two-week period in November–December 2015 we introduced the project to these women and heard their stories. We met them in three large groups in the main community centre in Miono, the office of an NGO in Bagamoyo, or a community building next to the care and treatment centre in Mbwewe. The women attended these meetings because Julius had told them that there was someone interested in making a film about their lives and who wanted to know if they would participate. They were also paid a small fee for their attendance. Each meeting followed the same basic structure: I introduced myself, Leanne, and the two translators who were working with us; I then introduced the project and told them why I wanted to make it, how it would work, and how they could potentially be involved; and I explained that the film was different from most films in that the consent forms they signed were to protect them and give them rights, rather than to take their rights away. I also took time to carefully explain the potential issues or downsides to being involved: potential stigma, people thinking that the women would become rich because they were working with a white woman, and the women not wanting to share their story with a local or international audience. This process was pivotal to establishing informed consent at the outset of the project.

Once I had introduced the project, I suggested that those who were not interested or who were previously unaware of the purpose of the meeting should leave. At this stage no one left, because they wanted to either hear more or share their story. To warm up each group I asked them some general questions about their lives and everyday experiences of living with HIV/AIDS. After the group conversations we invited those who were interested to stay and share their stories with us individually, and, again, anyone who did not want to do this could leave. Leanne and I then sat with women individually and a translator to listen to their life stories. We asked them general questions about their family (e.g., the number of children and grandchildren they had), their interests (e.g., music), and what they did or did not like about where they lived. Some of the women spoke at length, and some for as little as fifteen minutes. It was through a combination of the group feedback and individual stories that we were able to identify a general picture of the shared experiences of the women, particularly those from Mbwewe and Miono. Most of the women worked in the *shamba* (fields), engaged in physical farming, were HIV positive, and were mothers, and in some instances grandmothers, and many had been left by their partners or, as they described it, were "left ones." As work in the shamba was seasonal and informal, they were often left in a precarious position and found it hard to pay for basic necessities such as food or school uniforms. Life in Miono and Mbwewe was particularly hard. A number of women had health issues in addition to managing their HIV status. They worked long hours and then had to care for their children and family members. They appreciated the togetherness of some of the support groups they had formed and enjoyed the opportunity to watch television, but such opportunities were infrequent as they depended on the women having free time and knowing someone with a television and electricity. The women did not have hobbies, because they did not have any spare time outside of the paid work in the shamba and the unpaid work in the home. One resounding feature of these stories was that if the women just had some small money to be able to start their own business, things would perhaps get better: they would have autonomy of their labour, be able to keep their earnings, and be able to do something more sustainable than the hard work of the shamba. The obstacles to this were significant: capital, bureaucracy, patriarchy, education, and opportunity. The obstacles also spoke to the wider socio-economic risk that shaped the lives of women living with HIV/AIDS in low-income countries, as first presented in the introduction (Anderson 2015). The lives they depicted were similar to the lives of Tanzanian women depicted in feminist research from the 1980s and 1990s: informal, "tedious and time consuming" (Nkhoma, Muro, et al 1993, 7) physical labour in the shamba; less earnings than those of men for the same work, lack of access to resources to start one's own business, and walks of long distances to access work, food, and health care and to sell their produce (Mbilinyi 1986; Nkhoma, Muro, et al 1993).

The women in Bagamoyo had slightly different lives than those in Miono and Mbwewe. They were richer, and most did not work in the shamba but had a small business of the kind that the Miono and Mbwewe women hoped for. The women in Bagamoyo looked healthier, having benefited from a higher income, more regular meals, and a more advanced hospital and care and treatment centre in their town. Bagamoyo is also only one hour away from the centre of Dar es Salaam, so accessing more advanced treatment and employment is manageable. Leanne and I considered basing the story in Bagamoyo given the relatively practical ease of shooting there and the interesting locations. However, it was clear that the more urgent and human stories were to be found in the rural areas of Miono and Mbwewe. Those women were more isolated from the basic services to be found in Tanzanian society, and, as such, their stories were the ones that would go unseen. Bagamoyo life was familiar to a large number of Tanzanians, particularly politicians and NGOs, and therefore was often represented in depictions of the HIV/AIDS response in the country. Leanne and I therefore decided to work with the women in Miono and Mbwewe to tell the story of the life of an HIV-positive woman who was working in the shamba, looking after her children alone as a left one, and having hopes and ambitions for life.

Stage 2: Testing the Story

Leanne and I collated the stories and the recurrent themes that came from our meetings to sketch out the story for the film. We did this, eating the popular street food of *chips mayaii* at the side of the main road that runs from Tanga to Dar es Salaam in Mbwewe. We agreed that the story would be set over four days in the life of the main character, Pili. Pili would be a left one – a single mother of two children who is HIV positive and working in the shamba, with the ambition to have a small business as a means of getting a better life. At the start of the film Pili would have the opportunity to set up her own business, a small market stall. However, to realize this opportunity she would have to raise money for the deposit while managing her own health. She self-stigmatizes about her HIV status, does not take her anti-retroviral treatment regularly, and has run out of medication. We follow the agency of Pili as she tries to change her life and comes up against barriers to effect change, such as government bureaucracy, disease stigma, and an overburdened health system. Underpinning these barriers are structural issues of gender inequality, state gatekeeping, and bureaucracy and problems of informal labour and employment. The film builds the tension with every day as Pili encounters new barriers and risks and has to compromise as she tries to get what she wants, at risk to her health and the wellbeing of those around her. The character Pili would not be based on one woman, such as the real Pili whose life I detail in the introduction to this book, but would be the summation of the lives of the left ones who had shared their stories with us.

Film that focuses on content and the themes of international development and politics has been criticized for focusing on agency and individuals rather than addressing the wider structural determinants of poverty (Lewis, Rodgers, et al. 2014, 125). Leanne and I were acutely conscious of representing the lives of the women who had shared their stories and of not falling into instrumentalist tropes on agency that depict an unfortunate hero who overcomes the odds in order to succeed. A film on this basis would not reflect the lives of the women with whom we were working. Capturing and explaining structural drivers of poverty and inequality is a challenge for storytelling because dramatic films tend to follow individual narratives. There is a clear reason for this: people are interested in the stories and dramas of people's lives, and the personalizing explanations of seemingly dry issues – how a woman accesses health care – make such issues a lived experience that may (or may not) evoke a response in the viewer. Stories require protagonists to drive the drama or communicate the themes that are explored. However, the use of individual narratives when one explores issues of international development such as HIV/AIDS and rural poverty opens such stories to the instrumentalist trap. The instrumentalist trap suggests that, regardless of the structures of inequality that limit the everyday choices and experiences of the lives of women living in rural Pwani, these women have a resilience that will allow them to pull themselves and their families out of poverty. This trap is heavily gendered within international policy practice (Chant 2006; Ferguson and Harman 2015; Griffin 2006; Razavi 2012). Our intent for *Pili* was to challenge this agency-based narrative and instead explore the classic relationship in international politics between agency and structure – agency being the ability of an individual to act and effect change, and structure being the structures of society that limit, curtail, or enhance such agency.

The structures of poverty and development frame the drama and narrative of the film. The film is driven by the lead character, Pili, and the action shows how she encounters, bends, and jumps the structures of her everyday life. The film is arranged around three dominant structures of power. The first is the gendered structure in which Pili finds herself as a working single parent living with HIV. We see her balancing the competing responsibilities of productive employment and social reproduction with her family and wider community. The burden of such responsibilities has direct consequences for how she cares for herself and her health. The second structure of power concerns the state and the global politics of the health system. This structure relates to the everyday burden, boredom, and time involved in accessing treatment for HIV and to the stigma and shame that these can bring. The final power structure is that of the informal agrarian cash economy in which Pili works, and her ambition for autonomy and ownership of her labour. This was a consistent theme among the women engaged in preparing the story of the film and in doing feminist work in Tanzania (Mbilinyi 1986; Nkhoma, Muro, et al. 1993); most women engaged in the project stated that their main ambition was to own a small business as a means of earning more money and sustaining themselves and their families. While the women may not have depicted these social forces in the language of structural determinants, power, or agency; they all had acute awareness of the existence of these structures and how they shaped their lives, and they consistently brought them up when sharing their stories. The cycles of inequality and the way these structures permeate and reproduce themselves are represented by Pili and her social circle.

After Leanne and I had sketched out the main story spine, we tested it with a select group of women in Miono and a larger group of women in Bagamoyo to ensure that we had reflected their stories accurately, to test some of the difficult sections, and to get feedback and input on the minutiae of Pili's life. For example, we wanted to know how much they would receive for a day's work in the fields, how much a deposit for a market stall and the subsequent rent would be, and how *vikoba* (micro-lending village community bank) groups and tax systems worked. Our main concern was, Would this happen in real life? Is it realistic? We asked these questions at the outset of testing the story and throughout the main production, establishing a position that, if something did not sit right or felt unrealistic, the women in the film would let us know. This was a tricky balance because in general the women with whom we were working were keen to agree or say that something was fine. Working with the women, we learned to ask specific, rather than general, questions; for example, instead of saying, "Would this happen?" we would ask, "What would you do if you had the choice between [x] or [y]?" In the initial assessment of the story a common response we had from the women was, "Yes, it happens." This was positive because it was what we wanted to hear; however, we wanted to know what else might happen in particular circumstances, notably with the big decision that Pili has to make at the end of the film. When we discussed the decision and what Pili would do, the women asked a lot of questions, and as a group we explored why she might choose to decide one option or why she might not. This discussion focused on risk, the decisions women have to make when they are HIV positive, how these decisions affect other people, and the circumstances some women have had to confront. It was through joint discussion that we were able to explore the issue and the local realities of the choices that women like them had to make. The reality of the situation and the circumstances meant that we decided to challenge the audience and position Pili less as a member of the "deserving poor" and more as someone who had to make difficult decisions and compromises to get what she wanted.

There were three parts of the story of which I was unsure. The first was the involvement of children. The initial plan for the project was not to involve children because this required additional ethical safeguards that could be difficult to navigate. From a practical point of view and following guidance from my university's research ethics committee, I was keen to keep children out of the film or to minimize their inclusion as much as possible. However, to make a film about the everyday risk of HIV/AIDS in Tanzania without children would have been unrealistic and missing an important component of social reproduction and responsibility and a key story device as to why Pili takes the risk she does for the future of her children. To exclude children from the film would have completely misrepresented the lives of women such as Pili; children were everywhere, and the majority of women we met were mothers.

Fig. 3 The first meeting with women in Miono to explain the project and hear their stories, 2015.

Involvement of children in the project required a re-engagement with the ethical processes of the research. My university research ethics committee and I were concerned about how the children would be seen (as HIV positive) and about their inability to give informed consent. The committee initially suggested blurring their faces; however, this would not work in the style of this film. The compromise was to minimize the involvement of key child characters as much as possible and reduce the screen time of any other children. Their characters would not be HIV positive, and it would be clear that they were playing a role. Pili would have two children, a son and a daughter, and they would be the only main parts for children in the film. The children who played the son and daughter were the children of two cast members. This made sense practically because the cast had been fully briefed about the intent and proposed outcome of the film, which suggested a more thorough understanding of consent to their participation than if we had worked with children whose parents were not involved with the film; also, the cast had an established relationship with the children.

The compromise to include children in the film in a way that limited their exposure created the main tension of collaboration with non-academics in the pre-production, production, and post-production of the film. During the pre-production I asked Leanne to remove several scenes from the screenplay that involved children. For Leanne these scenes were integral to the development of Pili's character and tension in the story; therefore, for each scene I had to argue why it should be cut and restate the ethical compromise for the decision. Leanne initially suggested that the scenes stay and we then cut in the edit; however, foreseeing a problem, I maintained my position, and these scenes were removed. We had a similar discussion during the post-production of the film when extra scenes and close-up shots of children appeared in the first cut. The issue here was close-ups of actors who played Pili's children, extra children of the actors (whom I did not have consent to include), and, of most concern, children in school uniform in one of the HIV/AIDS care and treatment clinics. In the case of one scene, one child whom we did not have consent to show obscures their mother who is delivering a sensitive and compelling performance. It was a source of understandable frustration that such scenes had to be edited to exclude the children or cut entirely. For other scenes, faces were blurred or darkened in the grade process so that they could not be identified.

Compromises as to how children would be included in the film created additional tensions with the cast. The shooting schedule had been organized around school times to ensure that the children's education would not be directly affected by the film. However, as the production progressed, it became increasingly clear that some children did not attend school or, if they did, it was on an ad hoc basis. One of the production assistants reprimanded the family for this because primary education is free in Tanzania, and I had to stop the assistant from doing so. This created a tension between the assistant and senior family members, and between me and the assistant. Talking to the family members with a different production assistant, I discovered that the children did not attend school because they were ashamed of their worn-out uniforms and lack of books. They did not want to tell me because they were understandably proud of their family and felt embarrassed.

Aside from the issue of child inclusion, my second reservation was the inclusion of a micro-lending group from which Pili would try to secure a loan. Vikoba groups were common in Miono and Mbwewe, and the majority of women to whom we spoke about the story were either members of such a group or familiar with them and how they worked. The women tended to view them positively, thinking that they were a good opportunity in which to realize their wider ambition of starting small businesses. I was uneasy with this because of the wider debate in research on international development about the efficacy of micro-lending (Hulme and Arun 2009; S. Johnson 2005; Parmar 2003; The World Bank 2015). While aware of the transformative potential of such groups and how common they are in low- and middle-income countries, I was also aware of the cycles of debt that they introduce to local economies and the limited returns on investment. In including the vikoba as a source of money for Pili, I did not want the film to be used as an advocate of such lending. I was overruled by the women: vikoba groups were a common part of their life, and they believed that these groups did have the capacity to help them realize a different life. They believed that small loans could make a difference and that it was through small enterprise that they could make money to improve their lives. The vikoba groups therefore remained and became a pivotal part of the story in which both my concerns and the women's interests were reflected.

The third part I was unsure of was how isolated Pili would be – living alone, a single mother, keeping secrets. Although being a "left one" was common among the stories we heard from the women, few people are ever alone in the communities in which the film is based. Most people live in compounds with, or at least near, extended families or kinship networks. We would therefore have to balance a sense of isolation against a sense of community and solidarity among family and female networks that is apparent throughout Miono and Mbwewe. To address this we developed characters who tried to engage and care for Pili, but we also explored how such community links might make an individual want to seek greater privacy. The wider characters of the film, notably Ana, Sekejua, and Zuhura, would be pivotal in exploring friendship, solidarity, and the question of privacy in the film.

The priority of the film was for the story to show the lives of the women from Miono and Mbwewe; therefore, their preferences took precedent over my concerns. Discussing potential reservations or different views gave depth to the wider story. It was not one dimensional but combined the women's knowledge of their lived experience and everyday engagement with structures of poverty, gender, and health systems, my own knowledge drawn from academic research, and received wisdom on such experiences. In addition, with Leanne's ability to construct a narrative drama screenplay from this story, the co-production led to a story based on local and global knowledge in a way that would be accessible and of interest to both Tanzanian and global audiences. The stories and knowledge shared by the women involved with the film reveal empirical insight about the practical political realities of health systems, the medicalization of health security, micro-lending, social reproduction, informal labour, and bureaucratization of the local. Their lives are situated within wider structures of the international, from complex donor relationships that pay for the anti-retroviral drugs they access, to the pharmaceutical companies that produce them, to the ideas that originated in Bangladesh that are adopted for local-based lending. Security is immediate – food, health, existence – and contested through a range of gender norms. All aspects of the international can be seen as being applied and contested among such women and within such communities. The story of *Pili* is thus based on the lives of the women we met, triangulated with the findings of my previous research on the feminization of HIV/AIDS and global health (Harman 2011a, 2012a). The formation of the story is the first part of the method of seeing. Two quotes from one of the women from Miono, Sesilia, came to define and shape the co-production of the project during the initial story formation: "Pili is everywhere," and "We are with you."

Once the story had been tested and refined with the women, Leanne wrote the screenplay for the film. It underwent three drafts in response to feedback from filmmakers and academic colleagues. The screenplay was translated into Swahili by two of the production assistants and then circulated to all the main cast prior to the shoot. One week prior to production Leanne and I met and discussed the script with the cast. It became apparent that the majority of the cast could not read. When given the script, a number of the cast just stared at it and shifted uncomfortably in their seats, nodding along to what Leanne was saying through one of the production assistants. During the production those who could read became overwhelmed, thinking about their lines and what they had to say, rather than acting out the lines themselves. As a consequence we reassured the cast members that they could improvise the scenes with their own language, and we would leave them the scripts so that they familiarize themselves with them. This was both to reassure and to avoid any embarrassment caused by the cast's admission that they were struggling with the text.

In practice, Leanne worked with the cast and production assistants to talk through each scene prior to shooting and to suggest the key phrases they had to say to ensure that the narrative flowed.

The production assistants worked to ensure that the actors said the key phrases and to translate between the cast and crew. For lead actors, this worked well because they quickly and easily adapted and picked up direction. Some of the cast adapted to improvisation with confidence; others took more time to adjust to having the camera surround their conversations. The difference in language, confidence, and reading ability could be seen as a barrier to the production of the film; in practice it made the work more difficult, but it also strengthened the quality and authenticity of the film and what the viewer sees. The unscripted feeling of the characters elicited some of the most emotive performances and became one of the core strengths of the film.

Stage 3: Casting

The third stage of co-production was the casting of the film and the development of the other characters who would be pivotal in explaining some of the wider themes of the story. With the exception of Bello Rashid, who plays Pili, the main female cast was drawn from the groups of women with whom we had met to consult on the story. Sixty-five per cent of the total cast identified themselves to Leanne and me as HIV positive. We do not disclose which cast members are HIV positive. The characters developed in the story were based on either the people who played them or a theme or person living in the wider community. Leanne, a core group of women from Miono who had been involved in the story testing, and I collaborated on the casting; as director, Leanne had the final call on casting decisions. The core group of women helped to consult on who would be suitable for what part, to identify any potential cast members whom we had not met, and to recruit recommended friends and family as extras. Extras and smaller parts were often decided on the day of shooting as needed.

Pili was the last role to be cast. Unlike the other characters, the actor who played Pili had to drive the story, show emotional range, give an honest performance, take direction, and have a face that would connect with audiences. The actor had to look young enough but also to have a face that suggested experience and a drive to take risks. Pili was therefore the most difficult and important role to cast. Bello, who plays Pili, was cast on the penultimate day of Leanne's and my preparatory research trip to Tanzania in 2015. She attended an acting workshop with her sister and some of

Fig. 4 Neema Juma, Ansity Noel, and Bello Rashid at an acting workshop in
Miono on the first day we met Bello, 2015.

the other women who had already been cast in the film. Up to that
point we had met women who could take direction to act but did
not look the part (usually too old) or who looked the part but were
less confident or able to take direction. During the workshop it
became clear that Bello could take direction, could act, had a compelling face, had emotional range, and was clever. She picked up
direction quickly and understood what was required of her. We did
not know much about her life, only that she lived with her family
in a shared compound, was a single mother, worked in the shamba,
and ran a small tea shop with the rest of her family. Her ambition
was to become a nurse, and she wanted to be in the film to tell the
story of women from Miono and to use the experience to explore
different opportunities for her future. Other than these points, I
knew little about Bello; she was the one woman with whom we
worked the most, but she was also the most private of them all.
It was more luck than systematic scouting that Bello attended the
workshop and was subsequently cast in the role of Pili.

Bello's sister Sikujua Rashid was cast as "Zuhura," Pili's friend in the shamba. The character of Zuhura has to represent the change in Pili's life and the cycle of poverty and inequality. The beginning of the film depicts Pili as the left one; the end of the film makes it clear that Zuhura is the left one and that there are Pilis and Zuhuras everywhere. Zuhura has to make Pili and the audience confront their feelings about what Pili has risked and achieved and how the lives of the women in the film continue. Sikujua was one of the first women we met who shared her story with us. Like many of the women, she had lived in Miono her whole life alongside her extended family and worked in the shamba. Her name loosely translates to "I didn't know," as in "I didn't know I was pregnant." She has four children – three sons and a daughter – and was living as a single parent, but the father of her children would intermittently come back into her life. Sikujua told us that her life was hard, the ability to feed her children depended on how well the work in the fields was going, and she had a number of problems. She could not afford the basic necessities for her children, her roof leaked, and she had family medical bills she needed to pay. She said she would regularly go to bed hungry. We had initially explored the possibility of Sikujua playing the lead of Pili; however she was visibly relieved when we suggested the role be played by her younger sister, Bello.

The character of "Cecilia" is the only part to be named after the woman who plays her (on her request), Sesilia Florian Kilimila. Sesilia also had attended the first meeting in Miono and was noticeable as one of the women who asked the most questions about the project and fully engaged with what the film would be about and what the women would get out of it. At forty-two years of age, Sesilia was older than some of the other women. She was a single mother of four children, and a grandmother. Unlike most of the women, Sesilia was head of her household, farmed her own land, and sold produce at the local market. She was financially independent, was able to support herself and her young son, and acted as a mentor for other women in how to set up their own business. It was clear that a number of the women deferred to her on a range of issues. The character of Cecilia is important in showing that Pili is not isolated or alone but has people supporting her in the community in which she lives. Cecilia characterizes female solidarity, warmth, and care; the feminization of HIV/AIDS; and progress in living positively with HIV. Sesilia the actor was also an important intermediary between the women in the film and me. As someone independent of a man, an owner of land, and a local peer educator on a range of issues, she was respected and trusted. She became a spokesperson for the women, particularly when I was not in Tanzania, and I could trust her to question something or raise a complaint or problem, as she had done from the outset of the project.

In addition to acting as a spokesperson for the women involved in the film, Sesilia was useful in discussing casting choices with Leanne and me. Two key characters that Sesilia helped to cast were "Leila," the head of the micro-lending vikoba group, and "Ana," a peer educator and local gossip. I had had the idea for Ana in my mind for a long time, having observed the work of HIV/AIDS peer educators in various care and treatment centres over ten years. These volunteers provide an important service to the global HIV/AIDS response, often for free or for a small per diem to cover a meal and transportation to and from the clinic. They can be identified by their proximity to the clinic registrars or doctors and by the free HIV/AIDS T-shirts given to them by the NGOs that provide their training. They are a wealth of knowledge on how clinics function and who attends them, and they want to be involved in any conversation. It had always struck me that such volunteers also had the potential to use this information as power or exchange in the community, or, in other words, to gossip. This is not meant to denigrate the importance of their work or to suggest that they are not sensitive to stigma and the needs of people living with HIV/AIDS. However, their role posed a conundrum: here was a disease that many would want to keep secret; yet the people there to help them both wanted to encourage openness and acceptance and lived in the same community. Ana would be the worst realization of this conundrum: she would be a peer educator who was kind and wanted to help Pili, but she also could not help but gossip. Ana would challenge the problem of secrecy in a close-knit community and would also provide light relief and humour within the film. Siwazurio Mchuka was cast in the role of Ana one week before the main shoot. Leanne and I discussed with Sesilia and then the wider group the possibility of Siwazurio playing the part, and it was unanimous among the group that she was perfect for the role. Siwazurio was excellent at improvisation and comic timing.

The character of Leila represents the bureaucracy and gatekeeping of the modern Tanzanian state. Leila was created at the same time as the production encountered increased levels of bureaucracy

Fig. 5 Leanne Welham, Sesilia Floran Kilimila, and Bello Rashid at an acting workshop in Miono, 2015.

and gatekeeping by the Tanzanian state (explored in more detail in chapter 4); the greater the barriers created by government agencies, the more Leila's character took shape. Leila is the head of the vikoba micro-lending group from which Pili tries to get a loan. She sets up consistent barriers to the loan, highlighting the need for procedure, hierarchy, rules, and reciprocity. She bends the rules only because of the patronage of the character Cecilia and her relationship to Pili. This role had to represent the everyday barriers to setting up a business and the risk taken on by individual women in securing such loans. Not only did this address my reservation about the inclusion of micro-lending, as discussed earlier in the chapter, but it also explored the day-to-day grind and the way in which actors have to go around the gate when bureaucracy results in gatekeepers and gatekeeping. The part of Leila is played by Mwanaidi Omari Sefi. Mwanaidi has the gravitas of a senior woman in the community with a lifetime of experience and knowledge. However, I was initially hesitant to cast her in the role because of her positivity and tendency to laugh all the time. Sesilia assured me that she was ideal for the role, and, when we discussed the part, Mwanaidi rapidly adjusted her facial expressions to stern and serious. During the production she was living with her brother, preferred not to remarry, and sold produce from a small plot of land that she farmed with her family. She told me that she had acted in Bagamoyo when she was younger and loved to dance. She also told me that she would do anything we asked for the film because she believed that the film could help the women and people living with HIV in Miono to tell their story.

The film, for the most part, is marked by the absence of men. This absence reflects what the women told us. The role of male characters had to strike a balance between what the women told us about the men in their lives and their experience of living in a highly patriarchal society, and at the same time not contribute to the essentialist and often racialized metaphors about African men being hyper-sexualized, polygamous, uncaring patriarchs (Stillwaggon 2003). *Pili* explores how patriarchy and gender underpin many of the problems and issues driving the structural determinants of HIV/AIDS. However, in the same way, not all women living with HIV/AIDS are virtuous victims, and not all men are hyper-sexualized, irresponsible, and unconcerned for the rights of women. It was important therefore not to homogenize the male characters, in the same way that we did not want to homogenize the female characters.

The patriarchy and tensions between gender and HIV/AIDS are represented by "Mahela," the field manager, by the men who occupy the public spaces in the film as drivers and vendors, and crucially by the absence of men from the central narrative. The main male character, Mahela, uses his power – drawn from relative wealth, community reputation, and gender – over Pili to compromise her agency. Mahela is a controversial character but, according to the women whom we engaged on the story, not uncommon. Mahela is the only character in the film played by a trained actor, Nkwabi Elias Ng'angasamala, who is famous in Tanzania for his role in *Siri ya Mtungi* and for his work with the Bagamoyo Arts and Cultural Institute, TASUBA. It was a difficult decision to cast Nkwabi because Leanne and I had wanted the cast to be 100 per cent real people from the community. However, this casting was important for two reasons: we needed someone with experience and the required range to deliver the performance of a character who changes in a subtle yet powerful way, and, more important, as a trained actor from

Bagamoyo, Nkwabi had the distance from the women and community in Miono. Even though Bello was playing Pili, we wanted to avoid any accusations of her playing herself or misunderstandings to that end. Having a well-known trained actor helped reinforce to the community that it was not Bello the actor, but Pili the character, making these compromises or choices; that the story was a drama. On set, Nkwabi was a calming and reassuring presence (particularly to Bello), chatting away or catching up with emails and his German practice on his tablet.

The more nuanced understanding of the role of men as caring and understanding of the position of women living in rural Tanzania is depicted through the character of "Abdul" and two of the medical professionals. Abdul is Pili's boss at the shamba and is kind and understanding of her interest in a market stall; he is also concerned about her health and well-being. Dr Omari and the attendant at the clinic where Pili collapses both take time to look after and care for her. These three male characters are imbued with care and compassion, to show understanding and solidarity with Pili and to provide a contrast to Mahela. There is still a hierarchy between the men and Pili based on wealth, education, and authority, but it does not lead to an abuse or power over her.

The character of Abdul is played by Barry Issa Ally, who works as a field manager in the shamba where all the field scenes were shot. He lives with his wife and daughter in the fields and was pivotal in allowing us to film there and to use his house to film scenes between Abdul, Pili, and Zuhura. Barry was cast at the last minute after the initial person intended for the role pulled out. He knocked down one of his walls to let more light into the room where we were filming, delivered a sensitive and moving performance, and then went back to work in the field. He charged me £10 for the wall and took the whole thing in his stride. Like Bello, Barry was one of the many revelations we had in the casting of the film.

The role of the two doctors and the clinic registrar were played by a nurse, Catherine Mgimwa; the Miono clinic pharmacy manager, Justus Joseph; and a barman from Bagamoyo, Castor Alfred. We did not want to cast real doctors because of the demands on their time. The doctors based at the Miono and Mbwewe care and treatment centres are primarily responsible for the HIV/AIDS clinics and the maternity wards, which are in high demand; however, because these clinics are the only facilities with trained doctors in the town, they also serve as the second point of contact after the local pharmacy, should any member of the community become ill. The doctors were incredibly helpful, supportive, and accommodating of the project and, though not in the film, were fundamental in allowing us to shoot in the real clinics.

The other supporting cast members were drawn from the wider meetings we had with the women. All the extras and small parts in the film tended to be cast on the day. The plan had been to cast these roles earlier; however, in practice the person who was initially cast might have dropped out or the extras were not anticipated prior to the shoot and therefore were hastily recruited. Mwanaidi brought along her nieces and cousins to play the extra women in the micro-lending vikoba scenes (some of whom we had met in the earlier meetings when discussing their stories); Bello got her mother, "Mama Bello," and her friends to play the extras working in the fields; and the bus drivers we used were the drivers of the different buses. Everyone else in the film was cast because they were already on the bus, waiting in a clinic, playing pool in a bar next door, selling phone vouchers, or working in the shop in which we were filming (such as the chemist and the stationer). Even those characters without dialogue – washing children's clothes, calling out to Pili on the street, and waiting in a clinic to see a doctor – are emblematic of the poverty, inequality, and disease. The characters in the film both drive the narrative and provide depth of understanding of the everyday structures that contain agency. These characters explain key themes in international relations: navigating identity and statehood, gender hierarchies, and the complex relationship between agency and structures of inequality and disease.

Payment and Consent

After the main cast had been identified, specific conversations were had about the requirements of the film – shooting for five weeks, working six days a week – and the issues the cast members might want to think about regarding potential stigma in the immediate community, their exposure nationally and internationally, and the impact on their personal relationships, for example partners returning if they thought the women had money. All cast members were encouraged to reflect on these points between the research trip in November–December 2015 and the beginning of the main shoot in

February–March 2016. During this time they could raise any issue they might have via the production assistants. One week prior to the main production and the signing of the consent forms to their participation, these conversations were repeated and the various issues discussed at length. Throughout the process a number of the women looked bored by such conversations and my repetition of the issues, with the sense that they were committed and just wanted to proceed.

Consent forms are principally used to protect research participants, in this case the women in the film. As a consequence, these forms followed the standard university mechanisms of making provision for the women to withdraw from the project at any point without explanation or constraint. Such agreements would not occur with a usual film project, where contracts exist to keep actors committed to the full project rather than free to leave at any point. To organize film contracts around models of research consent would give all the power to actors rather than producers, thus potentially disrupting the whole production process. This was a difficult position to explain to the crew, that we could be four weeks into the shoot and any of the cast could withdraw at any point. However, it did also place a greater onus on the importance of ensuring that the cast members were comfortable and happy with all aspects of the process for the instrumental reasons of keeping the production going and ensuring that they were reasserting their consent to participate on every day of the shoot. Consent for the project therefore not only happened at the outset of the project through the formal signing of consent forms but was a sustained process throughout the five-week production.

One particular difficulty of ensuring informed consent was the unknown of what would happen with the completed film. All the women were informed as to the intention of the film: to secure a premiere at an international film festival, theatrical cinema distribution, and screenings to academics and policy-makers. Any money made from the film would go back to the women and community in Miono. The cast would potentially benefit financially; the crew would not. It was important that the women were aware of the intended plans for distribution so that they could understand the type of visibility we were aiming for, whether they wanted to be that visible, and the potential consequences for them. However, we also did not want to raise their expectations as to what the film could achieve. The film could be a great success, generating potentially transformative amounts of money for the women in the film, or it could generate no money at all. Any money raised would also take two to three years from the completion of the production to come through; therefore, in effect the women would finish shooting and then go back to work in the shamba. The balance struck with this particular dilemma was to inform the women of the intent for audience but to downplay the potential sums of money that the film could generate because there was no guarantee of this and it could potentially act as a perverse incentive for their participation. I would be held to account for my commitment to returning all funds to the communities in which the film is based through written public statements, oral commitments, and notification to both my university and the funder of the project.

The main ethical issue was external scrutiny over pay and the incentivizing of co-production. Payment for participation in research is rare in politics and IR, and, where it does happen, it is usually a small fee to cover the research participant's expenses, such as travel costs and light refreshments. Initially my university research ethics committee had some reservations about payment to participants: they did not want the women to be incentivized to participate or the money used to coerce them to continue when they wanted to withdraw. I insisted that the women be paid: (1) the film was work, the women would lose their daily income from working in the fields to work on the film, and at the very least this should be remunerated; (2) the long-term benefits of the film meant less to the women than did their immediate need for money to support themselves and their families; and (3) it seemed unjust that the British and Tanzanian crew members would be paid for their time and expertise, and the cast members who had arguably greater and immediate need for money would not. I came to an agreement with the ethics committee that I would pay for participation over the international poverty threshold of US$2.00 a day (even though many of the women were earning less than this) and would seek advice and input from NGOs working in the area to ascertain an appropriate rate – enough so that the women would not suffer from loss of earnings, but not so much that it would be a perverse incentive to their participation. The threshold of US$2.00 roughly translates to TSh4,000. On consultation with Tanzanian partners, it was suggested that I pay TSh5,000 per day because Tanzanian shillings are available in notes of TSh500, TSh1,000, TSh2,000, TSh5,000, and TSh10,000, and one note of TSh5,000 was seen to have higher exchange value than two notes of TSh2000 or four notes of TSh1000. This seemed straightforward, and I proposed the pay rate of TSh5,000 (US$2.50) to the women, plus one meal, per day – more than they were earning in the fields, more than the poverty threshold, but not so much that it would be a perverse incentive for them to keep going – thus keeping the ethics committee happy.

We discussed the pay rate with the women during the week before we started shooting, and they asked for more; they wanted to be paid TSh10,000 (US$5.00) a day. They suggested that, even though it was more than double what they received for working in the fields, some women earned more from the market or tea shops, and some women had to find child care on the days they were filming. The basis for such arguments were slightly dubious because I knew that the majority of children were looked after by extended family members for small amounts, if anything, and that only one or two women were successfully selling produce at the local market; most were not. If I had held firm at TSh5,000, I am confident that the women would still have participated in the film; it was still double their daily income. However, I also appreciated that they saw the film as a one-time opportunity: regardless of the potential long-term financial benefits their need was immediate. The rate of US$5.00 was considerably less than the crew was being paid, the women would be working for the same amount of hours, and their need was greater. I therefore agreed to their request. All adult main cast members were to receive TSh10,000 plus one meal and water; extras would not be paid but would have access to water, or, if they worked on the project for over an hour, they would be paid TSh5,000 plus lunch and water. Children would not be paid to be in the film.

Money was definitely a factor in the women's decision to participate in the film. They saw the film as an opportunity both to tell their story and effect change and to get out of the shamba for five weeks and receive a regular income. However, money alone does not explain their participation. The main cast members agreed to participate in the film before payment was discussed, and many signed consent forms when the proposed fee was TSh5,000. The ethical dilemma here was to not coerce or incentivize the women's participation and also to acknowledge the work the women would be doing, the inequalities in payment between cast and crew, and the everyday needs of the women and their families. As chapter 3 explores in detail, this ethical knot reproduced itself in different ways, because money can facilitate co-produced research, but it can also reinforce hierarchies within such a relationship as well as leverage on both the part of the cast and the producer. The knot was managed through a process of continued dialogue between me, my ethics committee, Tanzanian partners, and the women in the film, and by focusing separately on the processes of informed consent and payment.

PRODUCTION

Co-production was pivotal in the pre-production of *Pili* in order to use the diverse knowledge from women living in rural Pwani, filmmakers, and academics in shaping the story, cast, and themes of the film. The co-productive element of the main production of the film continued to draw on these sources of knowledge but expanded to include different aspects of the community in which the film was based. The involvement of the wider community was a necessary practicality and an important means of building trust, quality, and authenticity in the film.

The main production of *Pili* took place over five weeks, working six days a week, with a break on Sunday. At the outset of the production there was a discussion with the women as to whether the break should be on Friday given its importance in Islam and the Islamic faith of most of the cast; however, in practice Sunday is the main day of rest in Tanzania. The majority of the film was shot in Miono and Makole, with three additional days of shooting in Bagamoyo and two days in Msata. Shooting in real locations – functioning care and treatment centres, markets, and functioning meeting halls – required participation and input from various senior figures in the local community. As the beginning of this chapter discussed, such participation was facilitated by the driver Julius of Trans Tanz and through my position as a known trustee of that organization. Leanne and I suggested to the women that we should meet with the male elders to explain what we would be doing. The vocal women in the group did not see the point of doing so and suggested that the male elders knew we were in the town, and, if they wanted to speak to us and find out what we were doing, they could come to us. Involvement of local councillors, policemen, and doctors was a practical necessity – we could not use these locations without their permission – and became vital for wider trust in the community. Of crucial importance, such involvement also presented an additional oversight to my conduct and that of the crew when on location. Miono is a close-knit community, and the news of any ill or inappropriate behaviour would have reached senior representatives. In contrast to the national and regional governments (see chapter 4), none of the local senior representatives asked for or was given financial payment of any kind. What was more important was time: I had to spend time with them to carefully explain the intent of the project and how it would work and to answer any of their questions. Once satisfied, they were obligingly accommodating; for example, one local councillor held his weekly meetings under a tree outside his office so as not to disrupt a scene being shot in the meeting hall. I insisted that we could rearrange, but he refused. All the families who lived in Makole where Pili's house was based helped care for the actor's children between shots, to provide extra snacks for the cast if they were hungry, and provided small props at short notice. These families were paid a small fee for the use of one of their homes and for any incidentals.

The shooting schedule was organized around the concerns of cast experience (i.e., shoot the easy scenes first), the need to be as inconspicuous as possible to avoid any interference from the government or local thieves (see chapter 4), and the desire to avoid the early rains of the rainy season. Any scenes involving children were organized for Saturdays when they were not supposed to be in school, and we did not stay in one location for more than three days, to avoid any external intervention (again, government or rumoured thieves). The first half of the shoot comprised internal scenes with Bello on her own and scenes of work in the shamba and of walking; the second half of the shoot featured the more difficult group vikoba scenes and those involving large props such as a smashed-up car and an ambulance. The penultimate scene between Pili and Mahela was the last to shoot, given the performance and confidence it required from Bello. Plans naturally changed because initially we managed to get ahead of schedule; then they slowed because of issues with the crew, and death and illness among the cast, as discussed in chapter 3.

Shoot days changed depending on the scene and the light required. The average day was scheduled to begin with the crew being collected at 6:30 a.m., travelling to meet the cast, setting up, and being ready to shoot at 8:00 a.m. This rarely happened. The drivers would be late, breakfast would be late, or the cast members had not yet had tea. Tea is given not at home in Tanzania but at work, and no

work happens (or, at least, one has an unhappy team) unless everyone has "taken chai." Once everyone had arrived and taken tea, the
cast would change into costume. The costumes were the women's
own clothes. Despite the women, particularly Bello, being asked to
arrive in the clothes ready to film, they never would. As the cast
members were changing, Gary would prepare the camera, and Tom
the sound, while Craig discussed the shot with Leanne. I would be
working with the assistants to ensure that we had all the necessary
props, to finalize the lunch plans, and to think through anything that
we would need for the afternoon's shoot. Leanne would then spend
twenty to thirty minutes running through the scene with the cast and
one of the production assistants. Once everyone was happy, Tom
would put microphones on the cast, and Gary would put the camera
on Craig. Sound's at speed, camera's rolling, standing by, standing
by, action, cut. I would then take a note of anything Leanne said.
The numbers on the board were changed to indicate scene number,
shot number, and take. Gary would change the lenses between shots,
following Craig's direction; shots moved from one shot to the next
once Leanne was happy. Each scene would take from one and a half
to two and a half hours to shoot. Regular scenes would involve no
more than five shots and anything between two and twenty takes,
depending on the number of cast members per shot, the urgency of
the light, and the difficulty of the scene. The more difficult scenes
would take up to ten shots. On average we would aim to shoot two
and a half pages of the screenplay per day, with a one-hour break
for lunch. Lunch would be either in the main food venue on the high
street in Miono, which was next to the bus stop and the pool hall
and at the front of the main market, or by the side of the A14 road
in Mandera. The standard lunch was beans, rice, spinach or pump-
kin leaves, and goat or beef stew provided by one-woman catering
operations. Over lunch I would confirm the props for the afternoon
and any large props that we would need later in the week with the
translator–production assistants, and respond to any issues from the
cast and crew. This could range from a sick relative, to the need to
sack a crew member, to the sourcing of special juice for the children,
to having a chat with local police or town councillors.

The most difficult scenes to shoot were the vikoba scenes and the
penultimate scene at Mahela's house. For the cast, these scenes were
difficult because of their emotive content. We therefore gave extra time
and space to shoot these scenes and often did so with as few people

present on set as possible. For the crew, these scenes were difficult because they mainly involved shooting day for night. This was a problem for sound because the microphones would pick up the daytime sounds of poultry, children playing, people drinking in open-air bars, loud music coming from barbershops, and motorcycles and tractors passing by. Day-for-night scenes involved cardboard, old sheets, and tarpaulin (and lots of pins) being hammered against all the outside windows of the locations by the production assistants and me, thus creating the darkness and soundproofing required but also incredibly hot spaces for the cast and crew to work in. Once the interior was complete, I would then work with the production assistants to talk people outside the locations into being quiet or, failing that, to pay them.

The majority of scenes were shot in the day to make the most of the natural light and to not tire the cast and crew, who had become used to shooting in the day. For the few scenes that needed to be shot outside in the dark, extra provision was made for both cast and crew. Dinner was provided by one of the local lunch venues and often served from the back of Michael's car. One week into the production I was advised by Michael and Ally that "bandits" had heard we were filming and might try to rob us. Initially skeptical, I listened to their concerns and ensured that we changed locations every two days instead of the planned three. On their suggestion I reluctantly recruited two security guards for all night scenes and to accompany anyone travelling on the dirt road from Miono to the main A14 road after dark. The security guards came recommended by the Miono police station. When they arrived at the location, they told me they each carried a gun. I was not happy about this, given the number of children around, my responsibility for the cast and crew, a concern that guns could cause more harm than security, and a keen awareness of the research ethics of the project. I told them not to carry a gun in future. The faces of the guards suggested that they disagreed and that I did not know what I was talking about: guns were normalized for private security guards in Tanzania; therefore, if a security guard was hired, he would come with a gun. To ensure the idea of security for the crew with the guards on set, I compromised my own concerns and thoughts on insecurity and had to balance my ethical responsibility for the well-being of the cast and crew with what made them feel more insecure and their own perceptions of insecurity. I allowed the guards to be present for two night shoots.

The situation with the security guards posed an everyday security dilemma for a research relationship based on co-production. From my perspective there was no threat, and I did not want to hire the guards, especially not armed guards; from the perspective of my Tanzanian crew members the guards were a necessity. I thought that they made the cast and crew more insecure; the Tanzanian crew thought that they made them more secure. I had an ethical responsibility to protect the cast and crew from harm on account of the research, and the cast and crew thought that this was a good form of protection. Co-production meant compromise and trust in my responsibility to ensure the well-being of the cast and crew; however, such compromise and trust also generated insecurity.

Equipment

The equipment used to shoot *Pili* is emblematic of the co-productive elements of the film. *Pili* was shot on a Canon C300 camera, with 18 mm, 25 mm, 32 mm, 50 mm, 75 mm, and 100 mm lenses. The total kit excluding sound (the sound recordist, Tom, used his own kit) – main camera and lenses, sound extras such as monitors, microphones, and moose bars – was insured to the value of £250,000 and hired for £4,680. The complete hired kit list is detailed in full in the appendix to demonstrate the amount of equipment required to build the camera and shoot the film. At £4,680, the kit was hired out at a significant discount to the market rate. Accompanying the main kit was a range of small hard drives to record the dailies (the footage taken that day) and large hard drives to back up the full film. One hard drive was left in Tanzania, one hard drive was given to the editor, and the final hard drive I keep in a locked filing cabinet.

The electronic equipment was supplemented by a range of small and large props sourced from the small towns in which the film was shot. The majority of props were sourced from the cast and the crew or from the surrounding area on the day. Small props ranged from anti-retroviral pill boxes to fruit to beauty products to hoes to *mandazi*. Larger props were straightforwardly dependent on our willingness to pay and on occasional local patronage. We needed a broken front door: I had one made from scratch by the local carpenters in Miono for TSh60,000 (US$30) in under three hours. For Pili's market stall, we moved three unused stalls from one side of Miono to another in order to create a line of stalls for Pili to walk past, only incurring the cost of a small rental fee and the pick-up truck to collect and return them. The main challenge with props was trying to foresee what would be needed and, if we had to buy them, the dispute settlement mechanism required to obtain a fair price. With the exception of water, all products had a negotiable value that was inflated when I was interested in a purchase. To avoid any *mzungu* (white-person) tax, I would identify what was needed and ask Ally to buy it. This became problematic the longer we were in the community because more people knew who the Tanzanian crew members were and that they had mzungu money. Receipts are practically non-existent for purchases in rural communities in Tanzania. For accounting purposes I had my own receipt book in which I or one of the production assistants would write the value of a product and have it confirmed by the vendor through signature, but more commonly through initials or a thumbprint.

Throughout the shoot we used many different vehicles: pick-up trucks to raise up the crew or drive them along during filming; motorcycles to drive on the beach; an ambulance; a crashed car; and four different buses. I would work with the production assistants to identify what was needed and then check with Leanne that they fit. On one day of shooting, Michael and Rose had impressively sourced three buses. Leanne confirmed that they would be fine but took out her smart phone to show me a picture that might cause a problem: one bus bore a picture on the left window panel of Muammar Gaddafi, complete with bullet belt and machine gun, and a picture on the right of Osama Bin Laden. The bus driver explained that they were seen as heroes in Pwani, but he could cover them up if we wanted him to. I thought it would be interesting and authentic to include them, but I shared Leanne's concern that they might cause an unnecessary distraction from Pili's story; we decided to cover them with plastic sheeting. We were able to source some vehicles, such as a crashed car, from the local police station, and an ambulance from the health centre. Ambulances are not abundant in Tanzania and therefore tend to be in use and definitely not available for free for one to two hours of filming. Our initial plan was to use an ordinary vehicle and add a flashing light and siren; the scene would be shot at night, so hopefully the audience would not be able to tell the difference. This caused some concern for Leanne who was unconvinced that we could source a flashing light and siren. By chance, during the week of shooting the crash scene we discovered that the

Fig. 6 Miono care and treatment centre and the broken ambulance, one of the biggest props for the film.

Miono ambulance had been out of action for some time and taken to Bagamoyo to be fixed. Should I be happy to pay for a new siren, light, and minor contributions to its repair, we could use it for one hour on its way back to Miono. The scene proved so realistic that at one point a doctor driving past the crash pulled over to see if he could help.

Pili depended on the quality and type of equipment sourced in the United Kingdom and Tanzania. The UK kit was the type used on high-budget film sets around the world and allowed us to produce a high-quality picture that would be taken seriously by distributors, festival programmers, and audiences (see chapter 5). The Tanzanian kit provided quality and the authenticity that was important to showing life in Miono as it was rather than as represented on a set. The combination of quality and authenticity makes the film unique and is part of its appeal to audiences; it shows the potential of collaboration between filmmakers and the wider community in which a film is set. However, the sourcing and use of kit also show how working in close environments with a mixed crew and kit cannot be separated from the wider economic hierarchies they represent. The fully built camera, held by a white camera assistant, inferred wealth. Equipment sourced in the community came not only with an expected *mzungu* tax but also with a "tax" that was variable depending on existing patronage relations and the urgency of need.

POST-PRODUCTION

The post-production of *Pili* took place in the United Kingdom because of cost, equipment, and practicality. Post-production was more straightforward than the main production but had the potential to be a great strain on the budget because the quality, and therefore the potential audience, of the film increased at each stage. The women from Pwani who had been involved in pre-production and the main production were not directly involved in post-production. To suggest that this frustrates the whole co-production process because the person who edits is the one who shapes the story, is inaccurate. As this section explores, while these women did not participate in the edit, it was their involvement and their stories that shaped and enabled post-production.

Unlike documentary filmmaking, the edit of *Pili,* with one exception, closely aligned to the main story developed with the Pwani women. The film was edited by Kant Pan. Kant and Leanne worked closely over three months to achieve the final edit. Translator Kwame Otiende ensured that the subtitles were correct in the final edit. I only visited the editing room twice to ensure that all was in order and to see if there was anything I could do to help. The film underwent three cuts before there was agreement on the final cut. The women involved in the film did not have any input into the editing process, principally because of practicality; they were in Tanzania, and the edit took place in London. Leanne and I ensured that the edit both remained faithful to the central screenplay and stories of the women and balanced the ethical concerns and issues raised in the production process.

The first cut exceeded my expectations of what we had set out to achieve; however, I was unhappy with the additional footage of children, which was then removed from the final cut. The second cut we sent to external peer reviewers for feedback on the film: Did it make sense? What did they like? What did they dislike? What was missing? The reviewers were a mix of academics, film experts, and friends or family, of different demographics, and with little prior knowledge of the film and its themes. Both Leanne and I were initially unsure about the ending and the slow pace of the beginning of the film. The crash scene at the end did not make sense and fell flat after the powerful scene between Mahela and Pili that preceded it. Leanne therefore decided to move the crash scene to earlier in the film so as not to disrupt the tension built in the Mahela and Pili scene and to add additional risk and threat to the beginning of the film. I was unsure of this move but thought that the scene worked better there than at the end of the film. With the third cut, we again sent the film out for final feedback, and again I insisted on further cuts to reduce the shots of children. These were not additional cuts but the original requests I had made after the first cut. Leanne and I went through the entire eighty-three-minute film, negotiating every shot that featured a child.

Once the final edit had been completed to a "picture lock," the film was forwarded to the sound-edit team and to colourist Malcolm Ellison who completed the last stages of post-production. The sound edit was managed by Tom Jenkins through his post-production sound team, Audium Post, and involved two tasks. First was the actual edit, during which the sound was cleaned of cross talk and background noise to ensure the clarity of the dialogue, and general atmosphere noises and extra background dialogue were added. Atmosphere came from the wild tracks made by sound recordist Tom during the production or from film sound repositories of general stock. Additional background sounds were created in a studio by a Foley artist, someone who creates sound effects such as footsteps or the opening of a beer bottle to be used in the main film. The only English voices in the Swahili language film are those coming from the radio as Pili listens to the BBC World Service while she works. Instead of licensing material from the BBC, which would have been expensive, we used a combination of scripts written by journalist friends and stories written by Leanne and me, which were then recorded by actor friends of Leanne. The English voices on the radio are the only cameo I have in the film. The second part of the post-production sound was the sound mix, where the sound editor sat in a studio cinema and adjusted the levels so that the sound balance was correct across the speakers and blended well across the scenes. Different formats require different sound mixes because sound is played out differently in a cinema than via YouTube, for example.

One aspect of post-production and sound that I had overlooked was the inclusion of an original score and the music that would feature on Pili's radio. The original score for the film was provided by Tim Morrish and was included in the sound post-production agreement that I made with Audium Post. The score builds tension, heightens affect, and deepens the emotional connection between the audience and the characters. In addition to the score, I needed to source songs for Pili's radio, either by licensing existing music or by recording an original composition with an artist. To keep with the authenticity of the film, it was important to use music that Tanzanians listen to. Popular music in Tanzania is a combination of Congolese standards, gospel, American hip hop, rhythm and blues, country music, and Bongo Flava (Tanzanian hip hop, and rhythm and blues). Through high-profile artists such as Diamond Platnumz, Bongo Flava has global appeal and is heard in a number of smaller scenes outside of Tanzania. I reviewed various female Bongo Flava singers and identified Shaa as someone whom we could approach to use her songs in the film. A contact of mine in Dar es Salaam introduced me to Shaa's agent, who agreed to license two of her songs for use in the film for free because the film's profits were going to the women in the film. In addition to Shaa's music, the film features a song by Peter Msechu, the star of Tanzania's equivalent of Saturday-night singing shows such as *X Factor* in the United Kingdom and *American Idol* in the United States. Leanne wanted to use Msechu's song because it had been playing in Michael's car when we shot a scene in which Pili dances with her children. At first I thought this would be difficult because we had no idea what the song was or how to contact the artist. However, production assistant Ansity was able to identify the song, and we were able to contact Msechu through social media. Similar to Shaa, Msechu was happy to license his song for use in the film at no charge. Both artists signed licensing agreements and provided the necessary files for the sound team. The licensing of music turned out to be the most straightforward transaction in the whole process of making the film.

Malcolm's role as a colourist was to grade the film, by ensuring the smooth transition between shots to make it look like one colour, to frame or sharpen particular outlines of the characters (especially in the dark scenes), and to draw on the colour palettes that Leanne and Craig favoured in creating the aesthetic of the film. This was an interesting process, drawing on colour theory in film and the need to match the aesthetic to the narrative and themes of the film. For example, Leanne and I were keen to strike a balance between the warmth and lush beauty of the location and the starkness and self-isolation of Pili; we wanted the film to have a beauty, but we also did not want to depict the idyllic Tanzania of tourism promotion. Once the grade was complete, Malcolm finalized the post-production by adding the titles, formatting the sound and picture, and providing an online hard-drive digital cinema package (DCP) for use in cinemas. Then Leanne, Craig, Malcolm, and I watched the film played back in a cinema in Soho, London. On our first viewing, it did not look right, there was a static to the movements, and the sound was odd. On the second time, the film looked much better and was ready for sign off. The film itself was finished. What was not finished at this stage was the extra work required to deliver a film to distributors.

Table 1 provides a list of everything that was required to produce *Pili* across the three stages of production. It shows the hidden elements of work and expense involved in a project of this kind and provides a guide for those seeking to use film as method. What is telling about this table are the various elements and the specialist labour required to deliver them. It also showcases the expansiveness of the film's co-production. The main focus of co-production was the co-operation between me and the women who appeared in the film and shared their stories; however, particularly in post-production, it was also a relationship between the ways in which the women appeared on screen and the specialists involved in delivering particular elements.

While the women from Pwani were not directly engaged in the post-production process, it was guided by a commitment to their stories and to adding, rather than detracting, quality. All the key requirements to make a film were negotiated: some deliverables were given for free, and the actors reduced their fees because of the intent of the project and the commitment to giving the profits from the film to the communities involved. Thus, while not directly involved in every post-production decision, the women shaped these decisions and gave me the power to negotiate on their behalf.

CONCLUSION

The aim of this chapter has been to explore and demystify the practicalities of making a film and co-producing research. In so doing, it outlines the practical requirements of film production, begins to

Table 1 Filmmaking checklist

Pre-production	Production	Post-production
1 Crew (+ contracts) – Above line (e.g., director, director of photography) – Below line (e.g., driver, translator)	1 Four (minimum) hard drives of film rushes/dailies	1 First cut approval
2 Story / subject matter – Story spine	2 Second unit footage	2 Final cut approval and picture lock
3 Script/screenplay	3 Still shots of key people/characters	3 Sound edit
4 Shooting locations	4 Still shots of key scenes	4 Original composition
5 Shooting schedule	5 Receipts/vouchers for every spend	5 Music licensing
6 Film permits	6 Release/ethic approval forms for all people in film	6 Sound mix
7 Kit – See appendix	7 Production diary	7 Grade
8 Hard drives – 2 small, 4 large	8 Hidden extras (wrap party, participant fees)	8 Titles
9 Production insurance	9 Revised budget	9 DCP package + online link
10 Ethics approval	10 Sales agent (if possible; see post-production)	10 Festival Strategy
11 Crew release and copyright forms	11 Production notes for editor	11 Graded stills
12 Cast consent forms/contract	12 Production notes for director	12 Short clips/trailer
13 Hidden extras (flights, receipts, petty cash)	13 Behind the scenes pictures / making of footage	13 Final budget
14 Master budget		14 Sales agent
15 Set up of a production company (if seeking commercial distribution)		15 Copyright registration
16 Travel schedule		16 E&O insurance
17 Props (large and small)		17 Special purpose vehicle company
		18 Copyright and title report
		19 Social media and website

see the politics of co-produced research, and thinks about how politics can be visually represented through film. At the basic level, this chapter has provided insight into the general practicalities of how to use film as method, such as the sourcing of the crew, kit, contracts, budgets, and the minutiae involved in film. It provided an overview of the three processes of film production: pre-production, production, and post-production. In this way it highlighted the formal requirements of film production (summarized as a checklist in table 1) and the unseen dynamics, such as agents, negotiating kit rental, and the hierarchy of a film set.

The chapter also illustrated how co-produced methods work in practice, with specific reference to research design and pre-production. Co-production requires a previous and sustained engagement with the people, communities, and networks in which the co-production takes place and a clarity as to the ethical process and the encounters that the politics of seeing entails. The co-production of *Pili* was made possible thanks to my existing relationships within the community in which the film is based and the ten years of trust built up with that community and the wider network of NGOs, politicians, and health professionals working in the area. Without this, the relationship would have been principally transactional, and I would not have had the same access to the health facilities, networks of tradesmen, and, crucially, the women who participated in the film. This project was co-produced principally by me, the filmmakers, the cast of *Pili*, and the eighty women whose stories underpin the narrative of the film. However, that co-production also includes the wider community in which the film was based: the doctors who allowed the use of the care and treatment centres, the local politicians, the carpenters who built props, the cooks who provided the catering, the farm workers who allowed us to use their land, and the people in the communities of Miono, Makole, and Bagamoyo who acted as extras and provided small props or space in which to shoot key scenes. Co-production of knowledge involved formal knowledge – stories of living with HIV/AIDS, how to direct, how to use a Canon C300 camera, the structural drivers of disease – and informal knowledge of how local political structures work and how to access them. The chapter demonstrated how women's stories, community knowledge, academic research, filmmaking skills, and the experience of the film production itself combined to visually represent political structures and agents. It explored how politics and IR were written into the story of *Pili* through the characters (e.g., Leila as the state, Mahela as patriarchy), the locations (e.g., the shamba as informality and precarious labour), and the main story arc. The gatekeeping, patronage, and patriarchy involved in the story of *Pili* were also evident in the making of the film. It was not just the lived experience of the women in the film that shaped the story but the lived experience of making the film that fed into the wider themes, characters, and narrative of the film. Hence, co-production required formal and informal sources of knowledge from multiple sources to be able to see the politics explored in the film.

This chapter revealed the process of seeing and how the women came to be seen through the film's main production. In so doing, it concludes the first part of the book, which has documented why and how film can be used as a method of seeing and being seen in politics and IR. The second part of the book picks up on some of the themes of this chapter to explore what stops us from seeing and the wider politics of co-producing film as method. The next chapter reflects on the power relations between the women and me, what such power relations can tell us about transnational feminism, and how such relations curtail and facilitate the stories we see.

3

Seeing Discomfort in Film as Feminist Method

It is one thing to want to see politics differently, to confront how hierarchies of knowledge work, and to design a research project using film as a method and as an output of co-production that values different knowledge sources and their agency. It is another to put such intent into practice. As chapter 1 argued, there are many potential red flags for a project of this kind: a white lens or gaze that constructs the lives and bodies of black women through the narratives of white women; the editing of a film in a way that undermines the women's lives or does not reflect their reality; the privileging of one set of knowledge over another; and a financial benefit for the British producers of the film through profit or career progression, with no material or social benefit for the Tanzanian women in the film (Blackwell, Briggs, and Chiu 2015; Chowdhry and Nair 2002; Chowdhury 2006). Chapter 2 considered how I tried to navigate some of these issues through the research design process and at every stage of the production. The chapter showed how hierarchies and differences are unavoidable and played out in various ways in the co-production of the film. What is missing from the discussion in chapter 2 are the unseen politics of co-production that can have an impact on the successful completion of a feature film, and the political tensions involved in the use of film as feminist method. This chapter is interested in such unseen politics and the discomfort and difficulty of co-produced research.

Beginning the second part of the book, the chapter shifts the focus from the how and why of using film as a means of seeing and being seen, to the what – what stops us from seeing and what the process of film as co-production reveals about international relations. As outlined in the introduction, *Seeing Politics* is about not only film as a method and an output through which women such as Pili can see and be seen, but also what the process of making the film reveals about what stops us from seeing. This chapter reads particular events during the production and post-production of *Pili*, such as death, illness, and rotten tomatoes, to show how everyday encounters and informal political processes inform the ways in which co-production works in practice. In so doing, it considers the role of temporality, agency, and money in the co-production process and how these three factors underpin feminist method of this kind and potentially limit what we see. The chapter argues that agency needs to be seen as fluid rather than static throughout co-production: to acknowledge the agency of the research partners is not to establish methods of how they see and represent themselves, but to discern how this agency can be used to maximize self-interests over a project's life cycle. Time is a function of agency: agents can use time-constrained needs and expectations to frustrate and shape the research processes to their own ends in unseen ways. Finally, material concerns are unavoidable and ever-present factors in filmmaking and co-production; they both enable and limit what we see. There is a need to confront research taboos around money: to not see the role of money in the co-production process is to not see the importance it has for co-producers in shaping the research process. In sum, the chapter shows that the difficulty and discomfort arising from co-dependent agency, temporal differences, and material concerns all can be barriers to what we see. However, acknowledging discomfort with these dynamics can help enrich the understanding of co-production and feminist method in IR and strengthen co-produced knowledge.

POLITICS OF CO-PRODUCTION

Some of the tensions, criticisms, and problems with co-produced and feminist methods that were outlined in chapter 1 were evident in the production of *Pili*. While the project in itself was an effort both to allow the represented to represent themselves and to give voice and space to women from low-income countries, material constraints as to who held the money maintained hierarchies of knowledge and power within the co-production. These tensions and problems, however, should not be a barrier to conducting co-produced projects of this kind. Drawing on the work of decolonial feminists such as Desai,

Ling, Mohanty, and Carty (Agathangelou and Turcotte 2010; Carty and Mohanty 2015, 88; Desai 2007; Mohanty 1998; Ling 2007, 144), this chapter argues that such tensions and difference should be acknowledged as a way to expand knowledge and understanding in order to move forward in addressing inequality. This involves discomfort, tension, and a blunt confrontation of the interests and intent of the different parties within the relationship. It is by being attentive to hierarchies and seeing this discomfort and the mess of such relationships that transnational solidarity and reciprocity can be built (Hammonds 1997; Shohat 1998, 52). This does not ameliorate the political differences in such relationships but begins the thinking about how such political differences can be challenged and addressed in research method. This section focuses on the unseen politics of co-production by considering the role of wealth, hierarchy, and agency; temporal dynamics and differences; the blurring of boundaries; and expectations and transparency.

Wealth, Hierarchy, and Agency

The clearest issue that frames co-produced research of this kind is financial and includes the initial hierarchy between the person with the money and those without the money. This plays out between the principal researcher who controls the budget, the film crew who are paid to do the work, and the people who share and act out their stories for the film. The financial hierarchy was foreseen and in many ways inevitable: I had money to do the project, and the participants would be paid for their time and involvement in it. In Tanzania I am not "Sophie Harman" but "mzungu Sofia" (white Sophie), where my white skin infers wealth and the subsequent power and privilege that is seen to derive from white wealth. From the outset of the project there would therefore be an unavoidable perceived hierarchy on account of my skin colour and whiteness, my Britishness, and the money I had to do the project.

As chapter 2 discussed, appropriate accounting and ethical procedure from the higher education sector required me as the producer and principal investigator to have the participants sign consent forms, which formalized the hierarchy of me as the person in charge of the project and responsible for their well-being and the ethical standards of the process, and to pay them at the end of every day. This formal procedure, however explained, created several outcomes. Principally

I was seen not as the co-producer or researcher but as the boss of the project to whom problems should be deferred, and as the person who paid for everything, such as food, per diems, and props. This created a position in which I was seen more as personally wealthy, because I had possession and control of the project money, than as relevant for my knowledge as an academic or research collaborator. The signing of documents – consent forms, records of payments – formalized the hierarchical distinction between me and the women in the film. My experience of working in Tanzania is that people are often happy to meet, speak in interviews, and engage with research but are hesitant to sign anything official even if it is designed to protect them. Informal agreements and practices are the norm, while formalized arrangements suggest a lack of trust and a hierarchy in which the signatory is to be controlled by the person who owns the paperwork. There was therefore a tension between the requirements of sound financial accounting and ethical procedure for a university research project and my need as producer and principal investigator to gain the trust of, and a sense of collaboration with, both the women involved in the story and production of the film, and the crew.

This tension played out in minor ways. At the outset of the project the cast members felt uncomfortable sitting at the table with me at lunch time. This changed after the second week when they became used to everyone working together and the collaborative part of the project. However, any direct contact with me was particularly awkward for individual members of the cast. This meant that I had to adjust my own behaviour and rely on the translator–production assistants to check that everyone was okay or to identify any concerns of the cast; to ask them myself would have resulted in a *mzuri* (fine) with no eye contact. I paid each cast member at the end of each day in order to maintain my side of the agreement to pay them the agreed amount, on time, and to let them leave at any point. I had to pay them in an envelope, and they would sign or thumbprint to ensure proof of receipt. Some cast members would slightly bow or bob down in a form of curtsey that made me uncomfortable. I tried to mention casually that they did not have to do this; however, when I realized that it made some more embarrassed not to, I had to reconcile myself to it happening. These deferential aspects of the relationship did not apply to all of the cast; some were very direct in what they wanted from the project and were happy to tell me what they thought. However, as the production process continued,

I learned that some of the more direct women were hiding greater problems in their lives that they only introduced to me at the end of the project. This may have been because they trusted me at the end of six weeks, they were ashamed or scared to say anything in case it ruined their role in the film, or they saw the final weeks as the last opportunity to see if I could help.

The final outcome of the ethical research process was that it gave to the women involved with the film an agency in the research and production process. While I had a certain amount of leverage as the person who paid the women, the women also had leverage because they knew that the success of the film relied on their participation. This led to a co-dependent relationship in which I was dependent on the women continuing to participate, knowing they could withdraw at any time, and they were dependent on me to fulfill my ethical obligation to them. The ability of the women to withdraw gave them agency over me as someone who wanted to complete the project; once the film was half made, the women knew that it would be difficult to replace them and that, given the money spent, I would want to complete the project. We were mutually co-dependent in the relationship: they needed me to pay them, and I needed them to finish the project.

Three events that occurred during the production of the film starkly reveal how material factors reveal themselves in a project of this kind. The first was the willingness of one of the women to contract HIV to be in the film. This did not happen. It had been the result of a misunderstanding that was swiftly and strongly rectified. Some of the women in the film are HIV negative but play characters who are HIV positive. As part of the process of informed consent I had to explain to them that, by their acting in the film, members of their community might identify them as HIV positive and consequently stigmatize them. They should think clearly about this and not participate if they were concerned; we could think of alternative ways to include them. Therefore, there was no perverse incentive for them to participate. However, one woman took this to mean that if they were not HIV positive, they could not be in the film. Following my explanation of the risk of stigma, they paused to think and then responded by saying that they would think of a way to become HIV positive to be in the film. The opportunity to receive a small, regular income for five weeks and one meal a day was seen as advantageous to the extent that they would consider risking their health. It was made very clear to that particular woman that she did not have to and should not do this and that she could still be in the film or participate in the film process in other ways if she did not want to act in it.

The second event involved the purchase of tomatoes. We arranged all group shoots around the women's needs; however, on one day there was a misunderstanding, and a group scene was arranged to take place on market day. One of the women sells food at the market and was unaware of the shoot. She felt bad about this and torn about what to do. My solution was to offer the options of rearranging the scene to be shot on another day, buying her produce, or paying someone else to stand in for her at the market. She agreed to let me buy the tomatoes she intended to sell, and at the end of the day we settled the amount and discussed any other issues she had been facing over the previous weeks. The matter was settled, but I was unaware that another actor had seen me provide money for the tomatoes and thought that the woman was receiving special treatment and a different rate of pay to the rest of the cast. Despite an explanation of the purpose of the money, the actor demanded both extra pay for the duration of the remaining one-week shoot and back pay.

The third event concerned the role of children in the film. As detailed in chapter 2, it was explained clearly at the outset of the film that there would be no children in the film other than the two characters of Pili's children and that they would not be paid for their involvement. This was to avoid any incentive on the part of the parents to take their children out of school and bring them to the production on days they were not needed, or to create any inequalities between the cast members whose children were on screen and those whose children were not. Children under school age could accompany their mothers to the production. This only became inconvenient when certain children were upset to be separated from their mothers when they were shooting a scene and, in one case, burst into tears when they saw a white crew member. The production had to fit around the sleep, shower, and feeding times of the youngest cast member on the days we shot scenes with Pili's children. Although on some days this could delay the shoot, these were necessary pauses and only minor inconveniences. I agreed with one of the principal cast members that the production would pay for an aunty to look after her children when she was filming. I knew that her children were cared for by family when she worked in the fields – often without payment or for a small contribution to the household finances. However, I also knew that she was testing me to see if I was committed to her well-being and that of her children because a significant part of the film depended on her involvement. She and I both knew that for the production to work she would have to be content and that the aunty nanny was a test of the boundaries of her agency in this.

Despite it being clear that no child would be paid to be in the film, in effect the parents of some children used their position to accrue extra money. For example, one extra, "boy with the ball," was cast in a small role after informed consent had been established by his guardian. This had involved a long conversation and the signing of a consent form. Three days after the shooting of the scene I was approached by one of the translator–production assistants who told me that the boy's family had come by and were not happy, because they had not agreed to his participation. One man argued that he was the boy's father and that the boy should be paid to be in the film. I explained that we did not pay children to be in the film and that we had sought consent from someone who had identified as the boy's guardian. The man was not happy with my answer. To smooth over the situation I paid him a small fee, and the matter was settled.

These protracted negotiations were not uncommon during the production. Extras would often ask for extra money, food, or water – after having signed the consent form, and shooting was about to commence. They would air a grievance, I would be brought in to address it, and the easiest and quickest solution to the problem would be to pay them additional money. The extras used their agency to delay the production, aware that members of the crew were frustrated with the delay and that I would have to reconcile the crew's impatience and the extras' demands. However, given the availability of extra participants, I rarely paid the additional money requested. Most concerns, I found, could be alleviated with tea, *mandazi*, and fruits. This settlement would often frustrate the crew who just wanted me to pay the relatively small fee and get on with things.

An initial reading of the second and third events may suggest that some of the women and extras involved in the film were opportunistic. In the second event the woman knew that there was one week of filming left, that she was free to withdraw from the project when she wanted, and that, if she did, the project would not be finished. An initial reading of the first incident may suggest that the woman did not understand what she was getting into or its long-term consequences. However, in all incidents the women knew the situation well. They were enacting agency based on their immediate needs. In contexts of extreme poverty, the need for money is immediate: it is needed to feed families, fix homes, and pay for the everyday incidentals of life. This was evident in small ways throughout the shoot when children from the cast members' extended family would attend the crew lunches or I would be presented with receipts for reimbursement of family members' medicine. The long-term consequences – in the first instance, the health effects of being HIV positive and, in the second, the potential failure of the film and therefore the lack of future profits from it – were less concerning or important than the need for money in the immediate term. The short term was more important to the women, whereas the long term was more important to me. For co-production to work I had to acknowledge and reconcile the temporal differences between the cast and me that arose from the differences in our wealth. Their needs were immediate, and their involvement in the film was an opportunity to meet as many of these needs as possible. Co-production in this instance required mutual recognition of the benefit of the process to all parties, their different needs, and the ways in which agency adapted and changed throughout the process.

Temporal Dynamics and Differences

The temporal dynamics and differences presented the most significant challenges of co-production – from the expectations and immediate needs outlined in the previous section, to the working practices of cast and crew, to anxiety at the end of the production. The temporal working practices of such a diverse cast and crew required a number of adjustments to expectation so that everyone could work together. Crew members with experience working on professional film productions were used to the production needs being addressed at a separate time and space to the main shoot. However, because of the co-produced nature of the project, the production arrangements (e.g., extra casting, consent processes, prop identification) took place at the same time as the shoot when issues arose and had to be addressed. This led to some frustration among the crew who wanted prompt reconciliation of any production issues in order to proceed with the main shoot. Often this was not possible because of the academic ethical issues involved in some of the reconciliation, and the importance placed on sitting, explaining, and listening in Tanzania. Some crew members had to accept that reconciliation in the production process took a long time, and I had to accept that some issues would have to be handled promptly without compromising the ethical standards of the project. The production ran to the temporal preferences of Leanne as director but had to be managed by me as producer. The temporal intensity of film production was in tension with the slow process of academic research and adherence to ethical process.

The temporal intensity of film production was slowed by the norms of Tanzanian working practices. As chapter 2 explained, social norms suggested that no filming would take place until everyone had taken tea. Cast members would not arrive prepared for the shoot (in the appropriate clothing, as suggested the day before) and would take some time to familiarize themselves with the day and location. One translator–production assistant wanted to sleep when they were not directly engaged with the production. As all the food was freshly prepared, there would be a further delay if the lunch locations were changed or the timing of lunch was earlier than agreed. This slowed down aspects of the production and required an adjustment of expectations, but it did not prove to be a major disruption to co-production.

The issue of timekeeping was a source of agency for one of the drivers on the project. One driver was regularly late or sometimes did not arrive at all (see chapter 5). One driver was on time until the second driver suggested they delay. This situation could be read that one driver was just bad with timekeeping; however, that driver was on time for issues that directly benefited him. As the shoot progressed, it became clear that he was using time to exert agency over the production: his agency was to control the time that everything began or to attempt to disrupt the production's schedule and thus the completion of the project. He used time to make it clear to me in particular that he was able to exert control and power over the production. At first I tried to discuss the issue of time with the driver; however, little changed as it became clear that he had wider disruptive plans (which I discuss further in the next chapter). I therefore circumvented such disruptions by recruiting new drivers and arranging alternative transport plans.

The anxiety at the end of the production was expressed by a principal cast member in the final week of shooting the film. Such anxiety was expressed through introversion, isolation from the rest of the cast and crew, and clear unhappiness between takes. Initially, when asked about it, the cast member explained that the anxiety concerned an upcoming scene. This was something about which director Leanne and I were also concerned. Deciding that it would be best to separate me from the conversation as the person who paid the women, Leanne and one of the translator–production assistants met with the cast member to discuss her concerns and reassure her about how the shooting of the scene would work and what she would have or not have to do, and that she would never have to do something with which she was uncomfortable. The cast member seemed happy with this at the time but then repeated the same pattern of anxious behaviour. I then met with the actor with a different translator–production assistant. After some awkward silences and mutual staring out to sea, the actor explained that she was uncomfortable staying in the hotel where we were based. She thought that it cost a lot of money; she would rather stay somewhere cheap and have the money to give to her family. At the time we were shooting away from her home in Miono, and I had put all the crew and cast in the same hotel. The hotel was not expensive, but it was not the cheapest accommodation available. This was a clear oversight on my part: I wanted to treat the cast equally in where some crew members were staying, but, had I given it more thought, I could have foreseen that this would have made some members uncomfortable. I explained my intent and reassured the cast member that the hotel was not as expensive as she thought and that, if she preferred, we could move her to alternative accommodation. She seemed happy enough with my explanation and decided to stay. However, shortly after the conclusion of the conversation it became apparent that she remained anxious. I decided to meet with her again but with yet another translator–production assistant to see if that would help to get to the bottom of what was concerning her.

During a long conversation the actor explained the family burden and worries she had carried over the six weeks of working together, her ambition for the future, and her concern about what would happen once the project ended. Many of these concerns she had hidden from the wider cast and crew, and being away from her family amplified them. Compounding these short-term needs was the realization of the impending future, that the temporal space of working on a film would soon be over, and that she would be back working in the shamba. In focusing on the short-term needs and opportunities presented by the project, she had not encountered the long-term aftermath of what would happen when the co-production had finished and her life would return to normal. This was not a conversation that could lead to a reconciliation in the same way one could meet the short-term needs of some of the cast. It was a conversation that could not be reconciled, because it highlighted our asymmetry of wealth, positionality, and opportunity and how, combined, they led to different experiences of fear or hope for the future.

Temporality is a central issue to co-produced research and a potential barrier to the stories we see. At the outset of the production the cast members were focused on the short-term and immediate benefits and gains from the project, while I was fixed on the long-term consequences and any potential risks or benefits to them on account of their participation. As the production developed, the cast members shifted to think about how the present intersected with their future, an issue I could only reconcile in the immediate short term through conversation and clarity on what the film could do, but there were no guarantees as to how it would change their lives in the long term. Time had become a source of agency for both the Tanzanian cast and the crew over me as the producer and principal researcher on the project. Cast members knew that I had to complete the film in a specific time frame, and they were therefore able to use these restraints to gain small amounts of money through inflated child-care or loss of earning costs. Crew members knew that deliberate use of poor timekeeping could disrupt the production and served as a reminder of their necessity to the process. All the cast and crew members had different social norms about timekeeping and the aspects of production that required speed and those that required more time and temporal space. Adjusted expectations and collaborative rhythms of work are a necessary part of any co-produced project. The acute role of temporality in the co-production of *Pili* showed in how the short-term immediate needs for many of the cast members became confronted by their emerging future as the co-production was concluded. Here the blurring of present and future, and fiction and non-fiction, revealed the problematic nature of the work; it raised expectations and the potential for change in the story of the film and its short-term production, but at the end of the process it reiterated the past life of shamba work and low, irregular pay for the future.

Blurred Boundaries and Intimacy

The blurring of fact and fiction and the shifting temporal space of the production were compounded by the intimacy of working alongside women in the communities in which they lived. Such close collaboration began to normalize everyday poverty and to blur the boundaries between the researcher and the subject of the research throughout the film production. This is a positive factor, considering that poverty was the norm of the community in which the film was based and that the women acting in the film were also co-producing the research. Part of the intent of feminist method and a project of this kind is to blur the boundaries between the researcher and the subject of the research, and between the knower and the known, so that the represented can represent themselves and knowledge be co-produced. The research process became deeply personalized through shared experiences of illness, death, and humour. This generated emotional responses in me as a researcher in ways that previous research projects had not. As the women involved in the film had to make the sense of temporal shifts in their position, I too had to make sense of my position as an academic researcher and film producer and of the intimacy of an intense working experience.

During the five-week shoot two crew members and two cast members experienced the death of a close family member. Leanne and I attended the funeral of the cast members' sister and grieved with their extended family that we had come to know well from working together on the film. One crew member had kidney stones, and two cast members got malaria. One cast member who said she would never marry got married at the end of the production. One crew member became engaged and got married shortly after the film wrapped. One crew member became engaged to her long-term partner once the film was complete. In this sense, the short period of making the film – one year from pre-production to completion, including the six weeks of the main production – involved a microcosm of life and an intimacy between cast and crew, particularly as the crew became immersed in the lives of the cast. Death, illness, and marriage, with only birth missing. For five weeks Leanne and I thought that one cast member was pregnant as her stomach grew; however, it turned out that this was the result of her having a regular meal a day.

Intimacy arose through the shared experiences of death and illness and through everyday boredom and the repetition of working together. The British crew members all stayed in the same guest-house, seeing each other at most mealtimes because there was only one place to eat and not much to do in the evenings when they were not filming. The cast and crew all had mild health emergencies that produced embarrassing bathroom episodes. Humour played a role in securing effective working relations and patterns, and particular cast and crew members were effective at lightening the mood on set. One cast member gossiped that another was attracted to a crew member. One crew member confided that they were attracted to another. Much of this gossip was idle but passed the time and created bonding patterns and the illusion of intimacy at least across cast and crew.

The most intimate moments of the co-production were the shooting of emotionally difficult scenes. For such scenes Leanne would reduce the number of people near the shoot. Therefore, often I would be waiting with other cast or crew members away from the main production where I was not expressly needed. On two occasions members of the cast concluded a scene in tears and approached me for a hug. One was at the conclusion of a scene in which a character explained what it was like to live with HIV. The hug and tears were a great surprise to me because the cast member had always been so stoic in all the previous days of co-production. The second occasion was one of the group vikoba scenes in which Pili had to break down the other women and beg for their help and understanding. In this instance, many of the women wanted some time to themselves following the scene. A hug suggested a shared form of intimacy, because public affection or touching between adults, other than holding hands between friends, is uncommon in Tanzanian society.

The illusion of intimacy and the blurring of boundaries are important here because in many respects they were unidirectional. The crew members became immersed in aspects of the cast members' lives and their stories; however, the cast knew little about the life of the crew. They saw pictures and asked questions with regard to who was married (only one Tanzanian member of the crew), who had children (only two Tanzanian members of the crew), and who was religious (only the Tanzanian members of the crew). The cast knew little about the lives of the British crew, and what they did know they met with peculiar laughter or a confused nod. The cast members met my partner when I returned to Tanzania to show them the final film and expressed an interest in visiting the United Kingdom. However, beyond this, the women in the film did not become as intimately involved in my life as I had become in theirs.

Academic work is often solitary, and even as a feminist researcher I am keen to maintain boundaries between my professional life and my non-work life. The co-production of *Pili*, in contrast to my usual working life, required team work, always being around people, and intrusion on my non-work life. One issue with Pili's character is that she is isolated in a society where it is rare for anyone to be alone. As chapter 2 discussed, the intimacy and lack of privacy for the women living in these societies is one of the key themes we wanted to explore in the film. Working in such an environment was initially a challenge for me, as someone who often works alone, particularly as I had additional academic work to do outside of the main production, which meant that I had little time off. I found it hard to create space for myself to think about what was happening in the process of co-production and to take time away from the project. Consequently, even after returning to my home in London after the production had ended, I had difficulty not thinking about the film, the events in Tanzania, and the women. At a minor level it was hard for me not to think about the film when I would receive messages, early in the morning before I was awake or on weekends, from a variety of people in Tanzania. At a more substantive level I was concerned about the well-being of the women who I knew had health concerns and issues with their families and had returned to work in the shamba. This affected my sleep and my ability to relax and became a presence in my relationship with family and friends. I did not share this with the women in Tanzania, the crew, or my colleagues.

Instead of negating my academic ethical responsibility to the co-producers of the research, such intimacy and blurring of boundaries extended my ethical duty of care that the women come to no harm on account of being involved in the project. At the end of the film production I returned to my everyday academic life in the United Kingdom, and the women in the film returned to their everyday lives, working in the shamba and navigating immediate socioeconomic and health risks. However, we were bound by mutual concerns about our well-being and the final distribution of the film. The women wanted me to complete the film and secure a way to make money from it for them. I wanted the women both to trust that I would fulfill my commitment to return any profit to them, and to stay healthy – to assuage my own conflicted feelings should they fall ill. These conflicted feelings grew as my career began to change as the film got greater attention, and the lives and well-being of the women in the film stayed the same or, in some cases, worsened. I had an intimate understanding and had intruded on their lives; their lives had indirectly intruded on mine, but they had no means to understand this because I did not share it with them. The politics of temporality and difference involved in the co-production of research and the blurring of boundaries meant that my relationship with the women remained financial and long term even after their initial involvement with the project had ended.

"Have You Got Something for Me?"

The temporal and material dynamics of the co-production shaped the transparency and accountability of the project post the main production. As chapter 2 outlined, informed consent and opportunity to withdraw were introduced at the outset of the project and then reiterated at every stage of the production process. This was done in order to fulfill the ethical obligations of the research project to everyone involved and thereby be fully transparent about the intent and potential outcome of the research, and to be as accountable as possible to any issues arising. It was also done to ensure that the co-producing partners had given informed consent and that, as a co-producing partner myself, I could ascertain a commitment to the project and be sure of their motivations for doing so. I knew that these motivations were partly financial (they would be paid regularly everyday) and partly aspirational (they wanted to tell their stories to wider audiences). Upon completion of the film the women in Tanzania became more transparent about their interests, and I became less so. Transparency and accountability are not static but shift over the life cycle of co-productive, transnational relationships. This change is particularly acute in the shift from production to the expectation of reward and the distribution of profit.

The shifts in transparency were evident in cast anxiety at the end of the project, as outlined earlier, and in my own behaviour when I returned to Tanzania after the main production had been completed. During my visit to Tanzania in October 2016 to screen the film in Miono and Makole the women's and the community's interest in the film became increasingly transparent. *Pili* was screened to two audiences – a large audience of approximately five hundred people in the playing fields of Miono secondary school, and a smaller audience of thirty in Makole. The audience sizes reflected the time of day: owing to a technical difficulty with the first screening we had to move the second screening to the daytime rather than an evening; therefore, a large number of people were at work. I had organized the screenings with a Tanzanian fixer and his team, who would set up mobile cinemas, and with Ansity, the production assistant and translator from the main shoot. Ansity and I were the only original crew members to attend. Leanne had planned to attend but pulled out of the trip on the day before we left for Tanzania over fears of her own security in response to threats that had been made against us (see chapter 4). On my arrival in Miono I was the happiest I had been over the course of the project. I was physically and emotionally bowled over by cast members running up to give me a hug. I delighted in hearing the stories of how everyone had been. I was pleased to see that the walls of Sesilia's house were nearly finished. I was completely overwhelmed to see the number of people who appeared as if from nowhere to attend the film screening in Miono. During the eighty-three minutes of the film the crowd was illuminated by the headlights of buses or motorcycles arriving to drop off audience members. School children ran out to see what was happening after their late classes. People cheered upon seeing their friends and family on screen and at key points in the film.

As soon as the film finished, the field quickly cleared out. As it did so, I called the cast members to the front to applaud them and remind everyone that they were actors. We did this at the beginning of the film, with key cast members standing up; Bello and Sikujua told everyone who they were and that they had played the roles of Pili and Zuhura, respectively: they were not the characters. When everyone started to disperse at the end of the film, one of the cast members turned to me and said, "So, Sofia, have you got something for me?" At this point a number of other cast members looked to me. Ansity nodded and shrugged: "You know what they mean." I did know what they meant. I had arrived in Miono with small gifts for everyone, such as football shirts (Arsenal, the most popular team in Miono) for the children, and clothes for some of the cast, but I had not arrived with cash. The women who first asked about money were not members of the core cast, although their ears pricked when they heard the conversation. For some cast members, my arrival back in Miono was an opportunity born of a need for money.

The upfront request for money was not surprising and was sensibly opportunistic; all the women's previous interactions with the project had involved some amount of money, however small. I may have been returning to Miono as academic Sophie, but within the community I was still *mzungu Sofia*, the white, British producer with money. What had changed was that the women were open and transparent about their current interest and investment in the project: it was less about having their story told (though this still mattered to some of the key cast); it was more about the money that the film could make or I could provide.

As the women became increasingly open and transparent about what they wanted from the co-production relationship, I became more closed and secretive. I maintained my regular updates with the cast through Ansity, ensuring them that I had not forgotten them and was working hard to sell the film. Leanne and I would send them money from time to time. When we were accepted for our first major film festival, I thought it important to let the cast members know. I asked Ansity to communicate to them that we were in a festival, which, though it did not pay, was a big deal for us because it would give us exposure and help with distribution (see chapter 5 for more on this). When we won two awards at the festival, I excitedly sent Ansity a message from the theatre, and she replied, "Awww congratulations. Does that come with money?" When we signed a sales agreement, I similarly let Ansity know, but we agreed to not tell the women in Miono. Any money arising from sales would take months, if not years, to come through, and we thought it best not to raise their expectations. I wanted to share the good news, let the women know that we were working to get the film out into the public, and be as transparent as possible. However, as things progressed with sales and screenings, Ansity, Leanne, and I agreed that we would wait until the money started to come in before telling the women. They had been transparent about what they wanted; I became less transparent about what was potentially coming to them.

What was potentially coming to them was an estimated six-figure profit. The sales agent and the distributor would take their contractual percentage (different for domestic and international sales), 10 per cent would be allocated to Trans Tanz, and the rest would somehow go back to the community and the women in the film. I had never envisioned making a film that could make a significant sum of money; I therefore had to think carefully about how "the rest" would be given to the community. I decided that the split would be 10 per cent to Trans Tanz; 50 per cent to a "Pili Fund," from which the community could draw the money to spend as it saw fit; and 40 per cent to be divided among the main cast members to spend as they liked. I would not tell anyone how to spend the money, but I would help provide the infrastructure, such as bank accounts and potential savings plans, if the women wanted it. This decision caused concern for some involved in the project who questioned whether it was sensible to give away the money without some guidance, project, or purpose – in other words, without conditionality. They were concerned that the women would not know what to do with money, that family members might return and take the money, and that the women might be exploited by local politicians or opportunists, thus creating potential upheaval in their lives. A number of people plainly asked if I was really going to "give away" all the money.

The people who asked me these questions were a mix of crew members, academics, friends, and family. Part of me was concerned about the impact that such amounts of money would have on the community and the women's lives; part of me was thinking about paying off my mortgage. However, the money would go back to the community and the women involved in the film; this had been established at the outset of the project when there was no money. There would be no conditions attached to the money. I had spent the early years of my career conducting research that showed the problems of conditional aid lending, and now that I was in the position of lenders and donors such as the World Bank, I would not adopt the logic of the same bank that I had spent ten years criticizing (Harman 2009, 2010, 2011b). Moreover, I was not "giving away" money or aid money; the women and the communities in the film had earned it. I would also maintain my ethical responsibility to them to help avoid any foreseen harm caused by their involvement in the project, by providing guidance or by thinking through *with* them on the way to avoid any harm coming to them as a result of the money. I would recognize the women and the community as having their own agency to manage these harms and to spend the money where they thought it was important to do so or on what they wanted. The only thing I would control was when they would know about the money.

Material factors are an ever-present factor in transnational partnerships and forms of co-production, and shape the stories we see. Money can be divisive – who has money, who does not, who wants

money, who will give or withhold money – and can be productive as
the basis for enabling this kind of co-production. As this section has
explored, material concerns and their temporality can shape transparency and accountability within the transnational partnership. As
needs become greater, one partner may be more transparent about
these needs, which in turn can make another partner less transparent
about the ways in which their position or the project can meet these
needs. How money shapes transnational partnerships and co-production of research should not be surprising to anyone who has been
involved in any type of partnership or working relationship. Yet,
money remains a taboo subject that is seen to somewhat dirty transnational relations when conversations or concerns about money are
seen. While problematized, there is little taboo over feminists having
money from the global north to co-produce research or projects with
women in the global south; however, there is a taboo when women
in the global south make a claim to the money or how a project will
materially benefit them. As this section has explored, people are comfortable with the thought of women from the global south reaping
the benefits of a transnational project, when there are no benefits, but
when the monetary benefits become evident, questions arise as to who
should receive the money and how it should be spent. Questions are
framed in the paternalistic language of care for the impact of money
on poor women's lives but are underpinned by a notion that one side
of the partnership knows how to spend money better than the other
does. This fundamentally divides any notion of equal value of knowledge on both sides of the relationship and undermines the agency of
those receiving the money, by suggesting that they do not know how
to spend it or to safeguard themselves. For transnational relations to
thrive, the politics of money has to be seen in how it shapes transparency and different interests within the relationship. One party cannot
lay claim to knowing the best way to spend money. To do so undermines any notion of co-production and reinforces knowledge hierarchies and paternalist tendencies over the poor.

IMPLICATIONS FOR FEMINIST METHOD
AND SEEING POLITICS

The inevitable blurring of professional boundaries produced by a
research project of this kind reveals new insights and questions about
feminist method and the politics of seeing in IR. These insights and

questions inform my own feminist praxis that builds on the work of decolonial feminist scholars such as Desai, Mohanty, and Shohat. The co-production of *Pili* as a method of research builds on such work by demonstrating the importance of the mutual understanding of genealogies and the need for mutual reflexivity in the process of seeing, through direct and indirect ways. The discussion on the politics of co-production demonstrated that feminist method based on transnational collaboration is a "messy relationship" (Desai 2007), leading in practice to engagements with "discomforting truths" (Carty and Mohanty 2015, 88). The co-production of *Pili* shows that the politics of the past and the present continue to frame projects that want to change the future. There is no escaping that it was a project co-produced by a white, British, child-free, wealthy female academic who lived in a city and by black Tanzanian mothers who lived in rural villages and worked in low-paying, informal employment, and that the relationship was imbued with the politics of inequality, hierarchy, and colonial history. Fundamentally, however, it is the working through of such "discomforting truths" that generates critical reflections on the process of seeing; more than that, it is through this process that co-produced knowledge can be created and that hidden dimensions of such relationships – temporal, material, and agency – can be seen. This knowledge is not of the global south for the global north, but is of the global south and the global north and for a global audience. Discomfort does not mean that research of this kind is not and should not be done. To the contrary, I argue that it is through the inhabiting and revealing of the uncomfortable and messy politics of such relationships that transnational feminist praxis can continue to reflect and advance.

This chapter has shown that the co-production of film as method confirms what many feminists have already argued about transnational feminism and feminist praxis with regard to positionality, reciprocity, and long-term commitment. Positionality and acknowledgment by the researcher regarding gender, wealth, knowledge, race, and an issue not explored here but pertinent to such activity – sexuality – underpin feminist praxis and should be the basis upon which transnational relationships are developed. Depending on the type of transnational feminist activity, the most pertinent factor in this relationship is the issue of wealth, including the perceived notions of wealth and poverty, who owns the wealth, and who needs the money. However, as Mohanty (1998, 486) notes, imbued with the issues of positionality and wealth is the genealogy of the actors involved and the importance of understanding each other's genealogy and history. Hierarchies of wealth and differing genealogies do not have to be a barrier, but transnational feminist activity cannot be romanticized to transcend this. Instead, as Desai (2007, 5) argues, it is important to acknowledge the politics of dual possibilities: acknowledging the existing hierarchies and frameworks in which such interactions take place, and sharing a vision for a different future.

The reciprocal basis of research and knowledge creation, and the potentially transformative benefit of co-produced research, are of crucial importance. This point has to be mutually agreed upon and constituted throughout the project. However, some aspects of the benefits and pitfalls of the encounter cannot be foreseen or overstated. In practice research processes focus on the potentially negative components of engagement, which are in many respects rightfully overstated. In contrast, other than in risk assessments, such negative outcomes for the researcher are often *understated* because it is presumed that the researcher engages in such processes for their own gain and knowledge creation. Reciprocity shifts through the process of co-production as a form of transnational feminist activity. Reciprocal benefits and shortcomings therefore have to be as clear as possible at the outset of a project; in addition, there has to be a mutual awareness that such benefits are not linear. For co-produced feminist methods to work, there needs to be a collective commitment to reciprocal benefits and to the addressing of any shifts and changes in such benefits and reciprocity.

Finally, the co-production of *Pili* confirms feminist commitment to prolonged and sustained engagement as a core part of transnational feminist praxis. Short, time-bound projects are not representations of feminist method and knowledge creation. Such projects can produce some of the criticisms levied against the Western, material capture of transnational feminism. Any meaningful engagement requires long-term trust and a sustained relationship throughout the transformative plan, the project, and post project. This is a challenge to our perception of the research process as something that is done or completed. A feminist project is never completed; it is also deeply personal.

Positionality, *reciprocity*, and *long-term commitment* are all familiar terms to understanding feminist method, praxis, or relationships. Less familiar, and what the co-production of *Pili* starkly revealed, are the role of temporality, the shifting power and agency, and the role of money (which requires a frank discussion) in making these relationships function or dysfunction. Temporality frames much of the agency and mutual reciprocity in co-production and has the potential to frustrate collective ways of working if no attempts to engage in temporal dynamics are made. In the co-production of *Pili* it was the temporal issues that framed and at times frustrated the methods of seeing. Academic research is slow, and the realization of outputs from such research is similarly slow. However, the needs of some women, in this case the women of Miono, are much more immediate and material. The creation of knowledge in the long term is recognized as a good in the long term, but the everyday realities of women's lives mean that basic needs are essential and imminent. Temporal frustration in the project came from initial misunderstandings or the downplaying of the short- and long-term needs of all parties involved. Where this was unaddressed, it nearly led to the breakdown of the project. However, through the listening, conversation, and reflexivity of all involved, the temporal issues were understood and navigated in order to address the individual needs and the collective commitment to the shared project. It is by understanding the temporal dynamics of agency that we can fully see what the immediate and long-term needs and risks are for all women, as well as their agency in articulating, representing, and addressing such needs and risks. As the co-production of *Pili* demonstrates, feminist praxis and methods of seeing have to be cognizant of and adaptable to the shifting temporality of needs and change.

Related to the temporality and reciprocity of co-production are the shifting agency and power relationships during the life cycle of the co-production process. All actors had the ability to leave the project; this was particularly pertinent at the start of the process and was a powerful tool for the cast members during the main production of the film, but it shifted towards the completion of the film. At that time, the academic producer could physically leave the site of co-production but could not separate herself mentally from the project. The cast members were physically constrained by an inability to leave the site of co-production. Both the physical and the mental ability to leave a project constrain the agency of actors in different ways. For example, this could be acute for cast members who may be stigmatized in the communities in which they live or who cannot leave because of financial constraints, which in turn restricts their everyday agency. Less acute is how the researcher's agency is constrained by their inability to move on to new research and to think about new things, on account of continued relationships with the co-production partners and the time taken to manage the different relationships, expectations, and transparency involved in the project. Agency in the co-production of *Pili* became less about co-production and more about co-dependency between all partners: cast, crew, community, and me. The cast members were dependent on me to sell the film and manage the ethical commitment to reduce harm to them. The crew members were dependent on me to sell the film and ensure that it fulfilled their expectations. I was dependent on the cast and crew to maintain their support for the film and to maintain communication about the project. Agency during the life cycle of the project shifted from positionality and reciprocity to one of mutual co-dependency. This mutual co-dependency constrained the agency of actors in some respects (for example, the ability to leave the project) and enhanced the agency of actors in others (for example, using the co-productive element of the project as a unique selling point of the film to distributors).

Dependency, whether co-dependent or mutually dependent, is a word with strong, often negative connotations when used in reference to transnational relationships. A similar word with negative connotations is *money*, the money that divides and shapes relationships. The role of money or financial difference in research practices is a taboo in much of IR, the social sciences, and the humanities. Research is seen as a public good, and therefore research participants would want to participate in research for the common good. This is what we tell ourselves as researchers and those who participate in our research. In my past research projects the majority of interviewees or research participants have asked me what they get out of the research. I have explained to them that I would share the research findings and work with the participants to see how those findings were relevant to their own work, and in some instances I have offered my labour for free in other ways if it would be helpful to them. I have never paid research participants, other than to buy them a drink or a light snack if we are meeting in a public area. As chapter 2 discussed, co-produced methods of this kind that require regular labour and involvement over a sustained six-week period have to involve payment of participants to, at the very least, cover the cost of their lost earnings. The potential setback of such payment is the foreseen and unforeseen consequences discussed in this chapter.

The consequences of paying for involvement in co-production reveal two aspects. The first is that payment can produce new ethical challenges in the research process and presents an unavoidable frame to the co-production relationship. This frame occurs both with cast and crew and with their relationship to the academic researcher or film producer. The second revelation is that the obfuscation of this relationship or the denial that money is a factor (which should be ameliorated through effective co-production), conceals knowledge about how power works and reinforces the "othering" aspect of research. Money and material difference are an ever-present aspect of all types of research and shape the positionality of the researcher. It is something that any researcher from an institution in a high-income country who is conducting research in a low-income country will have to confront at some point in the research process. The extent to which this happens depends on the type of research and the degree of material difference. However, the issue of money is rarely confronted or discussed openly other than in ethical research processes about how not to incentivize research participation. Combined, the taboo around money and the need to conceal as part of the research ethics process reinforce both the barriers between the researcher and the researched, us and them, and the othering of research. This othering can be a convenient device for researchers to not confront or think through their positionality within the research process: researchers are somehow distinct or above the dirty business of money because of the ethical standard and common public goods frameworks within which we seek to work. However, researchers are not distinct from these material structures; we, like the people and processes involved in our research, are embedded in these structures. Co-production exposes such structures and involves a direct confrontation with them. Co-production and transnational politics require frank discussion over money that, while uncomfortable, allows us to develop our understanding of research positionality and ethics, feminist praxis, and transnational habits. This understanding could reveal the simple benefits of research to research participants, and how financial incentives or per diems incentivize and shape international diplomacy practices. Fundamentally, to obfuscate the role of money in shaping research and co-production conceals the very power relationships that we seek to explore in IR and the inequality that feminist methods seek to reveal.

CONCLUSION

Rotten tomatoes, rural funerals, and the use of children as leverage for money are not common themes of research method in IR.
They are, however, not uncommon for anyone conducting research
in rural East Africa or engaging in transnational feminist practices
where intimacy and everyday needs and risks have to be navigated and understood as key components of the research, project,
or movement. This chapter has critically engaged with the politics
of film as a method and as an output of co-production by reflecting on my position as the lead researcher and co-producer of the
film project and on the position of the women who co-produced
the film through their stories, acting, and locations. The chapter
explored what we already know about the limits, politics, and messiness of transnational collaboration and the potential and pitfalls
of this. Such exploration is vital to emphasizing a feminist praxis
that acknowledges genealogies, difference, and positionality but
does not use such acknowledgment as a panacea or justification to
acknowledge the issues and do it anyway. Instead, this chapter has
shown that through reflexivity in seeing and openly confronting the
messiness of such relations, feminist praxis towards change can be
advanced, new forms of knowledge can be created, and informal or
taboo forms of politics can be seen. Co-produced research requires
sustained relationships, intimacy, and contentious judgment calls on
a regular basis. However, it is by seeing this messy relationship and
the politics of co-production that new ways of collaboration, knowledge, and shared goals, such as co-producing a feature film, can be
realized. The key, as Desai argues, is to focus on the dual politics
of possibilities, "a pragmatic politics of what is possible within the
current conjecture and a visionary politics of what can be possible –
even as we recognize the power and complicity of some of us"
(2007, 5).

The chapter advances feminist praxis by showing the different
roles of temporality, agency, and money in the co-production process. Differences in temporal expectations, rhythms, and need all
frame transnational and co-productive relationships. These temporal differences can shift throughout the life cycle of a project and
can be deployed as a form of resistance or agency to the process.
Dependency and power asymmetries are not fixed to specific agents
within the co-productive relationship; they are in flux and change

according to the needs and interests of different agents. This is an important intervention as it challenges the notion that there is one agent, or a combination of agents, who has fixed power over other agents in the research relationship. While it is undoubtedly true that as the person with the money (*mzungu Sofia*) I held considerable power over the cast and crew of *Pili*; an emphasis on co-production in practice led to a co-dependency in which agency and power shifted between actors as the cast and crew used temporal, ethical, and material means to have agency over me. The role of money was fundamental to the co-production relationship. It is important to reiterate and show this. Money is unavoidable in the use of film as method: it is present in the visual aesthetic presented by the equipment and the process of paying people for props and by the resources necessary to produce even low-budget productions. Money is a taboo in the research process because of ethical concerns about incentivizing participation and the notion that research is a public good and therefore people should invest their time in it. To not see money and the role it has in positioning agents, framing the co-productive relationship, challenging participation, and shaping needs and interests overlooks the very division that stops us from seeing. Money, temporality, and agency all prevent women such as Pili from seeing and being seen (as well as enabling them to see and be seen) and shape the shifting agency and divisions between knower and known within the research process.

This chapter has explored the politics of what stops us from seeing, by deliberately focusing on the discomfort and difficulty of co-producing a feature film and on the ways in which co-dependent agency and temporal and material differences can restrict and enable the seeing of politics through film. The focus of the chapter has been on the practice of co-production by me and the women in the film. The next chapter continues to question what stops us from seeing, by focusing the analysis at the level of the state. Chapter 4 reflects on the role of the government of Tanzania and of gatekeeping at every level of state and society in restricting and shaping both the use of film as method and the politics we see.

4

Gatekeeping and Patronage
in the Politics We See

The politics of seeing is about what stops us from seeing and how film and film production help us see hidden and informal politics. This politics of seeing is most starkly exemplified at the level of the state, primarily with regard to how states engage in gatekeeping practices to control the stories that are told and the way in which women such as Pili are seen. However, film production does more than this; film as method opens up new ways of seeing the working practices of the state and how gatekeeping and patronage manifest at every level of society. In over ten years of working in Tanzania as a researcher and a trustee of an NGO I was never bribed by a co-worker, extorted by local immigration officials, asked for money, or detained at an airport by police. In the production of *Pili* all these things happened. This chapter details these events and situates them within the very specific context of film production. Film production reveals new insights on state behaviour that is born of a combination of the need to control the stories that are told and the way the state is seen, and the potential for personal, group, and state material gain. As chapters 1, 2, and 3 suggested, film as method has an aesthetic of wealth and the potential for audience and rupture; state and individual actors are aware of this and use formal and informal practices to negate and benefit from the process. Combined, these factors produce an acute form of state gatekeeping and patronage that can be seen and is reproduced at every level of society.

The intent of this chapter is to explore the role of states in preventing audiences from seeing women such as Pili and the way in which the process of film production enriches the understanding of the gatekeeping practices within the state, by seeing the informal and embedded nature of such practices at every level of society. In so doing, the chapter develops the themes of the previous chapter with regard to what stops us from seeing politics, the role of temporality and agency in the co-production process, and how film as method reveals new insights on traditional questions in IR. The chapter pursues this intent by first outlining the debates over gatekeeping and patronage politics and the way in which these concepts relate to the state in Africa in general, and Tanzania in particular. It then outlines the government agencies and structures that represent the gate, controlling the films and Tanzanian politics that are seen. The third section of the chapter critically examines how I navigated the gate to make *Pili* and how such gatekeeping exacerbated the cyclical nature of gatekeeping and the precariousness, risk, and distrust it involved. This section reflects on how patronage and gatekeeping work in practice and how the outsider is not distinct but is embedded in the practices of going around the gate. Finally, the chapter concludes with how the co-production of film advances the understanding of both state gatekeeping and the role of the state in controlling the politics we see.

GATEKEEPER POLITICS AND THE TANZANIAN STATE

States keep gates. These gates can take various forms – from physical borders that let people in and out of territories, to structural and network gates that let people access power and elected office, to financial gates that control the flow and taxation of revenue, to information and knowledge gates that control the politics seen. Gatekeeping politics has had particular resonance in the African politics literature with reference to understanding the African state and particularly the African state as a barrier to socio-economic and political development. African states have been labelled *quasi-states* (having legal sovereignty but failing to enact sovereignty; Jackson 1990), *extraverted states* (playing the international system to mobilize resources for their own ends; Bayart 2012), *governance states* (demonstrating "showcase status," as exemplary reformers, to foreign donors such as the World Bank; Harrison 2004), *instrumentalized disorder* (Chabal and Daloz 1999), *rentier states* or *petro states* (their political power being dependent on and defined by control of natural resources such as oil; Soares de Oliveira 2007), *fragile states* (having weak capacity in relation to the international system; Clapham 1996, 1998), *failed states* (lacking political and social infrastructure to provide basic services and public goods; R. Kaplan 1994; Rotberg 2004), and *neo-patrimonial states* (having democratic systems organized around patron-client relationships; Crawford Young 2012), among others. Without rehearsing all the debates around these different concepts here, what such labels have in common is that African states are somehow exceptional or particular in their relationship to the international through legacies of slavery and reparation, and colonialism and aid dependency, which in different ways have facilitated networks of patron-client relations as the operating principle of most states. For some, such international legacies and systems of patronage are seen as a central barrier to Africa's democratization, economic development, and, in some instances, agency in the international system because of aid dependency, and inequality or corruption, or both. To overcome such barriers, some suggest global restructuring of the world economy to address historical economic inequalities, while advocates of a developmental state emphasize restructuring the African state along the lines of East Asian state models that separate the state and economy from elite capture and excessive governmental control. However, as research on the African state has grown, so has the recognition that states are diverse and do not fit these different binaries or typologies. In addition, there is increased evidence of development gains being made by states that show clear evidence of international interference, patronage politics, and low-level corruption, leading some to add the term *hybrid states* to the list of African state typologies (Meagher 2012; Meagher, De Herdt, and Titeca 2014).

What I want to draw on in this chapter is the concept of gatekeeping and gatekeeping politics in the African state as a means of explaining the state behaviour of controlling the politics we see. Gatekeeping is seen as a pronounced feature of contemporary African statehood; whether refuted or reinforced, gatekeeping is still a practice with which scholars of African statehood engage. It is particularly relevant to this book because film as a method of co-production means at one point you have to navigate the state through film permits, location approval, and local power dynamics – the formal and informal gates to film production. This section looks in detail at how the concept of gatekeeping relates to the state in Tanzania. It does so first by engaging with the seminal work of Frederick Cooper on gatekeeper states and the various interventions made on this work, and, second, by seeing how such work can be applied to Tanzania. The section provides a detailed understanding of gatekeeping and how gatekeeper politics (rather than the gatekeeper state) becomes embedded in societies. It is this understanding that helps to read and explain the politics of film production in Tanzania and which, in turn, can be advanced by the practice of film production.

According to Cooper, the gatekeeper state is a legacy of the colonial period that "emerged out of a peculiar European-African history" and has significant repercussions for the modern postcolonial state. Colonial powers based their rule of African states on the monopoly of violence and an ability to control the flows in trade, finance, and resources in and out of the country (Cooper 2012). The ability to keep the gate of Africa's insertion into the global political economy enabled rulers such as Britain and France to maintain control while having illegitimate and precarious authority in their colonies. Authority was precarious on account of the weakened ability of the rulers to enter the social and cultural realm of the ruled (and vice versa) (Cooper 2012). Hence, while the colonial powers were able to keep the gate of the economy and the insertion of the state into the international, their domestic authority was made vulnerable by illegitimate rule and a distance from the ruled. Upon reaching independence from colonial rule, several African independence movements and leaders sought to define new forms of African state authority based in legitimate rule through consent of the people. However, as successors to the gatekeeper states, postcolonial state leaders saw that such gatekeeping practices could serve their own interests (Cooper 2012, 5), and thus adopted similar gatekeeping practices by working with old colonial institutions, cultures, and bureaucracies. The postcolonial state was inserted into the global economy through a dependency on international development and aid or, as Cooper calls it, on "a more recent form of colonialism" (156). Consequently, "once in power, African regimes proved distrustful of the very social linkages and the vision of citizenship upon which they had ridden to power" (159). The gatekeeper state in postcolonial Africa can therefore be depicted as one in which rulers "sit astride the interface between a territory and the rest of the world, collecting and distributing resources that derived from the gate itself: customs revenue and foreign aid; entry and exit visas; and permission to move currency in and out … Keeping the gate was more ambition than actuality, and struggles for the gate – and efforts of some groups to get around it – bedevilled African states from the start" (157). The ruling authority thus keeps the gate of what and who can or cannot leave the state but is also vulnerable to those who want access to the gate. Such vulnerability comes from internal threats to patronage networks and the external threat of loss of legitimacy within the international community.

The appeal of Cooper's gatekeeper state theory is its useful typology and means of understanding many African states. The typology fits many aspects of the colonial history and the postcolonial organization and behaviour of African states, which are revealed and understood through the application of the typology; it also aligns with much previous work on patronage politics in the postcolonial African states. Cooper's work chimes with considerable debate on the postcolonial, neo-patrimonial state and the depictions of de jure and de facto statehood in Africa and IR. The gatekeeper state has de jure statehood in that it has juridical recognition in the international, but, as Jackson would argue, suffers from a lack of de facto statehood, which heightens state vulnerability to internal dissent and external claims to legitimacy (1990). Neo-patrimonialism, as defined by patron-client relations where the state is organized around positions of loyalty, patronage to the president, and material gain for state officials, is also a key source of gatekeeper state vulnerability (Crawford Young 2012). Here, high-profile roles within the government or state bureaucracy are not attained through experience, expertise, or performance or because of a commitment to public service, but are given based on personal relationships and are conducted for status and personal material gain or, in this case, proximity to the gate or gatekeeper. For Crawford Young, the postcolonial state can be depicted as a hybrid mix of colonial legacies of patronage and authoritarian rule and of customary practices and efforts towards practising a Weberian ideal type of bureaucratic functionality (2012, 70).

Key to the bureaucratic functionality of gatekeeper and neo-patrimonial states is what Sklar depicts as the "managerial bourgeoisie" (1975). This managerial bourgeoisie is made up of civil servants, doctors, lawyers, military officers, and governmental leaders. Conventional wisdom from research on the postcolonial African state suggests that such a managerial bourgeoisie acts in its own interest – in this case to maintain its access and proximity to the gate – rather than that of the wider public (Tordoff 1997, 99; Crawford Young 2012, 45). For scholars such as Bayart, members of this elite managerial or bureaucratic bourgeoisie "were all the real worker-bees of the colonial hive" and "were instrumental in creating the foundations of the class which is currently dominant in Africa and in setting in motion the process of primitive accumulation from which the class was to benefit" (2012, 249). Thus, for Bayart, the group of elites at the centre of public office were in part a colonial construct that then imbibed such practices to constitute a specific class within postcolonial African society. It is this elite that is intrinsic to the maintenance of the gate by the ruling government: they support gatekeeping practices on account of in-kind benefits accrued through their proximity to the gate.

Gatekeeping practices have lasting legacies on the organization and function of state bureaucracies. First, there is at least the perception that public service leads to material gain and status within society. This can generate distrust among the public, frustrate their relationship and belief in public sector services such as health care, and attract people to work in the public sector for material reward rather than as a commitment to public service. Material benefit and public service do not have to be in tension with each other; however, an emphasis on material benefits can adversely influence the incentive for delivering better public services for a population. Second, such gatekeeping practices promote homogeneity in the public sector because those who are promoted or occupy senior roles tend to have shared backgrounds, experiences, expertise, and gender. Third, public administration is organized around individuals and personalities that can often change when they fall out of favour with the political establishment or become stale because they do not challenge the status quo. Fourth, gatekeeping restricts African agency as actors defer to key leaders within the bureaucracy or government, and those outside of the bureaucracy are limited by the rules and practices of patrimonial linkages. Agency is restricted as actors become unwilling to enact agency by challenging authority or suggesting change, which may limit their advantageous position. Fifth, gatekeeping enhances state vulnerability to international involvement and dependency and to national instability caused by the ruler's fear of relinquishing the benefits of gatekeeper control.

The appeal of Cooper's gatekeeper state is also the main source of its critique: that as a typology it becomes totalizing and homogenizing of all African states. This critique is perhaps unfair because it is unclear whether it was Cooper's intent to produce such a typology, and the detailed empirical analysis that underpins his *Africa since 1940* suggests an attempt to avoid homogenizing and totalizing categories of statehood. Wider critical engagement with Cooper's work falls roughly into three categories: the unitary intent of the gatekeeper state and the politics of assemblage; the gatekeeper state and the developmental state model; and the "African" nature of gatekeeper politics. Each of these interventions is not taken as criticism of Cooper's work but instead provides greater depth of the understanding of gatekeeper *politics*, rather than a model of statehood.

The first intervention on Cooper's work relates to the wider debate in IR as to whether states exist to be able to engage in gatekeeping activities or to act in unitary ways to maintain state interests around the gate. For scholars such as Death, drawing on the work of Dunn (2009) and Jessop (1990), African states are assemblages of practices and discourses. In understanding states as assemblages, Death argues that, contrary to Cooper's typology, "determining intentions and motivations is complex in any case and it seems unnecessarily and unhelpfully reductive and economistic to categorise African states" (2015, 15). The gatekeeper state is therefore unhelpful as a unit of analysis because this presumes a typology that becomes a catch-all in its application to African states, and it is impossible to suggest that African states act as unitary agents. To put it another way, given the internal and external factors that shape African statehood, and the multiple divisions even within political parties and elites, it becomes difficult to identify the interests of the state and if or how it keeps the gate; political actors within the state may keep the gate, but, as states are not unitary actors but assemblages of political actors, it is impossible to assign gatekeeping to a "state."

The second intervention on the relationship between the gatekeeper and the developmental state is based on the debate between Hillbom and Taylor. The developmental state model is predominantly based on the "East Asian miracle" of economic development that emphasizes good governance politics and institutional reform (C. Johnson 1982; Wade 1992). The key components of the developmental state, summarized here by Taylor, are "a determined developmental elite; relative autonomy; a powerful, competent and insulated bureaucracy; a weak and subordinated civil society; the effective management of non-state economic interests; and legitimacy and performance" (2012, 466–7). The economic success of East Asian states led both to a wider debate as to whether such a model could work in low- and middle-income African states and to various applications of the model by African governments in partnership with international financial institutions, such as the World Bank, and by development economists (C. Johnson 1982; Tan 2011; Wade 1992). Crudely, the wider debate and the relative success and failure of such applications have concentrated on whether the model can work in states that evidence patronage politics and gatekeeping practices. Hillbom's work argues that, contrary to the assumption that Botswana is a model of developmental statehood, the elite capture of institutions, the lack of a diverse economy, and a dual society between the formal and informal show greater evidence that Botswana conforms to the gatekeeper state model (2011). At best, according to Hillbom, Botswana could be characterized as a "development oriented gate-keeping state" (88). However, Taylor argues to the contrary, that Botswana exemplifies a state pursuing a hegemonic project of developmental statehood and that substantively the political-economic history of Botswana does not follow the typology outlined by Cooper (Taylor 2012). Hillbom's response to Taylor is that as an economic historian she thinks differently than a political scientist (Hillbom 2012). What is revealing in this debate is not who has the correct reading of Botswana's socio-economic development and statehood but that the Botswana state exhibits key characteristics of both typologies and, crucially, that gatekeeping practices are not necessarily barriers to development as is often assumed. Such arguments point to the "hybrid" model of African statehood that combines gatekeeping and patrimonial tendencies with development and democracy (Meagher 2012; Meagher, De Herdt, and Titeca 2014). This suggests that states do not have to fit a false binary between gatekeeping and developmental practices and that African states, as with all states, are complex actors framed by their socio-economic history and institutional development that can combine gatekeeping legacies and external and internal developmental trajectories; these, in turn, shape the workings and politics of state-based political actors. It is therefore perhaps more useful to see African states as engaging in gatekeeping politics as part of wider state practices rather than defining them as gatekeeping states.

The use of gatekeeping politics as a practice of African states, rather than gatekeeper states defining African statehood, draws on the work of Beresford. Beresford's work on gatekeeping politics in South Africa, and with Anderson in Sierra Leone, offers a third intervention on Cooper's typology: that gatekeeping politics is not an inherent or defining feature of African states but is a core feature of capitalist liberal democracies throughout the world (Anderson and Beresford 2016; Beresford 2015). Beresford does not directly use Cooper's model of the gatekeeper state as his unit of analysis but instead draws on the work of Hyden (1983) to define gatekeeping as "how political leaders in positions of authority within the ruling party or public office control access to resources and opportunities in order to forward their own political and economic ends. A cyclical relationship emerges in which resources and opportunities are distributed through patronage networks to regenerate the political power of the patron (or gatekeeper), and political power (access to state spoils) is in turn used to replenish the resources needed to maintain networks and 'purchase' the affection of the supporters" (Beresford 2015, 228–9).

Beresford identifies the two defining features of gatekeeping: "spoils consumption" or, in other words, public resources for private gain; and a "crony capitalism" relationship to public sector as a form of private accumulation (2015). Key to the practices of gatekeeping is not only the historical context to such political practices as exemplified by the work of Cooper and Taylor but the everyday political economy in which the gatekeeping operates (Beresford 2015, 230). Here Beresford demonstrates how the African National Congress (ANC) has been able to absorb and co-opt frustration and discontent with patronage systems in a way that maintains and feeds the power of the ANC and gatekeeping. The absorption of such discontent not only maintains but also reinforces the embedded nature of gatekeeping in South African society, as people use patronage networks to navigate everyday politics and political power. Beresford's overarching argument is that, while gatekeeping has not necessarily reduced developmental outcomes, it has contributed to "depoliticizing the inequalities and social injustice at the heart of underdevelopment ... while reifying the power of the ANC" and thus reducing the space for transformative politics (230). However, for Beresford, gatekeeping is not something particular to the ANC or South Africa; it is a feature intertwined with the development of capitalism that is in evidence to lesser and greater degrees in most liberal democracies (247). Hence, African statehood is not synonymous with gatekeeper states, but gatekeeping practices and politics can be seen as part of the practice of statehood to a lesser or greater extent in most capitalist economies.

What Cooper's work on the gatekeeper state and these three interventions suggest is that, though contested, gatekeeping and patrimonialism remain practices of pertinent importance to understanding the modern African state. While each of the three interventions takes issue with aspects of Cooper's theory, none rejects the concept and practice of gatekeeping altogether. Instead gatekeeping is seen either as a more universal phenomenon beyond Africa or as something political actors rather than states do. What is revealing here, and particularly in what follows in navigating the Tanzanian gate in the production of *Pili*, is how different political actors within the state practise gatekeeping *and* how gatekeeping is embedded within the everyday political economy of the state. These last two points are often overlooked in discussions on gatekeeping and patrimonial politics, in other words, how they work at the micro everyday level to shape political outcomes. As such, it is the everyday element of gatekeeper politics, who keeps the gate, and how it is navigated that further our understanding of this practice. Not only does film depict how gatekeeping works and is embedded within everyday life in communities such as Miono, but the process of making a film reveals how gatekeeping manifests through formal and informal power structures at every level of society.

Tanzania

Given the previous discussion, it is important to situate the understanding of gatekeeper, patronage, and developmental politics within the political-economic context in which the film was made, Tanzania. Tanzania is often seen as having a different postcolonial trajectory from that of other East African states because of *ujamaa* and the consolidation of power by the Tanganyika African National Union (TANU) (which later became Chama Cha Mapinduzi [CCM], following the unification of Tanzania and Zanzibar). Ujamaa is commonly described as a distinct form of socialism in Tanzania developed by President Julius Nyerere, in which, at least rhetorically, power was emphasized from below, with the people, and unified the population behind a Tanzanian identity that emphasized cohesion and postcolonial freedom (Hyden 1980; J.C. Scott 1998, chap. 7). The key political-economic aspects of ujamaa were villagization (the resettling and organizing of Tanzanians into distinct villages ruled by village councils and assemblies and engaged in collective agriculture); state-led industrialization through the nationalization of existing industries, and new parastatal industries; and the adoption of Swahili as the national language (Brockington 2008). The process was an attempt to decentralize power through villagization while consolidating these structures and the economic program of nationalization and state-led industrialization around the central party. Ujamaa was a large project of social engineering in which society could be organized into villages that would be productive for the common economy and social order. There are two common, positive narratives surrounding ujamaa: (1) the advances in basic literacy as part of the emphasis on primary education, and (2) the unifying impact on Tanzanians in building a nation-state that avoided the civil conflict and post-independence struggle seen in neighbouring states (Saul 2012, 121). However, these positive narratives overlook the substantive problems and struggles arising from the ujamaa period. At the most basic level the experiment was not seen to work: Tanzania's economic development became stagnant, and the process of villagization and common agriculture did not lead to greater productivity or the sharing of revenues among the poor and local farmers (J.C. Scott 1998; Sundet 1994). As James Scott argues, "like Soviet collectives, ujamaa villages were economic and ecological failures ... They had also forgotten the most important fact about social engineering: its efficiency depends on the response and cooperation of real human subjects" (1998, 225). The positive "unifying" narrative of ujamaa overlooked the wider issues of class struggle through enforced resettlement, occasional violence, the silencing and punishment of critics, and party political elite capture of local village authorities (Saul 2012; J.C. Scott 1998, chap. 7; Sundet 1994; Von Freyhold 1977).

Nyerere's legacy as *mwalimu* (teacher and father) endures in contemporary Tanzania. His iconography and speeches continue to regularly inform news and broadcast media content and are deployed by the CCM as evidence of the party's assumed right to rule. What is interesting about this legacy is its use by the CCM to reinforce its position as the natural ruling party, a party that is bounded within a political history of class struggle and discontent with ujamaa. As Brockington's work (2008) on contemporary village politics in Tanzania suggests, struggle and discontent with the political elite at the local and national level are not limited to the ujamaa period of the 1960s and 1970s. Brockington's study explores community members' understanding and discontent about the ways in which revenue was spent, accounted for, and illegally used by local officials in the village of Mtowisa, Tanzania. His work shows evidence of popular discontent but that this does not produce change: people can form communities through villagization, but accountability is only produced when it is won, not given (Brockington 2008). This is what Brockington poses as the core issue in village politics: "There is not so much a failure of accountability here, rather its absence. Politics and government here works without it" (122). Hence, one key legacy of post-independence ujamaa has been a state that produces systems of decentralized rule bounded to the lead party, in which patron-client relations are established but unpopular; yet such unpopularity does not lead to political change.

Gray's work on the political economy of Tanzania post-independence is particularly insightful on how ujamaa and the politics of corruption have shaped political trajectories within the state. Her earlier work in Tanzania demonstrates that both periods of socialist and liberalized industrial policy were shaped by the same political settlement of one ruling party, of even distribution of power among class groups within the state, and of "limited success" in both kinds of economic restructuring (Gray 2013; Gray and Khan 2010). Gray's close analysis of industrial policy and shifting approaches demonstrates divisions among the elite, private ownership of industry during the period of ujamaa, and how industrialization failed to address the constraints of the ujamaa legacy (2013). The limit lay in acknowledging the role of the private sector in the period of socialist reform and the constraints towards liberalization posed by a one-party system, which on the one hand suggests stability but on the other curtails competition (Gray 2013). This analysis is important as it reveals the constraining, path-dependent nature of the ujamaa period for institutional change. In addition, it aligns with the work of Harrison in demonstrating that, far from isolation, the ujamaa period was one of integration with the global political economy as donors such as the World Bank engaged with the process (Harrison 2004, 30).

Gray's use of Khan's political settlements theory – that a settlement is "the combination of institutions and the underlying distribution of power in a society" (Gray 2015, 4), and thus state practices such as corruption should be situated within the wider context of capitalist transformation – to understand corruption in Tanzania in her later work effectively opens up "the black box" of the Tanzanian state

(4). Gray argues that Tanzania's transition to independence and economic liberalization created divisions and factions among the elite within the party system and government. The struggle for independence "left the country with a muted experience of political mobilization" (14) that, in a view similar to that of Brockington's analysis, has curtailed accountability structures and demands. According to Gray, contrary to the situation in many African states and to patrimonial theory, power in Tanzania is organized not around the president or ideology but around the party and the education and employment networks, thus constraining the president's ability to act. The interventions that seek to address corruption by stopping aid flows are flawed because the fragmented political networks organized around the leading party, not leaders, shape power (2015).

Feminist research in Tanzania shows that women were involved in the independence movement but did not come to occupy positions of power within post-independence political networks. As Mbilinyi argued in her comprehensive study on women's employment patterns for the International Labour Organization in 1986, "women are systematically excluded from positions of power and/or prestige. They are relegated either to manual work or to work on implementation, but not on decision-making or creativity," and government decision-makers "tend to be prejudiced against women at all levels" (1986, 140 and 169). According to Shayo's work (2005), little progress has been made since this study; women do not hold senior leadership positions in government, in the ruling party (CCM), or in the other political parties and thus are at the margins of patronage networks.

Tanzania, in many respects, follows the model of patronage politics and gatekeeping that typifies much discussion on the African state: patron-client relationships are key to getting things done and opening up the gate to political influence and economic resources; such relations are shaped by the postcolonial institutions and political settlements that were formed during the struggle for and realization of independence; there is distrust among the population that positioned the ruling party in power; all of which is underpinned by institutional shifts and engagement with processes of capitalist transformation. However, what is notable about Tanzanian politics is the ongoing legacy and influence of ujamaa and post-independence state building. The Tanzanian state is organized around one-party politics, not the president. Thus, patron-client relations are dispersed among the political elite. The political elite comprises those within the party and those allied to the party in the private sector and international organizations. There is not a unified political elite but a divided elite organized around patron-client networks of education and employment rather than ideology and a legacy of struggle. The power of the elite through the ruling party, CCM, is not centralized in Dar es Salaam but draws on its decentralized base in local authorities. Power is therefore not based on one's closeness to the capital city but on the networks within distinct territories. Finally, as also perceived by Beresford in South Africa, there is an accountability conundrum in Tanzania where people are aware of and dislike the corrupt practices they see but do not use democratic structures to make change. At the same time, as similarly discerned by Cooper's analysis on gatekeeper statehood, the members of the elite themselves do not trust the population that maintains the ruling party's power. There is therefore a lack of trust between the ruler and the ruled. The ruling elite, in this case the CCM, absorbs this discontent within the system of rule through narratives of post-independence and of *mwalimu*.

Gatekeeping politics thus exists in Tanzania; however, it is dispersed among party elites and maintained by the structures of society that benefit the least from such structures. As the next section demonstrates, gatekeeping is practised at different levels of the state in Tanzania and reproduces division among the elite and distrust at every level of government. As scholars such as Death (2015) caution, there is little evidence of the state acting as a unitary actor; it is therefore more revealing to see which actors or assemblages keep the gates and what impact this has on the state and the ability to govern. If patronage and gatekeeping networks are rooted in the everyday political economy of Tanzanians, it is important to consider how the gate is kept, how people get around the gate, how this shapes their decisions, and how the gate attempts to keep stories of Pili within the state. As the next section shows, gatekeeping in the production of *Pili* was dispersed among government agencies and actors. The more formal the gate, the more informal the measures taken to navigate it and get the film made.

THE GATE

The principal gate to making a film in Tanzania is the Tanzania Film Board. Like in most states, the film board issues permits for filming based on the location of the film and on agreement from the representatives of that area. This requires the formal submission of paper-work outlining the intent of the film, the shooting locations, details of the main crew, the itinerary, and a fee of US$1,000. However, as this section explores, the formal procedure of securing a permit becomes adapted to the whim of the gatekeeper who changes pro-cedure as a means of legitimating and reinforcing their role and of asserting power over the film producer. The more I fulfilled the for-mal requirements of securing a permit, the higher the gate became. As a consequence, the formal practice of navigating the gate becomes subsumed to the informal and local structures of patronage: whom you know, what power they infer or offer in order to unlock the gate, and artificial directives presented as "procedure." This section explores how the gate operated and adapted at the national level in the securing of a film permit. It demonstrates the co-dependent but clashing relationship between formal and informal, central and local authority, state practices in Tanzania; that the state does not act as a unitary actor but through a system of doubt and mistrust; and how gatekeeping politics is reproduced and reinforced through everyday political practice and navigation of the gate.

An application for a film permit to the Tanzanian High Commission in the United Kingdom was made in October 2015; once it had been approved, a full application was submitted to the Tanzania Film Board via email in the same month and then in person in November. Email correspondence with the film board suggested that this would be a straightforward process. However, when I arrived in Tanzania to finalize the paperwork and pay the fee for the permit, the film board informed me that I needed a letter of support from the Ministry of Health and Social Welfare because the subject matter of the film related to HIV/AIDS. This was the first case of the gate being raised by expansion of the government's involvement with the project to include the Ministry of Health and Social Welfare.

After I had submitted the paperwork detailing the film synopsis, the passport details and biographies of the director and the pro-ducer, and ethical considerations and had spent three days sitting in the Ministry of Health and Social Welfare, the director of preventive services provided a letter of support for the project but noted that two members of the ministry would have to be present throughout the shoot, and their full per diems and expenses paid. Then the chief medical officer emailed a list of requirements that the film would have to meet to receive approval. The majority of these requirements related to project transparency and ethical responsibilities to vulnerable populations that would be expected of approval for any project of this kind. However, one pertinent problem was the proposed ministerial veto over the final content of the film and the supervision of the ministry in the film's production. This was the second case of the gate to making the film being raised: to have ministerial veto over the production and edit of the film and its content.

Once the letter from the Ministry of Health and Social Welfare was secured, the film board noted that, as the word *research* appeared twice in the synopsis, the application had to be referred to the government research agency the Commission for Sciences and Technology (COSTECH). One month followed, and the film board requested that the US$1,000 be transferred to secure the permit. When the money had been transferred into the account of the director of information services, the film board stated that, because the film included HIV/AIDS, the project had to be referred to the National Institute for Medical Research (NIMR). Written objections were submitted to the film board based on the fact that the film was not clinical research, none of the film crew or researchers involved were clinicians or had any experience in medical research, the film had already been presented to COSTECH who was responsible for social science and humanities research permits, and therefore the film should not be subject to NIMR approval or procedure. The film board was adamant in its need for the NIMR to approve the project, but had not formally notified the institute. Once contact had been made with the NIMR, an additional US$500 was paid to submit to them five hard copies (the emailed versions were rejected) of a letter of introduction, a letter of support from Trans Tanz, and a complete application form – most of which referred to clinical trials and was therefore not applicable to this project. Initially NIMR representatives expressed to fixers with whom I worked that they were unsure as to why they had to review the application because it was a film and not clinical research; however, when it was formally lodged with them, they would have to follow through with their procedure. The NIMR did nothing with this submission until it was followed up one year after the fee had been paid and all documentation had been submitted. Subsequent to the follow-up I was asked to submit a letter of support from the district medical officer of Pwani and the local doctors in Miono where the film would be based. Both of these documents were supplied, and the NIMR finally sent through its approval to the film board. However, similarly to that of the Ministry of Health and Social Welfare, the approval included the caveat that the final edit and publication of the film would be subject to NIMR approval. The film board had raised the gate for a third time by introducing an additional financial and institutional barrier to the project.

The raising of the gate to make entry to film production more difficult by additional institutional and financial requirements and delay tactics can be explained in different ways. The simplest explanation is that increased gatekeeping introduced additional revenue for the state. Introducing different requirements and institutions opened up formal opportunities to increase state revenue (the film permit plus the NIMR submission fee) and informal opportunities (for example, a request for a laptop computer or tablet). While revenue might have been part of the issue and aligned with Gray's notion of "petty pilfering" (2015, 2) within the state, the fees were one-time payments and not sufficiently large enough to warrant the amount of time and effort involved for all parties. An alternative explanation is that what I experienced was not an unusual form of gatekeeping but an established procedure necessary to make a film in Tanzania. The film does have sensitive content and involves a potentially vulnerable population (as discussed in chapter 3), and it is therefore not out of the ordinary for health authorities to be consulted in the project. The procedure outlined by the NIMR and the Ministry of Health and Social Welfare follows established practice on research. However, the film was not a form of clinical research, and, moreover, on consultation with a number of Tanzanian production companies, I found that the referral of my project was an isolated incident. No one had heard of this happening before. It was the norm for film productions to meet obstruction and new hoops to jump through, but the introduction of the NIMR and the research process was not. Perhaps the different treatment was on account of the film project being based at a university rather than a production company. According to the experience of other production companies, the initial response from the NIMR, and the fact that the film board decided to raise the gate after receiving the US$1,000 fee for the permit, suggest that much of what happened was not established procedure but was introduced as the process unfurled.

If my application for a permit did not follow usual procedure, the explanation for the obfuscation could be that the film board did not want me to make the film and therefore wanted to make the process

increasingly difficult so that I would give up. The government of
Tanzania does not want films to be made that challenge the state's reputation as having "showcase status" among donors (Harrison 2004,
39), reflect badly on the government, or address contentious issues.
Government agencies control what people see and how Tanzania is
seen by the world. The need to control film production, particularly
by foreign film producers, had become particularly acute following the
2004 film *Darwin's Nightmare*, which was criticized by the government of Tanzania for portraying the country negatively (Rice 2006).
The Tanzania Film Board could have been genuinely sensitive to what
I wanted to do and therefore introduced additional checks, balances,
and restrictions through government representation on the shoot and
final editorial control in order to minimize any potentially negative
connotations to the state. The film board's reaction to the film could
be read as an attempt to protect the people living with HIV/AIDS from
exposure or exploitation by a foreign film crew. This appeared to be
the official position of the Ministry of Health and Social Welfare and
the NIMR. On one level, such actions discriminated against people
living with HIV/AIDS by limiting their opportunity and choice to be in
the film in ways that people who were not HIV positive were not limited. The intent of the film was to *positively* discriminate in favour of
people living with HIV in Tanzania so that they could tell their stories.
Excessive state protection led to negative discrimination. However,
on another level, the actions of the state reflect a wider tendency to
view HIV/AIDS as an exceptional health issue. As the introduction and
chapter 1 outlined, exceptionalism is related to stigma, behaviour,
security, and celebrity, but it is also about the amount of money allocated to HIV/AIDS in global health that has resulted in the disease
being instrumentalized by governments and civil society in various
ways for material gain. This is not a new finding, but it corresponds
with work on the markets developed around HIV/AIDS funding by
community organizations (Harman 2010). The aesthetic of wealth
represented by the act of filmmaking – equipment, expertise, potential
profit – combined with the film focusing on a disease that had been
a source of donor income for the state, leveraged the importance of
the film.

The state's need to censor the film highlights an additional explanation of the protracted procedure: the need for civil servants to
protect their jobs during a period of instability and unease within the
Tanzanian civil service. In November 2015 President John Magufuli

was elected on a reformist mandate and began a series of high-profile measures to limit state corruption, waste, and poor performance. At the start of his term Magufuli publicly cut the budget for the parliament-opening state dinner from TSh300 million (US$150,000) to TSh25 million (S$12,500); he banned first-class travel for government trips for all except the very senior members of government; he suspended the commissioner of the Tanzania Revenue Authority over the loss of cargo containers worth TSh80 billion (US$40 million); and, to the delight of many Tanzanians, he became famous for appearing unannounced in various ministries and hospitals to question why people were not working and why equipment was out of order (BBC 2015; Monks 2016; Mwenda 2016). Such gestures initially prompted popularity among both Tanzanians and Kenyans who thought that their government could learn from Magufuli, as depicted by the social media hashtag #whatwouldmagufulido, and temporarily earned him the nickname "the bulldozer." However, the sacking of ministers and civil servants made government workers vulnerable, and the established patron relations obsolete. Securing a film permit thus became caught between the gatekeeping practices of controlling and regulating the stories told in Tanzania, and the second-guessing by officials of the president's next move in order to protect their jobs. Vulnerability exacerbated the perception of state regulation and gatekeeping and the need to control and censor the stories being told in Tanzania.

The final explanation underpinning all of this was that the state did not trust my intentions. Despite following the formal procedure, I had not followed the informal procedure of submitting an application to the film board via a known fixer. I had in effect appeared from nowhere with my paperwork and fees, without a letter of introduction or a Tanzanian fixer, and was therefore judged with suspicion. This was a basic error on my part of which I should have been cognizant, given my previous experience of conducting research in Tanzania; introductions, informal networks, and patronage structures are key to gaining any acceptance by the state. A common subtext to much of the discussion I had with government agencies was that they somehow did not trust what the project was about. This was in part perhaps because the paperwork highlighted that the film was initially conceived as a "docu-drama," something that is not easy to categorize, which led to confusion as the film developed. It could also have been over the unusual origin of the film – a university project rather than a film production company. However, it was also in part because all the paperwork was submitted directly without going through the known fixers who seemed to legitimize applications to the film board. Submitting paperwork without knowing someone who acts as a legitimizing agent produces distrust. I had prepared and submitted all the paperwork myself; it was only after the bottlenecks arose that I contacted a fixer. When fixers were introduced to help assist with the process, they were informally asked, "Who is this girl?" "What does she want?" in an attempt to demonstrate both hierarchy (with the repetitive use of *girl*) and lack of trust. Distrust emphasized the need for short-term gain and self-protection that in this instance manifested itself through bureaucracy, maintenance of hierarchy and power over (rather than power to), and obstruction.

The gatekeeping practices exhibited by the Tanzanian state were therefore a combination of the established norms of state revenue and patron-client concerns and a wider need for control of the representation of Tanzania and the stories told. Underpinning this was the need for civil servants to protect and leverage their own power within the state and the ruling party and to show a level of distrust towards me because of my failure to engage with the informal rules of the state; these rules suggest that I should have worked with known fixers and government insiders who would have made the process more straightforward for both parties. I did not initially do this, because I did not have the budget for a fixer, and, given my contacts in the area in which the film would be shot, I naïvely did not think that this would be necessary. The relationship between the formal gatekeeping practices and the informal processes that are key to unlocking the gate represents the co-dependent tension between the formal and the informal. As the next two sections demonstrate, the more formal the gatekeeping became, the more reliant I became on informal processes, which then ultimately undermined the legitimacy of the formal process.

The formal procedure suggests that all applicants are equal in the process of securing a film permit as long as they have the correct paperwork and can afford the permit fees. However, the informal procedure suggests that the formal procedure is dependent not on whom you know but on who knows you and will vouch for you as your patron. This puts an independent researcher like me in a bind because to produce a film of this kind I had to enter into a number of relationships as a client to a patron (senior health officials) who had no relationship to the project but would be required to write appropriate letters of support. However, it also presented an opportunity because my encounters with the state did not suggest that different authorities were operating in a unified or joint manner; I could therefore work with different aspects of the state to produce the film. As the next section explores, the practice of making a film required me, far from being a distinct, independent researcher, to navigate the gatekeeping practices of the Tanzanian state, and the higher the gate, the more I, like many Tanzanian citizens, went around the gate. This undermined the formal procedure for both me and the state: I had begun the process of making the film by carefully adhering to the rules of the state, but, as they changed, the gate became higher, and the rules seemed to be introduced or made up the more I navigated and went around the gate, playing politics with different state agencies, and in some respects transfiguring into a person not to be trusted. Substantively in navigating the gate and engaging in the wider politics of patronage, I exacerbated the very issue I was seeking to avoid. By the time the film began shooting in February 2016, the government of Tanzania had received US$2,000 for the project: $500 for five business visas for the UK crew, $500 for the NIMR application, and $1,000 to the Tanzania Film Board; formal submissions had been made to the film board and the NIMR, but no film permit had been issued. I finally received a film permit in March 2017, one year after the film had wrapped.

GOING AROUND THE GATE

The decision to proceed with the film production, though a film permit had been paid for but not physically received, was made in January 2016. Throughout December and January I had continued to work with a friend and two fixers in Tanzania to try and secure the permit. This involved drawing on all their networks in the Tanzanian government and film sector to see what the issue was and how it could be resolved. There seemed to be genuine confusion as to why the issue had been referred for medical ethical approval, but not surprise given the changes in government that were happening at the time. However, the more the issue was explored, the less likely it seemed that the film board would issue a permit or return the permit fee. At one point it was informally suggested that I resubmit all the paperwork and a new fee through a fixer company known to the film board.

Exasperated by the process and not knowing how to formally and informally progress the issue, I decided to proceed with the production. The crew was prepared, the cast was ready, and there seemed to be no sense in delaying the production in either the short term (any minor delays would mean shooting during the rainy season, which would be impossible) or the long term (no time estimate was given by the NIMR or the film board for the resolution of the issue; it could have been two weeks or two years). I decided to proceed by going around the gate where possible to make the film, while trying also to unlock the gate by continuing to work with a fixer to chase the relevant government sectors for a permit. My hope was that the permit issue would be resolved within two weeks of the start of shooting.

Contemporary forms of gatekeeper statehood are organized around the formal reification of paperwork and bureaucratic procedure and the patronage networks at multiple levels to enable ways of circumventing paperwork and excessive bureaucratic procedure. The two elements are mutually reinforcing and contradictory because each practice undermines the other. However, the co-dependent nature of these practices means that an actor needs both in order to navigate the gate. The first element – paperwork and evidence of bureaucratic engagement – was relatively straightforward to demonstrate. I had duplicate copies of the film board application, the NIMR application, the proof of payment to the film board, the proof of payment to the NIMR the letter of introduction from the Ministry of Health and Social Welfare, the proof of ethics approval from my university, and the letters of introduction on letterhead, and, crucially, I had evidence of all the formal visa applications and business visas for the UK crew members. In addition, I had evidence of payment made to every person and for every item connected with the project. The only paperwork that was problematic was a contract with one Tanzanian crew member who "forgot" to bring the signed contract from home in the initial weeks of production. Otherwise I had contracts and signed invoices or proof of payment from everyone else involved with the project. I therefore had a substantial package of paperwork to demonstrate that the authorities were aware of what I was doing, that I had submitted fees to the state, and that the letterheads and insignia on the paperwork inferred legitimacy or status.

Securing a patron at the local level was relatively straightforward given the combination of my ten years of experience working in the community in which the film was based, my white skin colour as *mzungu Sofia* that inferred wealth, my doctorate that suggested status and networks, and a film project that suggested potential future income. From the outset I was able to establish good relationships with the doctors working in the local care and treatment centres who were keen to support the project and allowed me to use the centres as locations for the film. Throughout the project the doctors and other medical professionals in the local clinics were the most straightforward and transparent people with whom to work; they asked for nothing in return, supplied paperwork on request, went out of their way to support the project, and saw the relationship more as a partnership than as a patron-client engagement. This approach contrasted significantly with that of the regional health officials, who through Tanzanian's decentralized health system had significant autonomy from the central government as well as power over the region. My first engagement with the senior health official for the region was straightforward; I had the letter from the Ministry of Health and Social Welfare so he was happy for me to proceed. As was often the case with regional health positions, the senior health official whom I met at the outset of the project was then replaced. The replacement was similarly satisfied by the ministry letter from central government. However, when the NIMR requested that his name be added to my film permit application as my Tanzanian point of contact, he asked for a laptop, then a tablet, and then pictures of me. I declined each request.

The other key to opening the gate at the local level was my relationship with Julius, the driver of the Trans Tanz bus. During the preparatory trip to Tanzania to obtain stories and cast the film I began to see posters of the driver in the ruling party's signature green and yellow colours all over Miono. He had sought and won a position in local office. Part of his election campaign had been to use the work he had been doing with the community through Trans Tanz to get elected. He had not informed the trustees of this. It was also clear that he was still taking his salary from the charity and then subcontracting the work to another driver who was unknown to the trustees. Some members of the community even suggested that Julius had used the Trans Tanz bus for campaign purposes (which he refuted). This presented a conundrum: I was effectively the boss of the local politician, which meant that I would be protected at the local level from any unwanted police or government interference during filming, but I was also concerned first that people would only participate in the project because of my link to him and their concern about the consequences of not participating, and second that he had frustrated the terms of his contract for which I was responsible. I therefore had to discuss with Julius what had happened and what could be the way forward, while at the same time distancing myself from him in a way that would not have any consequences for those participating in the film. We were mutually dependent as co-patrons: he needed me to keep his name involved with Trans Tanz, otherwise he would lose legitimacy in the community; as a trustee I needed to ensure my commitment to Trans Tanz, and as a film producer I had to act independently of the organization to ensure no unwanted interference from local authorities. We talked during the pre-production, and Julius avoided me during the main production; the only time I saw him then was when he sped past the crew's van on the back of a motorcycle as we arrived at a location. I tried calling him, asked people to see if he would meet with me, and spread word that I had no issue with him.

Similar to my relationship with the cast explored in the previous chapter, my engagement with local gatekeepers reflected the changing patterns of co-dependent patron-client relations: they are not linear (because the position of the patron switches), they do not necessarily involve money; and they are dependent on different levels and sectors of government. Fundamentally they can engender compromising positions that reproduce their informal nature and insecurity. Julius subsequently stepped down from his role; however, this had to be managed in a way that recognized our co-dependency so that he would not lose his lucrative position as a politician and the cast and crew would be protected in the community. In the case of the senior health official, I did not provide any material possessions or photographs, but I did have to add him to the NIMR form as a main collaborator on the project, with no intention of involving him. I had to navigate the informal power structures of patronage ("I give you my patronage if you send me a laptop") with the formal requirements of the state and my ethical obligation as a researcher. The formal requirements of national gatekeeping practices reinforced the informal patronage networks at the regional level, thus undermining both functions of the state. It was only at the local level where doctors were not seeking higher political office that the relationship worked as a partnership based on mutual benefits: I was able to make the film, the health centres would benefit if any profit was made, and the stories were explored in the film.

Going around the gate as a non-citizen introduced an additional element of risk: detention by the state of any non-Tanzanian crew member, and confiscation of the kit and the film itself. The only threat of detention was to me as the project lead and name on the paperwork. I assessed the risk as low to medium, given that I could provide the paperwork should I be investigated by the authorities. The threat to the kit and the film itself was more concerning. Should I be detained, I would be able to work through the process of my release; however, should the hard drives containing the film be confiscated, there would be no film. The kit posed an additional problem in terms of insurance and transit. Most film equipment is imported into states through an internationally recognized "carnet" system that provides ease of transit and ensures that no tax is paid on import or export. This is a requirement of all standard rental companies. However, Tanzania is one of the few states that is not a signatory to the carnet system, meaning that the importation of equipment depends on the Tanzanian Film Board's or the border officials' applying the formal or informal rules on its arrival and departure from Tanzania.

As chapter 2 outlined, the complete film kit was insured for the value of £250,000. However, standard insurance of equipment for university research projects and specialized film insurance do not cover confiscation by a public authority. Insuring against confiscation by a public authority usually pertains only to high-risk states where journalists may be under threat; Tanzania, a low-risk country, is not included in the list of political risk insurance providers. After four weeks of my exploring multiple insurance options, a specialist insurance firm was able to identify full cover for the kit just twenty-four hours before the kit departed the United Kingdom.

The most apparent risk to the project was the embarkation of the equipment. If the equipment could get through the border gate, the production would be possible, given the established networks I had in the locations where we would be filming (i.e., it was unlikely that those involved in the project would want to jeopardize it). The equipment was shared among the five British crew members, who passed through immigration one week apart and as individuals to avoid looking like a film crew. A camera that is not fully built looks like the camera of a keen amateur rather than that of a professional director of photography. The only kit that was questioned was one of the personal cameras of the director of photography; otherwise all the equipment passed through the gate without challenge. As soon as the film wrapped, one hard drive was stored in Dar es Salaam, and the others were distributed among the crew.

Bribery: Extracting Revenue from the Gate

Given the issues around the co-production of research discussed in chapter 3, my main concern in proceeding with the production without a permit was the potential impact this might have on the Tanzanian cast and crew. The Tanzanian state has penalized citizens for participating in films such as *Darwin's Nightmare* (Rice 2006); therefore, the long-term consequences and the responsibility of the production team to the Tanzanian cast and crew were the more pressing and important issues for me to address as a researcher with an ethical obligation to research participants. I had not foreseen the potential risk that the Tanzanian crew members posed to my own well-being and security. Protection of the cast was initially sought by involving local politicians in the area and establishing a support network between Tanzania and the United Kingdom. This was to help address any short-term issues, such as friends and family thinking that cast members had money because they worked on a film, and long-term issues that might arise from the film gaining an international profile, such as stigma and government profiling. The cast did not know about the issues of the permit; the crew members did. The crew members knew of the permit situation from the outset of the project as I went through the different stages required by the Tanzania Film Board. They were initially supportive and keen to solve the problem, and then they used the lack of a permit to attempt to blackmail me at two stages of the production.

The attempted bribery by the translator and driver Ally working on the project showed that the immediate risk in not having a formal film permit was to the crew rather than the cast. Ally showed early signs of disgruntlement when in the first week of shooting he requested that I pay him upfront the full amount for six weeks work. I refused, suggesting I would pay half at the beginning and half at the end. While this was not an established university practice (where people are usually paid at the end for their work), I had come to an agreement that I could pay Tanzanian crew members either half up front and half at the end of the project or on a week-by-week basis. This was because in some cases they would be paying some costs up front, such as petrol, and because of the temporal difference in financial necessity. The first half would be paid once Ally supplied me with an invoice for my university finance records. He was not happy about this and produced an incorrect invoice (for the full amount); after a tense conversation he produced a correct invoice, which I then paid. I was not concerned about this encounter, I understood that he had financial needs and was in a difficult position, and many of the conversations on set could be tense or unpleasant.

One week after this small pay dispute Ally informed me that local immigration officials from Bagamoyo had been asking questions about the UK film crew. I reassured him that all the crew members had business visas, so this was not a major issue; I suggested that he give them my telephone number and direct any questions to me so that he would not be compromised. I did not understand how they could have known about the film crew because we had been filming in remote locations and had not done any filming in Bagamoyo at that stage. Ally persisted and said that he knew the immigration officials so he could present our passports and visas to them and rectify the issue. I thought that this was a bad idea and that these things were better left alone; however, because I thought that he understood the system better than I did, I agreed that he should travel to Bagamoyo the following day with the UK crew's passports and visas. He called me during the middle of the day to inform me that immigration did not think the visas were business visas and there was some confusion. I reassured him that they were business visas and that I had the application paperwork with me; as they now had copies of our visas, they could contact me directly if they wanted to follow up further; he should return to Miono and leave it with me. At this stage my concern was to protect him from being dragged into a situation with which he should not have to deal and to protect the crew from this kind of interference when they were doing their jobs.

It subsequently became clear that Ally was using his knowledge to collaborate with local immigration officials in petty corruption. At the beginning of the fourth week another translator called in sick, with kidney stones. The crew members were all concerned for her well-being, given we had worked closely together for four weeks; however, Ally did not show any concern. He instead batted away concerns for her health and explained that immigration was asking questions again and he feared for his safety. I tried to reassure him and once again suggested that he refer the officials to me should they contact him; however, I could see that he would only be satisfied if I reported directly to immigration. I agreed to do so first thing the next morning, but I had substantive reservations about it, sensing that the local immigration office was playing games over the visa issue. Director Leanne agreed to attend the meeting with me. We were both concerned that the meeting was a bad idea; I felt supported by having Leanne with me but began to develop concerns about Ally's intentions. As soon as we arrived in the immigration office, Ally left, explaining that he had an important meeting to attend. Leanne and I told him that if he left, we would leave, but he told us to stay and then ran out of the door. We did not hear from him for a further six hours, and he did not return to the shoot for one week. He said that he had spent the day hospitalized for malaria and pleurisy. In effect, he had set us up with the immigration officials, who informed us that our business visas were not business visas (they were) and that I could rectify the situation by paying US$150 per UK crew member. We left the office without paying, thanks to Leanne faking an acute illness; we said that we would stop shooting (we did not), and reassured them that we would contact central immigration to rectify the issue (I did not because there was no issue to resolve).

In the sixth and final week of the project, Ally threatened me directly, demanding more money or he would create trouble with immigration. Ally was the only crew member not to have signed a contract; everyone else had. All but one of the Tanzanian crew members were paid a fee and given lunch; their pay did not include extra per diems or accommodation. Three days before the end of the shoot, Ally suggested that this was unfair and demanded per diems and accommodation fees for the next week, and back pay for the rest of the shoot, for two of the other Tanzanian crew members, otherwise he would inform the film board and immigration officials. He also wanted me to sign over a significant percentage of the film's profits to his NGO. Ally's claims were underpinned by racialized accusation: that I was treating the white British crew better than the black Tanzanian crew; that I was enacting my whiteness in my work as producer by telling people what to do and paying people; and that I was using Tanzanian labour for my own material gain and had no intention of returning any profit from the film to the community and the women as I said I would. When questioned, Ally acknowledged that such accusations were a threat. It was agreed under duress that the fees would be paid for accommodation of the crew members when they stayed away from home. On the final day of shooting a crew member presented a breakdown of the amounts claimed for accommodation; it included nights when the three crew members had stayed in their own homes and when they were absent from the production, and one crew member claimed for one week for which he had already been paid. I contested this and was then publicly threatened again and informed that I would be driven to a cash point every day for the four remaining days I was in Tanzania to withdraw money, otherwise they would deliver on their threat. I withdrew cash on the first day; on the second day I agreed to meet them at ten o'clock in the morning but left with the remaining crew members for Dar es Salaam at seven. On the fourth day the UK crew passed through immigration and security at Julius Nyerere International Airport. Three policeman and Ally arrived in the departure hall (note that Ally was able to go beyond the security check) and detained the crew in the airport police room. It took forty-five minutes before we were told what the issue was and that all the crew members were free to leave except me, who had to return to Bagamoyo to face charges. Once I heard the charge – the interpreter was claiming that I had not paid the Tanzanian crew (a significantly inflated sum) – I was able to provide documentation indicating that I had paid them; in addition, I had multiple receipts and invoices to show that I had been paying various people on time and for the sums agreed. The airport police were satisfied with this, and we were able to board our flight. I had known Ally for seven years. I had first met him in 2009 in his role as a local community worker and an NGO manager in the region. The length of time I had known him, and his prominent role in the community, meant that I had trusted him. Since returning to the United Kingdom I have learned that his behaviour was not an isolated incident but was part of a wider pattern that he had been engaged in for years.

The actions of Ally presented new problems to the project, from the safety of the cast involved in the film, to my return to Tanzania to screen the film, to those involved with the project. I was quickly able to ascertain that Ally had not followed up any of the issues with the women or even contacted any of them since the completion of the film. This did not surprise me, because they would only be of use to him if he could leverage funds from them or use them to obtain funds from me. When I returned to Tanzania in October 2016, I explained to the women everything that happened and told them to let me know immediately if he got in touch, and that he most likely would not.

When I returned to the United Kingdom after the main production, I had minimal interaction with Ally. I owed him a small amount of money that was the balance of his pay, and despite his attempts to jeopardize the project, I wanted to pay him so that he would have no legitimate claim that I owed him money. He agreed on the amount of money that was owed to him. I asked him to withdraw any police charges, he said he would, I paid him, and then he refused to withdraw the charges, instead reasserting that I owed him money – this time for another inflated amount. I did not hear from him again until one day before I was due to leave for Tanzania to screen the film to the cast, six months later. He began to send me threatening emails and messages, which I passed on to my university senior leadership for response. This was a deeply upsetting twenty-four hours: Leanne withdrew from the trip out of concern for her safety and well-being, and I felt scared and vulnerable to travel. My university, family, and friends tried to reassure me that I did not have to travel if I was concerned.

My return to Tanzania depended on paperwork to engage and satisfy the shifting bureaucratic and procedural requirements and a powerful patron. I had copies of all my original paperwork from the production, with the addition of subsequent correspondence with Ally, local police, a lawyer, and airport police. This provided the evidence base for clearing my name with the police. In addition, I employed the fixer with whom I had previously worked to try to secure the permit for mobile screenings of the film in Miono and to ensure that I was assisted at the airport should any incident occur, and in Pwani should I run into any problems. The fixer put me in touch with a well-known member of the Bagamoyo community who would be able to help address any problems with Ally. On arrival in Tanzania I met first the fixer and then his contact in Bagamoyo. Unbeknown to me, the fixer was a member of a wealthy family in Dar es Salaam with extensive contacts throughout Tanzania. This both reassured me in my immediate predicament and worried me about the sort of elite linkages I was making in the informal politics of the Tanzanian state. On my arrival in Pwani I learned that the

local contact had spoken to Ally, who was still insisting that I owed
him money. The contact had also dug up Ally's police record. He
recommended that he accompany me to the police station where I
could present my paperwork; he knew the police and could ensure
that I would receive a fair hearing. We travelled together to the police
station; the contact explained the predicament and who I was, I submitted all the paperwork, and, after he had explained my position
as a senior academic and his position in the community, we left. I
was reassured by both the contact and the police that there would
be no further bother. True to their word, the trip progressed without
any attempts by Ally to intervene or make contact. My fixer's contact at Dar es Salaam airport ensured that, when I left, I travelled
through check-in, immigration, and security with minimal problem
and passed through the fast-track channels.

At the end of January 2017 I was finally issued a film permit from
the Tanzania Film Board. This was sixteen months after I had begun
the formal application procedure and was the result of constant pressure from my fixer (who worked on this for free) on both the NIMR
and the film board, and from a professional civil servant at the NIMR
who apologized for the delay and addressed the issue promptly. I had
a permit to make my film, ten months after the main production
had wrapped. I did not have a member of the Ministry of Health
and Social Welfare on set, and I did not allow the ministry, the
NIMR, and the film board to have final say over the edit of the film.
This was to prevent government interference, high per diem fees, and
censorship. I had gone around the gate to make the film free from
government intervention, managed competing state agents at different
levels of government, become knotted in informal patron-client relationships, and exposed myself to blackmail as a consequence. There is
no way of knowing what would have happened if I had had a permit
from the outset, and there were no guarantees of a permit when I
decided to proceed with the film. However, in deciding to proceed, I
decided to go around the gate. In so doing, I directly embedded myself
within various patron-client relationships and compromising situa-
tions that had to be balanced against the wider ethical concerns for
the cast and crew involved in the project and my role as a researcher.
I had seen and was engaged in the everyday informal politics of international relations: navigating formal structures, informal rules, and
power hierarchies and balancing the interests of the project with the
wider interests of different aspects of the Tanzanian state.

FILM PRODUCTION AND EVERYDAY
GATEKEEPER POLITICS

Navigating the gate of the Tanzanian film board and research agencies corresponds to much received wisdom on gatekeeping politics: a "managerial bourgeoisie" keeps the gate to protect its own interests and to exert and maintain its power (the Tanzania Film Board); government service is a means of securing extra money through per diems (the immigration department); distrust is inherent at every level of political practice (the Tanzania Film Board, the immigration officials); and gatekeeping practices are embedded and reproduced by everyday practice (Ally, Julius, me). However, the production of a film also reveals new ways of seeing gatekeeper politics in Tanzania. The first corresponds to the need to open up the black box of the state to see how the state operates rather than assume that the Tanzanian state is a unitary actor motivated by a common strategy – in this case, the control of information and research production. The state functions through tensions and distrust at multiple levels, and agency is ascribed to political actors through relations to the president (not the party) and through expertise. The second is the shifting nature of patron-client relations between domestic and international entities, which produces greater agency for African actors. Finally, engagement with gatekeeper politics shows that such practices are by their very nature self-reinforcing despite having deleterious consequences for multiple actors. The temporal nature of African politics and agency explored in chapter 3 is again relevant here: there is little incentive to break gatekeeping practices when need is immediate. The greater the need or want, the more gatekeeper politics is reinforced.

The practices of the Tanzania Film Board, the NIMR, COSTECH, Bagamoyo immigration, and Dar es Salaam airport police suggest that the Tanzanian state either did not want *Pili* to be made or at the very least wanted to control the content of the story told by the film. However, there was little evidence that this was a combined, unitary approach taken by the state. To the contrary, many of the guidelines and procedures were ad hoc or reactionary and seemingly introduced at different stages to ensure that each agent was not leaving the gate open. The Tanzanian state did not act as a unitary agent, but elements of the state did exhibit common practices of distrust, procedure, and agency through non-action and keeping the gate shut. Actors working in central government had limited autonomy over decision-making, with a preference for moving the decision, or opening the gate, either across to other state agencies or up to higher authorities. The main role of the mid-level manager was inaction through procedure, with no autonomy to open the gate. At the local level, government agents – local politicians or doctors in charge of care and treatment clinics – had greater autonomy over decision-making and potentially greater immediate award for their own interests and needs. For the doctors this would be potential gain for the health of their patients, should funds be raised from the film, and for the politicians this was close proximity to a project that would be seen to have potential financial reward for the community. At the local level the political party, CCM, is the central location of power; however, at the national level the power is organized around the president. The closer to central government a political actor is, the less control, agency, or autonomy the actor has; the more local the gate, the greater autonomy and agency afforded to the gatekeeper.

The distinction between central political actors working in government ministries in Dar es Salaam, and local political actors working in local government and as health sector practitioners and managers, is important because of the differing autonomy over decision-making and because the central and local gatekeeping politics work in opposition to each other. The raising of the gate and the lack of decision-making at the central level push greater autonomy and agency to the local level. If people are unable to navigate the gate because of inertia, lack of a patron, or fear of the political actor at the central level, they navigate the gate by going around it at the local level. Pushing the gate onto the local level gives greater agency to local political actors because they are able to make direct decisions that maximize their own interests and, in some cases, the interests of the local population. Local political agents are more concerned about keeping on side with local party elites than with the civil servants of central government; hence it is not of immediate concern if they undermine central government decision-making. Although clinicians have less direct interest in aligning with party elites, functional relationships help their everyday practice. However, their interests tend to be aligned to regional health authorities and the immediate needs of the health centres in which they work.

The erosion of centralized authority through gatekeeping politics also pertains to the monopoly of violence or the threat of violence. The threat of violence encountered in the production of *Pili* was evident in the crew's detention by armed policemen at Dar es Salaam airport and in the threat of local bandits in the Pwani area as discussed in chapter 2. I was not directly threatened with violence in either incident; the threat was implicit in the *possibility* of violence – the gun on the table of the police room in the airport, and hearsay over the "armed" nature of bandits from outside of the region. However, in both cases the state did not have the monopoly of control of violence. The airport police were acting out the will of not the government authorities but a private citizen who had networks in local party politics. In the case of the local bandits, local politicians and police identified private guards from the military whom they recommended I pay to use when filming at night. Violence and the threat of violence were not owned by the state authorities but were available to those with the financial means and networks to pay for such a threat or for protection.

The higher the gate at the central level caused by a lack of autonomy and a fear of decision-making, the more people go around the gate at the local level, which then gives greater agency to local elites who have greater autonomy over decision-making. The impact of this is that central authority and governance is ultimately undermined because the rules established by the central state gate mean little if people can navigate around them at the local level. Therefore, the higher the central gate, the more insecure the central authority of the president. Insecurity and distrust become cyclical as the centre tries to consolidate control of the gate to reduce the power of local government elites, tighter consolidation pushes people around the gate to engage in local or informal gatekeeping practices, and this increases the power of local agents and the insecurity and distrust within the system. Instead of tightening the hold on central government authority, the cyclical nature of gatekeeping politics erodes it.

The second insight that film production as method reveals about gatekeeping politics is the flux between patron and client. During the production of the film I occupied the role of both patron and client to a range of different actors. I was patron to the local politician, film crew, and actors, and client to local health officials, politicians, and actors. Although it may undermine democratic state practices, the shifting nature of patron-client relations is the one space that ensures an element of accountability within gatekeeper state practices. In occupying dual roles, political actors have to be accountable to both clients and patrons given that this relationship is in constant flux. What complicates the picture, however, is wealth and agency. Accountability depends on the political agent recognizing and enacting its own agency and forms of accountability. This is similar to the problem identified by authors such as Beresford and Brockington: that, despite discontent with gatekeeping politics and corruption, citizens do not use their own agency to change the political system through democratic structures. This is in part because political systems absorb discontent, and the needs of the patron-client relationship are immediate rather than long term. However, it is also because of the large inequalities of wealth that frame most patron-client relationships. The flux of the relationship tends to be between those with financial or political capital: when both parties have one or both types of capital, the relationship fluctuates; however when one party has one or both, and the other has none, the relationship is static. Hence the electorate can gain more from politicians during elections – this is the one time it has political capital – but is unable to enact agency outside of election times unless its members have financial influence (can fund a campaign, deliver a public good for the community).

What is important here is to recognize that patron-client relationships, or patronage, are not a fixed component of African politics or "the way things work." Similar to the co-dependency that underpinned my relationship with the cast, as described in chapter 3, these relationships are in flux depending on the material and political capital and on the recognition by the political agent (at whatever level of central or local politics or of the everyday voter) of their own agency. It is this flux that offers the opportunity for greater accountability within patron-client relations and for change within systems of patronage. Moreover, this system of flux is a contemporary feature of most democratic capitalist systems. What makes the relationship more acute in states such as Tanzania is both the partnership with gatekeeping politics that reinforces informal networks of patronage, and the large inequalities of wealth. Inequalities in wealth narrow the opportunity for patron-client relationships to shift. As chapter 3 demonstrated, the agency expressed by the actors in *Pili* shows that it is not a lack of will on the part of citizens to act or exert political agency but the narrow opportunities they have to do so.

Gatekeeping politics is self-reinforcing with regard to the cyclical relationship between central and local authorities as discussed. However, it is also self-reinforcing through the everyday practices in society that recognize the changing barriers of the centralized gate and therefore localize and operate informally. The more the norm becomes the local and the informal, the greater is the distrust of formal procedures (e.g., contracts, written agreements) and of central authorities. This fulfills short-term needs and becomes embedded as a mechanism of how things work in practice. However, such informality and distrust heighten the precariousness of these processes and arrangements, particularly for the people with less financial or political capital to leverage or insure against long-term problems or need. Informality combined with patrimonial forms of gatekeeper politics exacerbates inequalities to the detriment of the poorest in society. The poorest in society are in a bind: they lack the financial or political leverage to engage in gatekeeper politics in an accountable manner and therefore have to go around the gate, which in turn exacerbates their position because they have no formal assurances or accountability measures of insurance for their-long term needs. As chapter 3 considered, where people have even minor access to political or financial leverage, they maximize their agency to optimize it within a particular time constraint. Gatekeeping politics is thus embedded within the temporal needs of the everyday in Tanzania. The majority of Tanzanians do not have the political, financial, or temporal capital to navigate the gate and therefore have to go around it; when opportunities present themselves, it is rational for the people to maximize their own self-interest in the short team. This embeds and reproduces the cyclical relationship between the central and the local, and the formal and the informal, within gatekeeping practices. The more people go around the gate, the more government actors tighten the gate, and this creates a greater incentive for people to look to other gatekeepers and informal practices – the cycle continues to the detriment of the majority of the population.

If the cycle of gatekeeper politics is to the detriment of the majority of the population and weakens the central authority of the state, it is important to consider whom it does benefit. In the short term, gatekeeping politics benefits those who are able to maintain the gate at the local authority level; they gain political and potentially financial reward. The benefits of gatekeeper politics are higher at the centre – greater financial reward, political prestige, and the lifestyle that both of these factors bring – but the risk is also higher. Where the gate is higher, there is also greater oversight from international actors, and competition for resources from different sectors of the state. The

cyclical nature of gatekeeping politics means that rewards and benefits need to be met quickly because distrust and informality generate
regular changes within the civil service and local government. There
is therefore an incentive to get what you can from the gate while you
have the political leverage to do so. This attitude permeates every
level of gatekeeper politics and the wider society. As the activities of
local immigration and Ally demonstrate in the production of *Pili*,
the need to gain rewards from the gate is immediate even if it may
potentially endanger long-term financial reward and job stability.
For example, had Ally delayed financial reward by not revealing
his corrupt practices, he may have been able to accrue extra funds
from the profit of the film that would have been channelled to his
NGO. Instead, his attempts to extract revenue failed in the immediate
term and had potential long-term consequences for his ability to do
so again. His position remains that he did nothing wrong; he just
wants the money he thinks he deserves as a gatekeeper within the
local community. Gatekeeper politics benefits short-term need over
long-term gain for the individual, the state, and wider society. The
cycle of gatekeeper politics and its embeddedness within the everyday politics of society mean that such processes become consistently
reproduced and in many respects unavoidable.

Given the cyclical nature of gatekeeping practices and the limited benefits to the wider state and society, engagement by an independent researcher with such processes is best avoided owing to
issues of ethical responsibility and clear accountability. Ethically, the
researcher seeks to do no harm to those involved in the research and
thus wants to maintain a critical distance from the political practices that reinforce systems of patronage and exacerbate inequalities.
Practically, researchers have to be clear about their actions to public
authorities, research participants, and research funders. However, as
the practice of co-producing a film demonstrates, these practical and
ethical concerns become challenged when the researcher is trying to
navigate gatekeeping practices. When the formal structures of the
state did not work, I took recourse to the local authority structures
and informal networks. To get things done I had to leverage my
limited political capital (relationship to a local politician) and material capital (money to make a film) to legitimize my actions in the
community in which I worked. Going around the centralized gate
by operating in this way fulfilled my short-term, immediate need to
complete the making of the film. However, as outlined, this created

greater problems in the long term. It exposed me to manipulation and extortion by the informal processes in which I had engaged with Ally and which ultimately threatened the completion of the film. I gave the Tanzania Film Board a reason not to trust me: I had proceeded without its formal permit, which meant that I would have to be careful in how I navigated the gate to secure the final permit. I paid private guards to protect those working on the film, which exacerbated tensions over private and public security. Finally, engaging in local gatekeeper politics compromised my personal safety in Tanzania and my ability to return to the United Kingdom. Not only had I engaged in gatekeeper politics, but, as the majority of Tanzanians find, my actions then reinforced the cyclical nature of such gatekeeping practices to my own long-term detriment. In the short term I made a film and had enough political (British, mzungu, and academic) and material (research budget and personal wealth) capital to find a solution to a problem. However, in the long term I compromised both my ability to return to Tanzania and those who unlike me could not break the cycle of gatekeeping politics by getting on an airplane and leaving the country.

To make a film meant practising international relations and engaging in domestic politics. My experience shows how someone with the critical distance of an external researcher or a foreigner, with prior knowledge of how gatekeeping and systems of patronage work, can become embedded within those very systems. Regardless of the political and financial capital of the agent, the structures of gatekeeping politics are so deep rooted in the everyday that they are an unavoidable part of the research process. My engagement with gatekeeper politics suggests that the researcher is not somehow abstracted from the social research they seek to investigate but is deeply embedded and intertwined with the political practices they engage and want to understand. It is important to maintain ethical principles of research, but this should not be to the detriment of recognizing one's own positionality and influence on political processes. To ignore this not only ignores the politics of the research process but also depoliticizes the researcher who can have both positive and negative, intended and unintended, outcomes on the subject of the research.

Finally, my engagement with gatekeeping politics provides a useful corrective to such politics being labelled as distinctly African or something "other" in which non-Western states or people engage;

these practices are universal. As Beresford (2015) argues, gate-keeper politics is not a uniquely African phenomenon but is found throughout liberal, capitalist democracies, and, similar to Cooper's thesis (2012), the origin of gatekeeping can be found in colonial practices. Gatekeeping practices are common to most political systems. However, gatekeeper politics becomes cyclical and exacerbates inequalities where extreme inequalities exist between who has access to political and/or financial capital and who does not. Where financial and political capital are more dispersed, gatekeeping practices are less; where there is greater inequality in accessing or gaining such capital, gatekeeping politics becomes more entrenched and harder to navigate. It is the extremes of inequality and the concentration of political and financial capital in African states such as Tanzania that help embed gatekeeping politics as practice within the everyday structures of state and society.

CONCLUSION

Gatekeeping, patronage, and the formal and informal ways in which they played out in the process of making *Pili* are represented in the film itself. The process informed the portrayal of bureaucracy (the vikoba group as the Tanzania Film Board), patronage (between Pili and the women in the vikoba group and the character Mahela), and how the bigger the gates get (in the case of Pili trying to secure a loan), the more the actors have to engage in informal practices and take risks to get what they need. The final film, *Pili,* is a means of seeing how patronage and gatekeeping can manifest within everyday encounters in small, frustrating, restrictive, and risk-taking ways. As Pili has to take risks to get what she wants and to bend to the informal and formal ways in which gatekeeping and patronage operate, so I had to do the same to get the film made. Given the gatekeeping at the central government level, I decided to go around the gate by engaging with local politics where I had greater political capital (existing relationships with senior members of the community). At first Pili fulfills the formal obligations of the vikoba committee, and, when this does not work, she draws on personal relationships, favours, and emotional appeal to get what she wants. To complete the film I had to take a set of risks, balancing the well-being of cast and crew, my ethical obligations as a researcher, and a commitment to finishing the film; for Pili to get her market stall, she has to risk her health and the health of her children and to balance short-term immediate risk with long-term gain.

This chapter has shown that the politics of seeing is about how states control the stories we tell and the politics we see in formal and informal ways. Moreover, it has provided unique insight into how these political structures operate at every level of the state. The combination of film as method and the inference of wealth and visibility created a specific form of gatekeeping and patronage politics. Gates exist in different ways when research is being conducted: the securing of a research permit, the access to interview participants, or the payment for use of a data set. These gates are always in evidence but can be navigated through research budgets, partnerships, and avoidance. What was unique in this use of film as method and output was the co-production of research with a range of actors in Tanzania, the need to control representations of the country, and the wealth aesthetic represented by film equipment and crew. As a researcher, the producer of the film, and *mzungu Sofia*, I was not a distinct observer of politics but was embedded with the everyday politics of the community and seen as wealthy, and therefore was subject to national- and local-level gatekeeping.

Exploring how gatekeeping and patronage worked in practice across government agencies and by individual actors offers new ways of seeing such politics and the state in Tanzania. While the findings of this chapter identify key trends and processes within the Tanzanian state – distrust, bureaucracy, patronage – the activities outlined cannot be attributed to the state's acting in pursuit of a specific strategy, but instead indicate a divided state with different practices depending on the level (central or local) and the hierarchy of the political actor. Like in most states in the world, those in the senior civil service, or senior politicians at the local government level, had higher autonomy over their decision-making. In practice, it is the low-level or middle managers who are keen to maintain the gate out of fear of leaving the gate open. This chapter therefore concurs with much of the existing literature on gatekeeping in showing that divisions between central and local authorities and the informal and formal structures of power perpetuate gatekeeping practices.

This chapter has advanced understandings of gatekeeping politics with regard to the ways in which gatekeeping is reinforced, first, by inequality in access to financial and political capital and, second, by temporality and the prioritization of short-term and immediate need.

Gatekeeping politics will continue to flourish where there are greater inequalities of who can access the gate through political or financial capital, and where poverty makes immediate need the priority. Gatekeeping is not a peculiarly Tanzanian or African phenomenon, but gatekeeping politics is more acute and therefore more in evidence in everyday transactions in societies with stark systems of inequality and poverty. Gatekeeping is exacerbated by the temporal dynamics of poverty and precariousness. The immediate needs of people without proximity to gatekeepers or patrons means that they will prioritize immediate gains and opportunities when they are presented with them. This makes gatekeeping cyclical and exclusionary because it simultaneously reinforces the very structures that distance everyday people from resources and decision-making while embedding those people within such structures. The more embedded people become within these structures, the more they go around the gate and exacerbate their own precariousness. As chapter 2 explored, cast members prioritized their short-term needs over their health; in this chapter, crew members prioritized their wealth over the risk of exposure for bribery and petty corruption, state officials prioritized their current employment in a time of political upheaval, and I prioritized the production of the film over my long-term ability to return to Tanzania.

States regulate how we see politics in different ways. This chapter has offered one particular way in which parts of the state of Tanzania attempted to restrict the ability of the everyday life of a woman living with HIV/AIDS to be seen through the co-production of a feature film. In so doing, the chapter has offered an analysis of understanding state practices with regard to gatekeeping and patronage. The focus of the last two chapters has substantively been on the pre-production and production of the film in Tanzania and has begun to explore the politics of co-production from the local and state levels of analysis. The next chapter shifts the analytical lens once more to post-production and the global political economy of distribution. It provides a detailed account of the system of film distribution and the ways in which, despite *Pili* being an academic-based project that was made on a budget and co-produced with a rural Tanzania community, the film is still subject to the same Hollywood-based rules, norms, and legal structures that govern distribution and consumption. In so doing, the chapter develops the thinking on what stops us from seeing, by considering global structures and systems of gatekeeping audience.

5

The Global Governance of Seeing

To secure an audience and make the invisible visible requires an engagement with the commercial structures of film sales and distribution and the wider political economy of global film governance. The politics of audience – who controls what and how films and knowledge are seen and consumed – points to a key distinction between reading and writing visual politics. Reading international relations (IR) through film, aesthetics, and art has pointed to the disruptive, transformative potential of visual politics (Bleiker 2009a, 2009b, 2015). As chapter 1 explored, for authors like Shapiro, film and cinema have been at the forefront of such ruptures – through either the affect and impact of moving pictures and sound on the viewer or the difficult political questions posed by film festivals to governments and citizens around the world (Shapiro 2009, 2013). Scholars engage in the social, political, and economic context in which art is produced but overlook the context and structures that limit or allow art to be consumed. Consumption is often considered with regard to the high arts, for example Renaissance painting or the opera, but less with regard to the popular arts such as film. Similarly, decolonial feminist debate has considered how the ways in which knowledge is produced can reproduce hierarchies (Mohanty 2003), but has focused less on how that knowledge is then used and consumed. Art can have transformative affect. To use aesthetics and art as part of plural methods by which to understand the international, it is important not only to read the aesthetic but to situate the aesthetic within the political-economic context in which it is consumed. The material structures that configure the way art is consumed is thus a missing component of the aesthetic turn in IR and decolonial feminist method. Art and aesthetics are not separate from, but embedded in, the political-economic structures in which they are produced and consumed. This is particularly acute for film. In operating within these structures, film and aesthetics may reproduce the very structures that stop the invisible from being seen.

If we are to understand the potential of visual politics, aesthetics, and film in IR, it is vitally important to understand the wider structures and hierarchies of film distribution and consumption that shape the stories we tell and the stories we see. Distribution and getting an audience are the final parts of the story in understanding how you see politics through film. As discussed in the previous chapters, the gatekeepers, new economic agents, and informal power structures all shape how films are displayed, marketed, and distributed to audiences. Films commonly receive financial backing based on their prospects of generating revenue for the production or distribution company. As such, there is a range of intermediate agents in the film industry who ensure that films are sold and distributed to audiences in order to make money. The actors, language, and codes of conduct around film distribution and exhibition operate within a system of global film governance that has Hollywood and the US film industry at its core. These agents and structures have a common interest – to get an audience and make money from the film. For a film from the industry's periphery such as *Pili*, the problem lies in navigating the racialized and gendered hierarchical structures of global film governance to secure an audience without reproducing the same structures that keep Tanzanian women and their stories invisible.

The analytical focus of this chapter shifts from the everyday local level in chapter 3 and the state level in chapter 4 to the global. The chapter explores the workings of the global political economy of film and its governance, the practicalities of how to distribute a film, and the ways in which *Pili* found an audience. To do this, first it situates the process of distribution within the global political economy of film governance. Second, the chapter outlines the practicalities of getting a film distributed to audiences. This section introduces the role of film festivals, government agencies, and sales agents as key political actors in the independent film world. Third, the chapter focuses on how *Pili* secured distribution, with reference to the informal and formal practices and opportunities that made it possible. Fourth, the chapter considers how finding an audience confronted the original aims and intent of the project with regard to visibility and co-production. This section highlights the ways in which the balancing of co-producer interests led to immediate challenges that were ultimately beneficial to the project. The chapter then draws together its main argument that to understand the power of the visual it is vital to understand both the political-economic context in which the visual is seen and how the parameters of this context can be challenged through new methods of co-production as a way of seeing.

THE GLOBAL POLITICAL ECONOMY OF FILM GOVERNANCE: *PILI* AND THE PERIPHERY

Chapter 4 considered the relationship between the state and film by exploring the ways in which the different parts of the state keep the gate to the films that are made and the stories that we see. The chapter touched on the political-economic relationship between the state and film production, from film as a potential revenue stream for states, to states' control of the stories and the perception of a country such as Tanzania, to the political-economic factors that shape the gatekeeping practices determining who can make a film. What is notable is that the gatekeeping and political-economic relationship between the state and film production is not specific to Tanzania. Regardless of the budget, origin, or type of film, the political economy is a fundamental part of film and film studies. Money and engagement with state structures and processes are key components of the ways in which films are made and distributed to audiences. However, they are an aspect of the process or art form that the majority of film studies prefer to ignore (Wasko 2003). While cultural studies and communication studies (which are distinct from film studies because of their differing positions on aesthetic value and the subject) have grappled with aspects of the art-money relationships (S. Hall and Whannel 1964, 70; Turner 1998), film studies continue to focus predominantly on film as an art form and on the aesthetic, technology, and authorship of the form (Wasko 1982). For scholars interested in the political economy of film such as Wasko (1982, 2003), Gomery (1998a), and Balio (2013), this is a major oversight because, for them, film is a commodity shaped by the industry in which it is made. As Guback argues, "film is a commodity, and exchange value sets the broad parameters that determine not only how the medium will be used, but also the shape of the industrial structure that makes, distributes, and exhibits it" (1982, xi).

There is therefore an overlooked but important relationship between political economy and film production and distribution. The political economy of film refers to how economic factors shape the politics of which films are produced, distributed, and exhibited, and how such films reinforce and reproduce economic inequalities and political hierarchies. The economic factors are the role of industrial capital in the early era of Hollywood, the contemporary role of debt and equity capital in financing global film production (Kellner 1998, 354; Wasko 1982), and the relationship between production finance and distribution. For example, the US film industry is underpinned by capital investment in productions and shareholder stock from Wall Street. Table 2 shows a breakdown of shareholders for the top companies in the United States as listed on NASDAQ (Sony Pictures Entertainment is not listed).

As table 2 shows, the main institutional shareholders of major film production and distribution companies are Wall Street money managers, with most holdings located in two-thirds of the same asset managers, namely Blackrock Inc, Vanguard Group Ltd, and State Street Corp. As with any major corporation, this exposes the major media corporations to fluctuations in the stock market and, at worst, subjects them to risk during times of financial crisis. The financial crises of the 1930s Great Depression and 2007–08 both had major impacts on the film industry (Wasko 1982). The consequences of the 2007–08 global financial crisis still have repercussions for contemporary US filmmaking, with major companies becoming more risk averse on creative projects or independent films, and investing in big blockbuster, comic book, or action hero movies with subsequent franchises (Balio 2013). Financial crises not only limit the money for making films but have long-term impacts on the willingness to take risks in creativity or ideas for films that do not have pre-established audiences.

The political economy of film also refers to how politics shapes the economics of the film industry and how film contributes to nation building and state ideology. Film is a strategic form of foreign policy and international relations. To varying degrees, governments have an active role in the regulation and development of domestic and global film industries. Governments can incentivize film production through tax breaks for production companies, low location fees, subsidized film festivals, and direct investment in training and education within the creative film sector. Such governments recognize the utility of film to the domestic economy and the cultural

Table 2 Institutional holdings of Hollywood media corporations

Company	Top 5 institutional shareholders
Time Warner	8% Vanguard Group Inc
	7% Blackrock Inc
	5% State Street Corp
	5% Dodge and Cox
	5% Massachusetts Financial Services
The Walt Disney Company	10% Vanguard Group Inc
	8% Blackrock Inc
	7% State Street Corp
	4% State Farm Mutual Automobile Insurance Co
	3% FMR LLC
Comcast/General Electric	8% Blackrock Inc
	8% Vanguard Group Inc
	6% Capital World Investors
	5% State Street Corp
	2% FMR LLC
News Corporation	16% SOF Ltd
	10% Blackrock Inc
	9% Sterling Capital Management
	7% State Street Corp
	6% International Value Advisers, LLC

Source: NASDAQ summaries of institutional ownership as of July 2017

representation of a state. Regulation or incentives can enhance or restrict the stories that are told within a particular state. For example, as chapter 4 suggests, the Tanzania Film Board was interested more in the restriction and censorship of film to ensure its control of the stories coming out of Tanzania rather than in the incentivization of foreign investment in the domestic economy. In the political economy of film, films are not only a commodity to be bought and sold around the world but also a wider vehicle to sell other commodities – from American products abroad to ideology such as the "American dream." As Woodrow Wilson famously argued, "trade follows film" (Wheeler 2006, 7).

Censorship and propaganda are two powerful tools used by governments to produce and distribute films that adhere to a particular political ideology. Censorship and propaganda can be used in extreme ways, such as the use of film as propaganda by both Allied and Axis powers in the Second World War, and as censorship during McCarthyism in the United States in the 1950s. Less extreme examples of government influence can be seen in films with national interests, such as war hero films, Cold War spy films, and films that seek to maintain specific social norms or state "values" like the predominance of the white nuclear family as "all American." Government interests seek both to build a sense of national identity within the domestic population and to export an idea or representation of the state to the wider world. Such powerful tools are enabled by domestic legislation, government film offices, regulatory bodies, and close personal relationships between filmmakers and governmental officials. It is through the close relationship between government bodies and representatives of the film industry that governments can extend their own ideological and economic interests via film, and the film industry can ensure that the government protects its interest and position in global markets (Miller, Govil, et al. 2005, 111; Wheeler 2006, 167).

Political-economic factors therefore drive where and how films are made and seen, the stories told and the norms they perpetuate, and the cast and crew that are selected; and shape the use of film as a wider tool of foreign and domestic policy. For experts on the political economy of film such as Wasko, rather than being avoided or obscured as an uncomfortable reality, the political economy of film should be made transparent and thus open to scrutiny and accountability (Wasko 2003, 10). Transparency helps to explain which stories are told and seen or go untold and unseen, and provides scrutiny of the ways in which political-economic factors drive inequality within the film industry. However, such inequalities and political-economic relations are not just governed by states or government interests. Domestic film markets exist within a wider global political economy of film governance that shapes what is seen and how. Not all governments or domestic film industries have the same leverage in international markets. Global film governance is an established hierarchy that is organized around the core of the US film market. As the following discussion demonstrates, this hierarchy is racialized and gendered and structures the systems of distribution and audience that are the central determinants of power in the political economy of film.

To understand how the global political economy of film functions and the position of *Pili* within it, it is useful to see the film industry as a system of governance embedded within the global capitalist economy. Drawing on Immanuel Wallerstein's world-systems theory, film is organized around a system of governance with Hollywood and the US film industry at the core, which interacts and shapes global film distribution and consumption practices in the semi-periphery (Europe, Bollywood) and the periphery (Nollywood, Swahiliwood, Africa). Wallerstein's account of the evolution of the world economy from an understanding of sixteenth-century capitalism in Europe may seem a stretch for understanding contemporary forms of film distribution, and both advocates and critics of world-systems theory may be wary of its application to what is a more recent phenomenon within the world economy. Wallerstein emphasized the *longue durée* of understanding the world economy and how it functions as a social system (1979, 37; 2004, 19). However, he stressed that the role of the scholar was to interpret the world through capturing global realities and adding abstractions to a comprehensive analysis (1979, xii). Drawing on world-systems theory illuminates the context and helps to understand how this industry functions and shapes audience consumption of art and film.

Wallerstein defines a world system as "a social system, one that has boundaries, structures, member groups, rules of legitimation, and coherence" (1974a, 347). The system functions through its own logic and the tensions between the core, semi-periphery, and periphery within the system of a capitalist world economy. Hence, all social action takes place within this entity and provides the legal and political framework in which agents operate (1974a, 5; 1979, 155). For Wallerstein, the capitalist world economy "is a system in which the surplus value of the proletarian is appropriated by the bourgeois. When this proletarian is located in a different country from this bourgeois, one of the mechanisms that has affected the process of appropriation is the manipulation of controlling flows over state boundaries. This results in patterns of 'uneven development' which are *summarized* in the concepts of core, semiperiphery, and periphery. This is an intellectual tool to help analyse the multiple forms of class conflict in the capitalist world economy" (1979, 293). The core is the location of industry, ownership, the bourgeoisie, and advanced methods of production (38). States that occupy the core tend to have strong forms of governance that maintain a national identity to justify inequalities within the wider system (Wallerstein 1974a, 349). The core is able to maintain its position through monopoly over industry, which means that the semi-periphery and periphery are always at a disadvantage as "there is a constant flow of surplus-value from the producers of peripheral products to the producers of core-like products. This has been called 'unequal exchange'" (Wallerstein 2004, 28). A monopoly allows large gaps between the (low) cost of production and the (high) costs of consumption (26). The semi-periphery is the key intermediary between the core and the periphery and as such is central to the functioning of the world system; in so doing, states in the semi-periphery are a buffer to political pressure from the periphery to the core and are dependent on the core for comparative advantage over other semi-peripheral and core states (Wallerstein 1974a, 350). States within this space can fluctuate between the core and the periphery dependent on changes in the wider global political economy (Wallerstein 1979, 89). The periphery is characterized by the absence of a strong state, low autonomy from the world system (Wallerstein 1974a, 349), and the weak outcome of unequal exchange. For Wallerstein, African states are located within the periphery (1974b). Writing in the 1970s that the one potential alternative to Africa's peripheral position was Tanzania, he suggested that Nyerere's project of ujamaa held a potential resistance to external pressure (1979, 81).

Within the world system the expansion of the core weakens the periphery, and unequal exchange becomes enforced by the core on the periphery (Wallerstein 1974b, 414 and 401). The system is maintained by military strength within the core, ideological commitment to the system of capitalism, and divisions between and within the lower and middle strata (404). Crucially for understanding the film industry in this way, advances in technology help consolidate and expand the power of the core by changes to the means of production (to make them more cost effective), new uses of natural commodities (e.g., coltan for mobile phone production), and new areas of industry and production (Wallerstein 1974a, 350). For the world economy to function to the benefit of the core, capitalist markets should only be partially free in order to protect core interests and monopoly of the surplus value within the system (Wallerstein 1979, 66; 2004, 25).

The strata of core, semi-periphery, and periphery and how they reinforce each other within the wider world economy reflect the divisions and mechanisms of film governance. Although the political economy of film does not reflect the sixteenth-century model of England at the core, Venice in the semi-periphery, and Poland in the periphery (Wallerstein 1979, 39), or a world economy underpinned by military strength, it is a form of governance underpinned by an ideological commitment to the economic value of film and the profit imperative and by divisions within the lower and middle levels of the industry. Such divisions are maintained through technological advancement and a monopoly of the surplus value of the industry between the core and peripheral states.

At the core of global film governance is Hollywood and the US film industry, referring both to the major film corporations and to the parallel independent sector. The core controls the mechanisms through which the governance system works and maintains its position at the centre of the film industry, using a combination of the following factors. First, the core is the centre of film capital where wealth is consolidated. Such wealth allows for both the production and marketing of products to audiences and the use of advanced technologies and skilled workforces to produce high-quality popular films or mass-market blockbusters. The concentration of capital in the United States is the consequence of the deregulation of the communications market in the 1980s; the loosening of anti-trust measures that led to "vertical" integration and mergers of film companies (Balio 1998; Wheeler 2006); and a strategic "horizontal" expansion into new markets around the world, supported by the US government's advancement of Hollywood's interests in the 1996 Uruguay Round (Wheeler 2006). As Gomery puts it, a small handful of corporations that formed in the 1950s "still have hegemony over the creation of the movies and the distribution of them throughout the world" (1998a, 251). Second, and related to the consolidation of wealth, is the role of new technology in advancing the skills and aesthetic of film production to new and wider audiences. The film industry both drives innovation because of increased competition and demand for the new among audiences and responds to it as new technologies emerge. Innovation has driven the Hollywood film industry since the arrival of sound and film financing from companies such as General Electric (Wheeler 2006). Third, the core is the centre of cultural capital within the film industry. *Cultural capital* here refers to the film critics and film festivals that legitimate films for audiences and are part of the wider marketing and mass appeal of the core industry. The majority of gatekeepers – sales agents, exhibitors, marketing executives – operate within the core or between the core and the semi-periphery. Audience – the crucial aim in both the production of film and the impact of aesthetics – is maintained by the core and disciplined by the codes of conduct of those actors that benefit from the core. The core is hegemonic through consent and participation; it maintains power, control, and influence to and over the global film industry, and such power, control, and influence are reinforced by actors in the global film industries in the semi-periphery and periphery.

The semi-periphery supports the core because it is close enough to benefit from the system, and the periphery is too distinct to effect change. Industries in the semi-periphery maintain and extract revenue from their own productions; this can be a significant industry such as Bollywood, which some actors see as having more of a core position or being a potential rival to the Hollywood core. The semi-periphery is often the site of low-cost location options for the core. Semi-peripheral states benefit from the location fees, the support structures, and the below-the-line crew roles involved in the production of core films in these states. While these states often do not own the means of production or take a capital share, the direct and indirect impacts on local economies are enough to support and maintain the core. Simply put, instead of competing with Hollywood, a film industry in, say, Ireland seeks to support Hollywood to gain a slice of a bigger pie. The semi-periphery states have their own film industries in which both cast and crew may train and develop their skills to then ultimately work in the core.

Peripheral states are identified as such because of their low-revenue or non-existent film industries, the marginal position of audiences, and the low technological innovation that limits both the production of films and the consumption by audiences. Such states already exist at an economic disadvantage to the core: their domestic film markets are saturated with low-quality Hollywood films that are cheapened by piracy; they lack investment or skilled labour to keep pace with technological change; and the soft power of cultural capital is limited at best to a region of the states rather than to the world. The peripheral aspect of these states is further reinforced by the lack of film production by core or semi-periphery industries in these states. Tanzania fits into the periphery of the film industry: low-skilled labour; lack of access to technology, particularly new technologies (other than drones, which are used by all major production companies); domestic and narrow diasporic audiences; and the predominance of pirated American films in the market. As chapters 1 and 2 discussed, the relatively low status afforded to the Tanzanian "Swahiliwood" or Bongo film industry, on account of the aesthetic quality of output, storytelling, and limited technological innovation, means that the audience for Tanzanian-based films tends to be (but is not limited to) the periphery. They do not gain international audiences outside of the Swahili-speaking diaspora or the legitimacy of awards and critical acclaim outside of Africa. Such hierarchies suggest that African film, stories, and audiences are somehow secondary or irrelevant to film production and viewers. Underpinning such hierarchies is a set of racialized assumptions or "coloniality of power" (Quijano 1993) in which the stories of women such as Pili are either constructed through the lens of Europeans (see chapters 1 and 3) or seen as inferior to films from North America and Europe.

Assumptions regarding a "coloniality of power" point to a central critique of Wallerstein's original analysis: it privileges class without fully attending to the ways in which the system is racialized and gendered. This critique is fundamental to analysis of how film is governed. As Grosfoguel has notably argued, world-systems theory offers a Eurocentric point of view, wherein "class analysis and economic structural transformations are privileged over other power relations" (2007, 215), particularly gendered and racialized hierarchies. Drawing on the seminal postcolonial work of Quijano (1993) and its conception of coloniality of power, Grosfoguel asserts that race and racism are the organizing principles of the world system (2007, 217; Quijano 2000). Race, racism, and racialized hierarchies explain the division of labour within the international system and become ordering principles for the capitalist world system (Grosfoguel 2007). As Akram-Lodhi suggests, capitalist markets as forms of social power were constructed in the colonial period and continue to be reconstituted in the postcolonial period; they are therefore embedded and reflect particular hierarchies (2018). Feminist political economists make a similar argument, noting the intersections of race and gender as operating principles that underpin and structure systems of global governance. Feminists such as True articulate the relationship between gender and governance in the following way: "'gender' is also a social structure that organizes the allocation of productive and reproductive labour within and across 'public' institutions such as governments and markets, and 'private' institutions such as 'family households' and shapes and sustains systems of global governance" (True 2014, 329). As Prügl argues, structures of governance regimes, exemplified here in the political economy of film governance, both reflect and construct gendered process of power (2004). What is important here is not the privileging of one structure – that is, class over gender or race – but attention to these structures and understanding of how they intersect, maintain, and reproduce hierarchies and inequalities.

The insertion of gender and race into the ways in which world systems are created, maintained, and reproduced is crucial for understanding the structures that limit and enable how a film such as *Pili* is seen and gets to be seen. The core, semi-periphery, and periphery are gendered and racialized. Ownership of the production, distribution, and exhibition companies is predominantly by white men operating in the core. This dominance is not only in ownership but also in who directs, shoots, sound edits, and stars in film. According to the *Women and Hollywood* blog and the Center for the Study of Women in Television and Film, as of 2017, in the highest-grossing US films women comprised only 8 per cent of directors, 10 per cent of writers, 2 per cent of cinematographers, 14 per cent of editors, and 24 per cent of producers (Lauzen 2018; *Women and Hollywood* 2017) – despite women making up 52 per cent of US movie audiences (*Women and Hollywood* 2017). In 2016, only 29 per cent of protagonists in film were women, and 76 per cent of all female characters were white. Women of colour within the film industry are subject to the double discrimination of race and gender and were even less represented in leadership roles and the stories told. For example, data from the Center for Study of Women in Television and Film on the top 1,100 grossing films between 2007 and 2017 demonstrates that 95 per cent of these films had male directors, and only four films had black female directors; only three films had Asian female directors (*Women and Hollywood* 2017). To emphasize this lack of representation: that is four black female directors and three Asian female directors – two broad, diverse, and encompassing categories – over a ten-year period.

Stark gendered and racialized inequalities are not just limited to Hollywood. An analysis by Women in Film and Television UK of the British Film Institute's (BFI's) filmography showed that between 1913 and 2017, only 4.5 per cent of films were directed by women, and less than 1 per cent had mainly female crew (Women in Film and Television UK 2017). On the one hand, data from such a large period of time will be slightly skewed given the advancement of women in work and the introduction of domestic equality legislation. On the other hand, the data also shows how in some instances gender inequality has become worse, not better; for example, in 1913, 31 per cent of the cast were women; in 2017, 30 per cent were women (Women in Film and Television UK 2017). According to the *Celluloid Screening Report* (2017) of the Center for the Study of Women in Television and Film, representation of female leadership in film declined between 2015 and 2017 (Lauzen 2018). The data on inequality is even more stark with regard to racial inequality: as the BFI highlights, "5.3% of the film production workforce, 3.4% of the film distribution workforce and 4.5% of the film exhibition workforce were from Black, Asian and minority ethnic backgrounds in 2012," and 40 per cent of the British public thought that ethnic minority characters in film were tokenistic (BFI 2018). However, the greatest source of under-representation was people with disabilities, who made up only 0.3 per cent of the film workforce in Britain (2018).

Diversity in representation, ownership, and leadership of different aspects of film production and distribution is important for equality as an end in itself and for creativity, innovation, and the telling of new and different stories. It is also important as a means of addressing the extreme end of gendered power relations: physical, sexual, and mental abuses such as those brought to the fore by the #MeToo movement in the wake of the 2017 accusations concerning Harvey Weinstein. In October 2017 the *New York Times* published a story about how film producer Weinstein had sexually harassed women in the film industry for over thirty years and paid for their silence (Kantor and Twohey 2017). Within one month of the story Weinstein had been fired from his company, banned from the Producers Guild of America, stripped of numerous honours and medals, and investigated by the UK Metropolitan Police (BBC 2018). As of October 2017, eighty-five women had come forward with stories that accused Weinstein of harassment and assault (Moniuszko and Kelly 2017). The impact of the Weinstein case was not just the extent and level of the alleged abuse but that it had been an open secret in the film industry; people knew the rumours or had heard the stories but continued to invest in and honour Weinstein (BBC 2017). Weinstein was not an anomaly; multiple accusations of abuse against other high-profile males in public roles followed (Almukhtar, Gold, and Buchanan 2018). Such accusations suggested that abuse was endemic within the film and entertainment industry; but, as the #MeToo social media trend revealed, it was not just endemic in film but throughout society.

The Weinstein scandal and subsequent #MeToo campaign are important here. Weinstein was not a rogue predator but symptomatic of a global gendered and racialized hierarchy of global film governance that operated to the detriment and abuse of mainly women. Gender politics is not only the act of male abuse of women but also the act of male abuse of men, the emphasis of male power over people, and the shaming and financial structures within the global film industry that have maintained silence about the abuse. Weinstein represented the workings of power in the film industry: he used his power over women to allegedly coerce them into sexual encounters; he allegedly paid for their silence (Kantor and Twohey 2017); and collaborated with former state intelligence agencies to spy on these women (Farrow 2017b); and female victims still worked with him because they lacked individual power over him as a dominant male producer (Farrow 2017a). The political economy of film governance shows an extreme form of inequality because of the finances involved, the concentration of financial power around key actors, and the gendered and racialized norms it promotes. Fundamentally, the scandal was important in that it triggered demand for change: change in the rights of cast and crew; change in transparency; change in equal pay; change in representation; and change for the types of stories told in film. Campaigns such as Time's Up and #MeToo spurred both a wider reflection and global attention on the gendered and racialized dynamics of global film governance, and a change towards seeing and believing women.

Pili sought distribution at the height of the Weinstein scandal and the #MeToo phenomenon and was in production during the 2016

#OscarsSoWhite campaign (although the hashtag was originally created in 2015 by April Reign, it gained momentum in 2016). *Pili* was produced between the semi-periphery and the periphery, featured a cast of African women, and was led by women, but it still had to engage in the processes and structures of audience maintained by the core and in the racialized and gendered hierarchies privileging whiteness, men, and masculinity. For *Pili* to attain distribution and a worldwide audience, it would have to engage with the norms, codes of conduct, and practices established by the core. The production of *Pili* seemingly put it at a disadvantage: distance from the core, minimal networks and access to gatekeepers, and ostensibly the "wrong" gender leadership and cast to successfully navigate the governance of film. However, the marginal production of the film and its female leadership operated in a period of flux and change in the film industry. Time's Up, #OscarsSoWhite, and #MeToo had created a unique opportunity structure in which film distributors and audiences publicly claimed to want to see women and diverse stories. Operating within this opportunity structure, the issue in gaining a distribution deal for *Pili* was whether a commitment and public interest in such change were translating into the formal and informal practices of film distribution.

HOW TO DISTRIBUTE A FILM

The system of global film governance shapes how films reach audiences. The way to distribute a film and have an audience is diverse, anarchic, and changing; however, the way to commercialize a film through distribution remains narrow, hierarchical, and rooted in accepted industry practice established by the US film industry. Such practices discipline when and where a film can be seen (a world premiere at a festival, closed screenings, subsequent exhibitions), the different types of actors that are able to engage in the process, and the behaviours that pass as accepted etiquette. They involve a variety of actors, from festival selectors to sales agents to buyers to distributors who keep the gates and determine which films reach an audience. The system of distribution is principally organized around the commercial interests of film. The artistic endeavour is presented as the important and legitimating aspect of film that is celebrated at film festivals and awards ceremonies. However, the artistic endeavour is monetized as a mechanism by which to increase the profit from a film. While "blockbuster" films are marketed to large audiences, have built-in product endorsements, and are nakedly ambitious in the pursuit of profit; independent films use the artistic or auteur aspect of filmmaking to leverage profit.

Distribution is regarded by experts in the political economy of film as the key to power in film, and Hollywood in particular (Wasko 2003, 56). This is because distribution companies are instrumental to both the films that are exhibited or screened to audiences and the films that are made. Distribution companies often finance films from the "package stage" of production, that is, when a film has a script and big-name actors attached. This has led to a degree of blurring between the production, the distribution, and the exhibition of film, which, from 1948 to the mid-1980s, had been distinct practices so as not to limit competition across sectors. The blurring of these processes and the growth of media conglomerates mean that most films are only made if they can be marketed for distribution and guaranteed returns. This point is the key to distribution company power and maintenance of the core: the "majors" are able to occupy and define the space for both distribution and exhibition of films, crowding out competitors who cannot rival them financially in both the purchase and the marketing of films. Small distributors lose out because they cannot compete, and small producers lose out because they do not have the leverage to negotiate favourable deals with exhibitors (e.g., cinema chains, online platforms such as Netflix) (Wasko 2003). The main route to distribution is therefore to get a distributor to finance a film from the outset or to get a "negative pick-up" where the distribution company distributes the film without any prior investment. These two routes are the dominant methods of distribution for mainstream film used by the majors.

For independent films or "indies" – i.e., those films not made by a major, often with small production teams, without major distributor support, and self-financed (Balio 2013) – the main method for distribution is via film festivals and markets, or private screenings to distributors, or by doing it yourself (Balio 2013). Indies are not separate from accepted practices of distribution and exhibition, and, for authors like Wasko, such films run parallel to the mainstream or majors (Wasko 2003). Although the lack of large financial backing may constrain aspects of indie filmmaking, indies tend to capture the attention and praise of both film critics and award panels that can convert artistic merit into commercial success (S. Hall and Whannel

1964, 359). The goal for indies is to secure a short exhibition run
in cinemas, a "theatrical release." Even though most indies only
have short runs in large cities such as New York, Los Angeles, and
London and little financial return, theatrical exhibition "lends an
aura of cinematic legitimacy" and establishes consumer interest and
market value for other forms of exhibition (e.g., DVD or on demand)
(Balio 2013; Wasko 2003). Most major film awards stipulate theatrical release as an entry criterion. Without exposure in film festivals
or a theatrical release, at best a film can be seen as a flop, or at worst
production companies can go bankrupt because the film is not seen
to have commercial value (Balio 2013, 115).

One way of avoiding the mainstream political economy of film
and the commercial aspect of distribution is self-distribution. The
most straightforward way of screening a film like *Pili* would be to
add it for free to an online viewing platform such as YouTube or
Vimeo or to an alternative independent platform. This would make
the film open and accessible to anyone in the world, particularly in
East Africa where there has been a rapid growth in mobile phone
technology and the use of phones to watch online material. The
appeal of such a platform would be bottom-up access to the film
that does not discriminate on the basis of ability to pay; in addition, it cuts out various parts of the film industry and reaches a
broad and diverse audience. Audience responses can be quantified
and engaged through comments and data records from the websites.
For these reasons, such accessible online formats would fulfill the
aims of this particular project: audience and impact. However, such
a format would mean that the film would generate limited income
(through a pay-to-watch service, for example) for the beneficiaries
of the film (the women and communities in Miono) and would not
have a theatrical release, which was the main aim and source of
recognition for the filmmakers who had collaborated on the project.
A film distributed for free on an online platform is akin to selling
a self-published book: the content may be of a high standard and
quality, but the quality is assessed by peers on the basis of the type of
output or platform. To distribute the film for free and online would
diminish the careers of the filmmakers and generate less income for
the women in the film. Although a do-it-yourself distribution is an
acknowledged method in the film studies literature, most research
cautions against this because of expense and time. To self-distribute
you would have to set up your own distribution company, develop

independent linkages with exhibitors of the film, and compete with the established major distribution companies. Hence, while authors such as Beaupre acknowledge that do-it-yourself distribution may be an attractive way of avoiding distribution companies – "the presumed manglers of a film and embezzlers of its profit" – ultimately "self distribution is a trap for the unwary" (Beaupre 1986, 203).

The traditional route for indie film distribution is therefore as follows. First, one has to secure a world premiere for the film at an international film festival. This is the initial encounter with hierarchy and gatekeeping practices. There are different tiers of film festival. The first tier comprises the top five festivals: Sundance, Berlin, Cannes, Venice, and Toronto (Balio 2013). Related to the first tier are prestigious but slightly smaller festivals such as Edinburgh, London, San Sebastián, South by Southwest (SXSW), and Tribeca. The levels then continue to include smaller and more obscure festivals depending on location, audience, and attendance by industry actors. The main African film festival is FESPACO in Burkina Faso; established and well regarded as the premiere festival of the continent, it tends to be ranked as a lower-tier festival that is not well attended by buyers and sellers from the major markets. African festivals such as FESPACO give global platforms for African films and have been central to their global appeal and recognition (Magombe 1996). Festivals are open to any film that can pay the fee (which varies from US$70 to US$100 per entry). However, selection is a political process of getting the film in front of the right selectors, and a balance of the type of films that have been submitted. For example, it is unlikely that a festival would select two British films that focus on HIV/AIDS in Africa in the same year. Selectors are the gatekeepers to film festivals, as Wasko argues: "The selection process of film festivals often relies on personal trust, long-time friendships, and subjective opinion. While there are usually festival selection committees, gatekeepers or political lobbyists have emerged on the festival circuit. These characters operate between filmmakers and festival heads, influencing the films that are offered and chosen. While big titles by well-known directors or films from the US majors rarely are affected by these manoeuvres, international exposure can be crucial for smaller or independent films" (2003, 208)

Film festivals are both an opportunity and a risk for film producers. The opportunity is that the film is selected and bought by distributors. The risk is that no one attends a screening or the film has a poor response from critics. Compounding both factors is the expense of attending, the inflated economy around the festivals (this is particularly high at the big festivals in transnational elite cities such as Cannes and Venice) (Schamus 1998), and the financial commitment to networking, lobbying, and showcasing the film to buyers. To navigate the selling of film, most indie film producers work with sales agents. Ideally, sales agents are involved in the film prior to a festival premiere. They can help negotiate festival fees, ensure that the right people see the film, and, importantly, lobby selectors to screen the film. If the producer does not have an agent prior to a festival, having a world premiere at a good festival will help in securing one. The job of the sales agent is to market, sell, and license the film to distributors and then collect on the agreements (Schamus 1998, 97). Sales agents represent the film at festivals and the major buyer markets that are organized around the Berlin and Cannes film festivals in Europe and the annual American Film Market in the United States. They arrange all the promotion and contracts with distributors and take between 15 and 25 per cent of profit plus any upfront costs for marketing the film and for film festival campaigns. The costs of marketing and delivering a film to a sales agent can reach up to or above US$500,000 before the film even has a distribution deal (Schamus 1998). Some sales agents arrange additional collection agents, who take a fee of 1.5 per cent to increase transparency in the process.

For a producer or a sales agent to sell a film to a distributor, a distributor to sell a film to an exhibitor (e.g., a chain of cinemas), and the combined actors to sell the film to an audience, involves marketing. Marketing includes film reviews, awards, multimedia advertising, social media campaigns, and media engagement generally. The marketing of film changed in 1975 with the advent of the blockbuster and the release of *Jaws*. *Jaws* changed the way that Hollywood films were sold to the public by introducing a saturated marketing campaign across television and outdoors (Gomery 1998b). Following the success of *Jaws* at the box office, the majors adopted similar mass marketing methods, which became the norm for selling a film to the public. This in turn inflated the costs of film marketing and the market value ascribed to a film before it was made: if the film is not marketable, it will not receive financing from a distribution company. The role of marketability pertains to indies as much as it does to majors. The relatively large, but now discredited (see the section on Weinstein) (L. Ryan 2017), independent distribution company Miramax changed the role of marketing in the indie sector in similar ways to those used for *Jaws* that had an impact on the major Hollywood blockbuster. Miramax became known for running high-level marketing campaigns organized around critical success and acclaimed industry awards. By securing Academy Awards, or "Oscars," for independent films such as *The English Patient* through sustained industry marketing campaigns, Miramax was able to turn critical success into commercial success. However, Miramax is also a model of caution for smaller independent distributors when marketing costs outstrip gross revenue. For example, as Balio demonstrates, the film *No Country for Old Men* was awarded four Oscars and grossed US$75 million in the US box office but lost money because of the marketing and distribution costs associated with the film (Balio 2013).

Once a film has been premiered at a festival, licensed to a distributor, marketed to audiences, and then exhibited, revenue is generated. The exhibitor, distributor, collection agent, and sales agent take their fees first before the final money is allocated to the production company, which in the case of *Pili* will then be allocated to the women and community in the film. It is those actors that were less, if at all, involved in the production of the film that reap some of the highest percentage of the film's profit. In the case of *Pili*, it is those who need the money the most who are the last to be paid.

HOW *PILI* SECURED A SALES AND DISTRIBUTION DEAL

As with the production of *Pili*, it was the navigation of the intersection of informal and unseen power relations within the formal governance of the film industry that secured the film's sale and distribution. The process of distribution was governed by the formal practices outlined earlier, by the informal, unseen codes of conduct, by relationships, and by the language of such practices that shaped the decision-making and outcomes of how the film would be seen. I knew little about film sales or distribution at the outset of the project and lacked any networks or contacts in the film industry. The thought of attracting a sales agent or a distributor at the early stage of production had not occurred to me as a possibility or a necessary advantage in getting an audience for the film. The distribution of *Pili* therefore started from a position of perceived disadvantage: a film set in the periphery; female leadership and cast; a non-English "foreign language" film; and a producer with no networks. This section details how *Pili* transferred from being an academic co-production project to being an established indie film with a sales and distribution agreement.

The distribution of *Pili* roughly adhered to the process of a negative pickup over an eighteen-month period. The day that post-production was completed on *Pili*, director Leanne sent a password-protected link to her agent, who passed it on to a friend who was a selector for the Sundance Film Festival, and then Leanne got in touch with a key contact at the British Council Film Programme. The British Council Film Programme has a mandate to promote British films and has established relationships with film festival selectors. The British Council took a keen and early interest in *Pili* and over the course of six months screened the film to selectors from the Sundance, Berlinale, Cannes, and Toronto film festivals. It had an internal selection process and then charged for the screenings. The screenings were pivotal for *Pili* because they provided an opportunity for selectors to see the film in a proper cinema, narrowed the field, and gave the film its first entry point into the festival circuit.

As a consequence of the film's quality and the endorsement of the British Council, *Pili* was shortlisted for the Sundance and Berlin festivals but was not selected. The game changer for the film was when it was shortlisted by selectors for three different categories at Cannes: Director's Week, Critics' Week, and in competition for Un Certain Regard. It is rare for an unknown film to be shortlisted for three different categories, and the shortlisting alone for a festival as prestigious and well-known as Cannes raised the profile of the film within certain sectors of the film industry. This was not by accident but by a direct intervention from the British Council, which, sensing we had little contacts or patrons to promote the film to selectors, emailed the shortlisting news to various sales agents.

It was at the Cannes short-list stage that Leanne and I were approached by a number of sales agents who were interested in representing the film. We agreed to work with one agent prior to finding out about Cannes' final selection. If *Pili* was selected, we could potentially negotiate a better deal with a different sales agent; however, given that selection was not guaranteed and the offer was a standard deal with a well-respected company, Leanne and I decided to accept it. However, as a consequence of delays in negotiation, internal politics in the company, and our film's not being finally selected for Cannes, the initial deal fell through. This was a significant blow for all involved, which was made worse as our entries to other festivals such as Venice, Toronto, and London followed a similar pattern: early interest and excitement, and then nothing. It was becoming increasingly apparent that we needed more industry influence, patronage, and support not only to get selectors to watch the film but also to network and lobby effectively so that *Pili* did not become an easy film to drop. The film was receiving attention because of its quality, but it was falling down because of its academic and peripheral origins.

The breakthrough for the film came when it was selected for the 2017 Dinard British Film Festival. The selection was enabled by the first sales agent whom we had encountered at the Cannes stage and who took a strong personal interest in *Pili*'s success. The agent's intervention helped us get into the festival and ensured that the film was placed in competition. To be in competition raised the profile of the film within the festival to both the film industry and audiences and increased the number of screenings that would take place. Given the twelve months of opportunity and disappointment with regard to festivals, Leanne and I attended Dinard to enjoy ourselves with minimal expectation. However, mindful of my commitment to the women in the film and the filmmakers who had yet to see the benefits of their involvement, I was keen to use the festival as an opportunity to network and promote *Pili* as much as possible. Although the festival was seen as more relaxed and less industry focused, it was one of the few opportunities I had to meet agents and distributors and, at the very least, industry advocates, advisors, and patrons for the film.

The first inclination I had that the festival could be a turning point came after the judges screening of the film. The head judge approached me at lunch to tell me that the film had moved her deeply, and then two major distributors from France sat next to me. Fortunately I was also sitting with our first sales contact and a representative of Film London who had taken me under their wing; they said all the right things, nodded at me when to stop talking, and made strong eye movements when I revealed too much – principally how much the film cost to make and that I would not have to pay back these costs. These are two major mistakes in the film

Fig. 7 Sophie Harman and Leanne Welham receiving the audience award for *Pili* at the Dinard British Film Festival, 2017.

world: the first rule of selling a film is to not reveal the budget, and the second rule is to never reveal how much has to be paid back or that the money is going to poor women in rural Tanzania. The second inclination occurred when people approached me to say that they had heard *Pili* was being talked about as the dark horse of the festival and that audience numbers were good. Prior to the judges screening of *Pili*, these people had been friendly and courteous but generally ignored me during the festival. The final inclination came in the question-and-answer sessions with local film groups. These groups seemed very engaged with the content and characters of the film, wanting to know what was happening with the women in the film and whether we would make another.

The major turning point came when *Pili* won the Hitchcock Public Award (the award voted for by audiences), and the screenplay received Special Mention by the judges. The audience award was the best award we could have won: it demonstrated that there was an audience for this type of film and that it could therefore make money. After the awards ceremony I was approached by several sales agents and distributors, and I made contact with a number of senior producers who gave me useful advice about distribution, said I could contact them with questions in the future, and, in one instance, offered to produce my next film (see chapter 6).

On returning to London I spoke to several sales agents and distributors and confirmed a UK distribution deal and international sales agreement. This agreement was between the distributor and an independent company that I had to establish to hold any potential liabilities for the film. *Pili* was then screened at a number of festivals around the world, such as the East End Film Festival in London and the Pan-African Film Festival in Los Angeles, had its sales debut at the Berlin sales market in February 2018, was screened to select audiences in partnership with Stop AIDS in London and UNAIDS in Geneva, and reached an agreement for a UK theatrical release. Over eighteen months the film has secured distribution and exhibition and therefore potentially financial return for the women in the film, prestige for the filmmakers, and audience for the widespread impact of the key themes and issues in the film. This was made possible through individual networks and supporters of *Pili* who leveraged the artistic quality and importance of the film to have the formal structures of the film industry engage and take notice. This was then compounded by initial audience feedback to demonstrate that the film could make money. Once again it was the intersection of informal and formal politics that generated the desired outcome. The small opportunity – to be in competition at a festival – with a democratic voting system among the public generated crucial success for the film.

THE POLITICS OF DISTRIBUTION
AND CO-PRODUCTION

The outline of how *Pili* gained distribution suggests a straightforward process, once informal patterns and codes of conduct had become clear, interspersed with occasional disappointment and chance opportunity. What it does not reveal is how this process challenged the initial aims of the use of film as method (outlined in chapter 1) and generated problematic issues arising from tensions between the academic and film worlds. This section reflects on these tensions and how the objectives of the project – to use film as African agency and feminist method, to have affect and impact, and to allow women who are unseen and unheard to represent themselves – were challenged in the process of distribution. The issue concerned engaging in the global political economy of film governance in order to distribute and exhibit the film without reproducing the hierarchies that silence invisible voices. This section shows that tensions are inevitable when attempts are being made to break new ground in both academic research and filmmaking through co-produced methods. Such confrontation is not only about the artistic endeavour versus the commercial aspect of the film but also about a balance of competing interests in the outcomes as well as the aims of the film. While being challenging and at times leading to individual professional setbacks, the tensions of co-production are not detrimental but are beneficial to the long-term overall success of a project, the advancement of knowledge, and new ways of seeing politics.

The Audience That Matters

The first challenge of balancing competing co-production aims is to determine who sees the film first. As outlined, the standard practice for film to reach an audience is to premiere it in a high-profile film festival. Film festivals want exclusivity, and therefore the film cannot be screened ahead of the festival. The privileging of high-profile festivals challenged the research aims and intent for the project in two ways. The first was with regard to film as African agency, as outlined in chapter 1. With the exception of FESPACO in Burkina Faso (Diawara 1992), African film festivals are rarely considered by global buyers and distributors and therefore remain on the lower rungs of the film festival hierarchy. It would therefore be commercially foolish to host the premiere of a film at an African film festival. However, given that the intent of the project was to use the film as a source of agency, and the film was set in Africa with an African cast, an African premiere would contribute to an intention towards building African agency.

I wanted to screen *Pili* at the Zanzibar International Film Festival. The film was selected for the festival in July 2017. The screening would give an opportunity for the women in the film to attend, alongside the musicians who had licensed their music for the film for free, and for a celebration with some of the Tanzanian crew. However, Leanne strongly disagreed and argued that to screen at Zanzibar would affect selection at larger, more prestigious festivals

and that it could wait until the following year. I compromised by
suggesting that I would wait to hear from another, larger festival to
which we had submitted, and, if we were not selected, I would proceed with Zanzibar. Our disagreement meant that we did not speak
directly for over a month. By the time I heard from the other festival
(that *Pili* had not been selected), I only had ten days to organize a
trip to Zanzibar. Organization would involve travel for the women
and one of the crew members, my own travel, a press conference,
and a party with the cast, crew, musicians, and representatives from
the UK government in Tanzania and the NGO sector. I concluded that
organizing this on my own in such a short space of time might be
possible but would come at a personal cost. The decision of balancing the African component of the film with the commercial imperative, and the disagreement with Leanne, had begun to take its toll
on me. In addition, cast members were messaging me for money for
their teeth, stomach, or children's clothes; estranged crew members
were asking me for money because they had fallen on hard times;
and I had a professional setback. So I decided to take a short break
from the project. I pulled the film from the Zanzibar festival and had
a productive engagement with the selectors about screening it in the
following year.

The second way in which a prestigious film festival challenged
the intent of the project was the way in which the film could be
screened to policy-makers, academics, and students. To reach policy-
makers, opinion formers, key target audiences working in HIV/AIDS
and global health, and academics and maximize the impact and visibility of the film, I had planned a number of screening events. I
had secured a screening of the film at Ciné-ONU (United Nations
Cinema) in Geneva, planned a parliamentary screening jointly hosted
with an all-party parliamentary group on HIV/AIDS (which subsequently did not happen because of the 2017 UK general election),
and arranged a panel showing at an international academic conference for scholars of IR. This was my first line of screening plans; my
second line was to arrange events in partnership with NGOs such as
the International HIV/AIDS Alliance and Stop AIDS, a tour of the film
in Tanzania where I would set up mobile cinemas in collaboration
with the Tanzania Commission for HIV/AIDS, and other events about
which people had approached me, such as the 2018 AIDS Cultural
History Month that would run alongside the International HIV/AIDS
Conference in Amsterdam. The problem was that all these screenings

could jeopardize the world premiere and any commercial contract reached with distributors. Initially I was advised to have academic audience members sign non-disclosure agreements to watch the film (I declined), and to push back the UN and parliamentary screenings. The additional screenings were secondary and thus not even considered as an option. This meant that the academic dissemination of the film, which was crucial to both the delivery of funding commitments and scholarly recognition, came second to recognition in the film industry and commercial gain.

The significance of specific audiences became less of an issue once *Pili* had premiered at the Dinard British Film Festival in 2017. At this stage the new distributor and sales agent for the film saw the link with the United Nations, NGOs, and academic screenings as major assets to the film: these networks could be used to leverage interest and build a community around the film. A community or network around the film would then help with the wider campaign to secure an audience upon the film's release. One of the key tensions within the co-production had arisen not in the balancing of everyone's needs and wants for the film but in the temporality in which these needs and wants were met. The tension also lay in establishing mutual recognition of what everyone wanted from the film and of the different aims and intentions for it. My aims and objectives for the project, as set out in the introduction and chapter 1, did not necessarily align to those of the filmmakers (critical recognition, film festival premiere, distribution) or the cast (making money) and, even if shared at the outset, shifted over the life cycle of the project. These aims were not mutually exclusive but in practice were mutually reinforcing; however, as with all politics, the tensions regarded what goals were prioritised, when, and how. Crucially the realization of these aims depended on working with people, such as *Pili's* UK distributor and sales agent, who recognized and understood how such aims could be mutually reinforcing.

Whose Story Is It Anyway?

The concept of co-production does not fit with the hierarchy and authorship of film. As chapter 2 explored, the idea of co-produced film as method contrasted with the hierarchy of a film crew's work on set. With film distribution, hierarchies manifest through authorship and ownership of the film. The credits of the film do not directly reflect the input of the stories of the women outlined in chapter 2. The credits simply state: "Story by Sophie Harman and Leanne Welham," and "Screenplay by Leanne Welham." The credits reflect who wrote the story and who wrote the screenplay, but they negate the input of the women in the process. The majority of the marketing, media coverage, and publicity for the film ascribes authorship to Leanne. This is a common and accepted practice of independent, auteur cinema. However, again this practice undermines the co-productive aspect of the film and the notion that film gives space for the under-represented to represent themselves. Ascribing authorship to the director was in many respects unavoidable, given that this is a standard code of conduct in film governance; however, I attempted to work within these parameters to reflect the co-production element. Work within these parameters included stressing the role of the women's stories in the trailer and the production notes, emphasizing the collaborative nature of the film in talks and screening question-and-answer sessions, and not having any named individual on the publicity materials for the film.

Working within the parameters of standard marketing practice created two tensions. The first was that, in emphasizing the co-production element, I was in effect reducing or undermining the role of the director. Authorship and public recognition of such authorship is important to directors as they establish a body of work under the director's name. This is particularly acute for new directors; given that *Pili* was Leanne's first feature film, reducing her authorship of the film in effect reduced her potential recognition in the wider film world. Authorship is less about who owns or writes the film (though this is also important and a tension in and of itself) but more about a mark of prestige and legitimacy, and evidence that a filmmaker is to be noticed and is commercially bankable. Not privileging the role of director was a way of aligning both with the co-production element of the project and with the range of academic input (my own) and new research and stories (of the women from Miono, Mbwewe, and Bagamoyo) that went into the film; however, to do so was in contrast to the established practices of film marketing and thus potentially detrimental to the way in which Leanne would be seen in the film world. Although this decision reflected the intent and aims of the project, it stood in tension with the established practices and codes of conduct and with the expectations of a pivotal co-producer of the film, Leanne.

The second tension around co-production existed in how the stories of the women in the film became instrumentalized to sell the film and how Leanne and I came to represent them through the publicity campaign. Films are sold based on the cast, the director, and the critical reviews or stories. Given that *Pili* was a film with no known actors, with a first-time director, and with a producer who had no industry networks, the selling points of the film came to focus on the lives of the women and their involvement in the film. These selling points and the stories of the women were reduced to an ensemble cast of untrained actors sourced from the community in which the film was set; 65 per cent of the cast self-disclosed as HIV positive; and a unique collaboration between the filmmakers and the community of Miono. These selling points were not misleading and emphasized the collaborative element and agency of the women in the film; however, they also reduced the women and their lives to their HIV status. This blurred the distinction between actor and character (with many audience members wanting to know how "Pili" was now, conflating Bello with the character she played) and led some to assume that all the cast members were HIV positive or would be familiar with the issues of a woman living with HIV rather with than the broader themes of everyday life in rural Tanzania.

Cast members were not directly involved in the film's promotion. Flying cast members to the United Kingdom would include practical requirements (obtaining passports for them, organizing travel from Miono to Dar es Salaam to the United Kingdom, arranging support for them in the United Kingdom, and supporting their families in Miono while they were there) and a financial commitment to pay for their travel and loss of earnings. It would also involve expectation management: they would arrive in the United Kingdom for a publicity campaign that would be relatively glitzy, and perhaps would expect that the film had therefore made money – before the film had made any money. These factors were not insurmountable; however, considering the feelings of guilt and financial need that had arisen in travelling from Miono to Bagamoyo (as discussed in chapter 3), it was highly likely these feelings would be heightened should the cast members travel to the United Kingdom. They would leave Miono to come to the United Kingdom, and their families would be in Miono; they would take an expensive flight when they would prefer the cost of the flight to be spent on their families. Money spent on flying key cast members to the United Kingdom would be subtracted from the film's final profit; in other words, it would affect the final lump sum they would receive. The emotional, practical, and financial costs of the trip would outweigh the potential benefit of their participation in the publicity campaign. The public relations team, the distributor, and I therefore decided to reduce the cast's involvement in the marketing campaign. Once the film made money, I would return it to Miono, and, should the cast members decide they wanted to spend it on travel to the United Kingdom, I would help facilitate that; however, it would be their decision to do so. Not involving the cast in the marketing and publicity for the film meant that in effect Leanne and I spoke for them in the question-and-answer sessions and interviews about the film. These exchanges were about the experience of making the film, the stories the women shared with us, the lives of the women today, and the future of the film. *Pili* was the story of the women and communities in the film and a medium in which the under-represented could represent themselves, but the narrative around the film was told by Leanne and me.

The instrumental use of the stories of the women in the film was not all problematic. The publicity for the film helped leverage and communicate key aspects of the women's lives to wider audiences. The film itself was valued for its co-productive aspect; for example, the judges at Dinard noted that the way in which the story evolved was a key factor in awarding *Pili* the Special Mention for its screenplay. Audiences responded positively to the fact that *Pili* was a universal story that showcased the complex lives of women who had been previously unseen on screen. Those aspects of the film that could have potentially worked to the detriment of finding an audience – non-English, from the periphery, an all-female cast and leadership – all worked to its advantage. The film was released at a critical moment in the film world as people realized the need for diverse stories and female-led filmmaking. The female-led aspect of *Pili* was therefore not a disadvantage to the film's success, because the film was gaining exposure when the gendered and racialized structures of the political economy of film were coming into question. *Pili* was in part able to advance within the parameters of global film governance as the norms and codes of conduct underpinning such parameters were being forced to reflect and adapt. The co-productive elements of film production did produce tensions; however, it was the combined strength of each of the co-producers that resonated with audiences, gained distribution, and ultimately made the film a success.

Universities Are Not Production Companies

The process of gaining distribution of *Pili* presents a cautionary tale for producing work of commercial value within the university sector. The intellectual property of and any potential liability for *Pili*, as a university research project, was initially owned by the university for which I worked. This became a problem when I was negotiating the first sales deal offered for the film. It is standard practice in the film industry for a production company to hold all liabilities and indemnities for a film. However, as there was no production company in this instance, the university would have to hold such liability; as a charity, the university did not want to do this and wanted the sales agent to change the established, standard practice of the film industry. I cautioned the university's negotiating team that it would be impossible to change established practices, especially not for a film of this kind, and one option would be to set up a company either within or independent of the university to hold such liabilities. The differing position of the university in contrast to established film industry practice resulted in a two-hour meeting between the sales agent, the university's innovation, business, and legal representatives, and me. The meeting ended in a suggested compromise, followed by a protracted stalemate, during which time *Pili* was unable to enter a tier-one festival and the agent with whom we were working decided to leave their company. Combined, these factors led to a collapse of the agreement and a sense that misjudgment and mishandling of the negotiation had caused the loss of this significant opportunity for the film. I was able to use the mishandling as justification for the university to assign the intellectual property of *Pili* to an independent production company that I established. This meant that both the university and I would be protected against any future liability; I would be able to negotiate future contracts independently of the university; and the university would not receive a percentage of the film's profits, a request that it had introduced in discussions over the initial sales deal.

The problem with this episode is that the process could not have been avoided; if a film is being produced as part of a research project, the project will most likely occur within a university, and the university therefore has a commercial interest and claim to the intellectual property. The intellectual property for the product was released *only* when the university failed to secure a positive outcome. This story is important for understanding the use and outcome of new methods and the production of research with commercial value. In the immediate term, a lack of understanding of the research and the type of agreement can contribute to a lost contract and great disappointment for multiple parties involved in the co-production process. This in turn can have a negative impact on personal working relationships. Over the long term it has implications for how universities work with non-scientific "inventions," as commercial outputs tend to be labelled. Most arrangements between universities and researchers for commercial outputs are framed by science models of the "inventor" rather than by the different needs of social science and humanities research outputs. To conduct new research methods, and for social science and humanities scholars to produce commercial outputs, university business and innovation teams have to adapt guidelines and practices to accommodate these goals better.

To break ground in using film as co-produced method in IR means you also have to break ground in film being seen as a research output in IR. In parallel to the issue with the sales agreement, it also became apparent that the university saw *Pili* as a side project concerned with public engagement and impact rather than as a major research project in and of itself. In a promotion meeting the film was not even discussed – only in passing reference to the ongoing social-impact benefits of my work. Many colleagues within and outside my university were incredibly supportive of the project and recognized its research contribution; however, the film itself was not recognized by my employer's indicators of success. There was little to no awareness of distribution as a mark of success, or of the difficulty in securing distribution of a film. This led to an odd position in which some parts of the university wanted to use the film to showcase interesting, innovative, and international research, and for me to teach specialized postgraduate courses on film as method; other parts of senior management downgraded the value of the film from one of research output to one of public engagement. What became apparent was that I had to justify the use of film not only as a method of co-produced research but also as a legitimate and important research output. Film is not simply a form of translating research to a wider audience; it is a complex research output with equal value to other forms of academic publication. The quality of the output should be judged on the film's content, with markers such as distribution and exhibition being used as similar indicators to publication and citation in written work.

Publication and citation indicators are not without fault and are subject to unequal power relations, in the same way that this chapter has shown that distribution and audience indicators are subject to unequal power relations. Although the indicators may be problematic, they do not discredit the research.

The Master's Tools

The balance between successfully distributing *Pili* as a means of securing visibility for the stories of the women in the film, and doing so in a way that does not reproduce the structures that rendered these women invisible in the first place, brings to mind Audre Lorde's famous statement: "The master's tools will never dismantle the master's house" (1984, 110–13). Working within the structures and parameters of global film governance to distribute a film does not challenge the hierarchies and inequalities within those structures. This is true to an extent with the distribution of *Pili*: as the process of distribution developed, the space for the women in the film to represent themselves was reduced, and European and American audiences were prioritized over African audiences. This suggests an unequal relationship with regard to the audiences that were prioritized (European over African) and the persons who were able to impose a wider narrative or voice around the film (Leanne and I as director and producer, respectively, rather than the women in the film).

The aim of *Pili* was to make the invisible visible and to use film as a method of co-produced research that explored power relations around the everyday risk of HIV/AIDS. The aim was not to challenge or dismantle the structures of film governance. Engaging in one political act – here, making the invisible visible through film – may generate or reproduce other forms of political-economic inequality. To make visible through large, global audiences requires engagement with the structures and political economy of film governance that generate and attract audiences. As discussed earlier in the chapter, other methods of self-distribution, while possible, limit audience numbers and are not seen as a benchmark of quality. Consumption and audience for visual politics is governed by material structures and practices. This suggests that, although visual politics and aesthetics have transformative power in one respect – here, making the everyday risk of living with HIV visible – in many ways aesthetic forms are governed and constrained by the very systems they seek

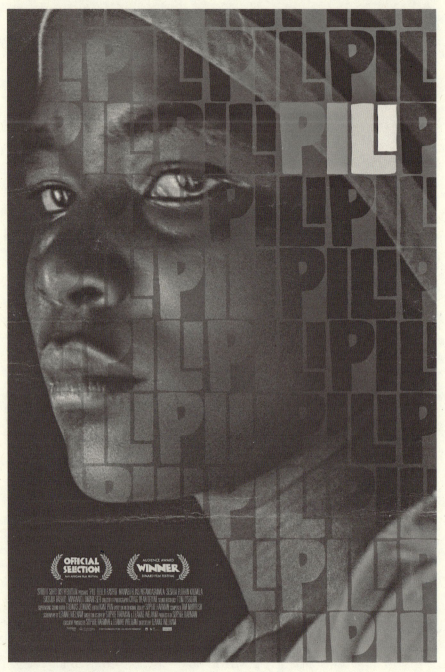

Fig. 8 Official poster for *Pili*, 2018.

to challenge. Seeing *Pili* and finding an audience through distribution required a direct engagement with capitalist systems of film governance. This chapter has shown that it is important to think about not only how knowledge is produced when one is thinking about decolonizing epistemology and methodology but also how knowledge is consumed. Navigating the existing structures of film governance requires a trade-off between seemingly incompatible aims: you either gain an audience, visibility, profit, and recognition by operating within the structures of global film governance, or you operate outside of such structures but minimize the potential for audience, profit, and artistic recognition. Attempts to reconcile these incompatible aims by pushing within established parameters produce the types of tension between co-producers explored here.

Pushing these parameters can generate positive and negative outcomes depending on the aims and interests of the co-producer. Aspects of *Pili's* production and distribution did challenge and push the parameters of established film governance; however, for distribution to be effective in terms of audience and profit, it had to work with the tools and structures of the master's house. The intent of *Pili* was to use different tools (film as research method) to dismantle a different house (the production of research and knowledge in IR). As chapter 1 outlined, part of the reason to use film as co-produced method was to challenge the aesthetic of HIV/AIDS. This is a significant challenge, and one film alone cannot do it, because one film cannot change the structures of film governance that have been in place for over one hundred years and are embedded within the global capitalist economy. What the distribution of *Pili* does do is open up space for a different presentation of the everyday risk of HIV/AIDS and make the case for more female-led, African cinema in worldwide independent cinema. *Pili* does challenge specific conventions in film governance – female leadership, unknown actors, no profit for the producer, Tanzanian story – and it is these modest challenges that made the film appealing to distributors during a period of flux in the film industry.

CONCLUSION

Audience consumption is fundamental to understanding visual methods and the way we see politics, in terms of how political-economic structures and conditions influence the impact and potential of the aesthetic. Visual politics is a two-way process between how the visual can have an impact on politics and how politics shapes the content of the visual form. By 2018, *Pili* had been screened in several prestigious film festivals, at the United Nations in Geneva, at several universities, and in special collaboration with organizations such as Stop AIDS. The film had both a UK distribution deal and an international sales deal. A film made in rural Tanzania, with unknown actors, a first-time director, and an inexperienced producer, had navigated the political-economic structures of global film governance to obtain an audience. This fulfilled the aim of making the invisible visible to a range of targeted and general audiences. Moreover, it fulfilled the differing but mutually reinforcing aims of the different co-producers: audience, visibility, and clear research output (my aims); legitimacy and recognition in the film world (the aims of the crew and filmmakers), and sharing their stories and making money (the aims of the women). The distribution and exhibition of *Pili* to a range of audiences shows what is possible to achieve in the use of film as output in IR.

Fulfilling the principle aims of the project and gaining an audience is only part of the story. This chapter has shown the other part of the story: managing the aims and interests of co-producers with regard to the outcomes of the film, and reconciling the seemingly incompatible aims over visibility. The first issue – the different aims and interests of co-producers – manifested in different ways, with long- and short-term consequences for those involved in the project. Balanced against short-term setbacks, frustrations, and the navigation of informal power dynamics, the issues involved with co-production ended up working as an asset rather than a detriment to the film's distribution and exhibition. The origins of the story, the marginality of the women involved, representation issues, and audience prioritization all became mutually reinforcing and beneficial to the wider goal of seeking a global audience. On first reading, these issues may seem problematic: less space for the voice of the women, commercial interests taking immediate priority over academic inputs, and universities discounting film as a research output. However, to label such issues as problematic overlooks the temporal and material concerns of the co-producers of *Pili*: for example, when and in what spaces the women want to be visible; the cast's interest in profit over participation; and, in the exploration of the ground-breaking use of methods, the need to change established mindsets about what constitutes research method and research outcome. The co-productive element may have produced short-term setbacks, but these were perhaps an unavoidable part of the process of doing something new and creating new ways of working in both the academic and the film world.

The second issue concerned the relationship between visibility and invisibility and the political-economic structures that shape this relationship. It was inevitable that taking the stories of one group of women and triangulating them with my existing research and the crew's expertise in narrative filmmaking would produce a specific story and narrative. *Pili* is not, and does not claim to be, the single story of women living with HIV/AIDS. In taking this one story and making it visible, the film does privilege the visibility of this story over others. Some stories are told, some are not told; some reach audiences, others do not. This has always been the case and has always been shaped by political hierarchies of wealth, education, gender, race, and ability. As this chapter has shown, stories that are told in the film world exist in a hierarchical framework of governance controlled by formal and informal power structures with the US film industry at the core. These power structures can be accessed if you have money, a commercial story, or the ability to access and navigate informal power structures. *Pili* was able to penetrate these structures because of the story of the women, the quality of the film, the money I was able to source to make the film, and the initial informal networks in British film that then snowballed. It is not beyond the ability of Tanzanian filmmakers to access these networks; however, the informality and positionality of the networks and the racialized and gendered hierarchies of global film governance make this difficult. For the cast members from Miono this would be impossible without co-productive partnerships. Engaging in established film structures potentially reproduces the hierarchies and systems that keeps Tanzanian filmmakers and the women from Miono from having equal access to global distribution networks. However, in showcasing the co-productive potential, talent, and stories from Tanzania in film production and the use of film as method *and* output in IR, films such as *Pili* can push the parameters of both the film industry and IR research.

6

Seeing Politics

If the discipline of international relations is serious about the importance and potential of visual politics, the will to decolonize sources of knowledge, and the need to make visible the domestic and everyday power structures that underpin global politics, then we need to change how we conduct and disseminate research. An impetus to see the invisible, to reveal what is not known, or to see an old problem in a new way is fundamental to research and knowledge. As chapter 1 demonstrated, scholars have emphasized the need for pluralist method, visual method, co-production, and a will to change how research is produced in order to recognize and work with different sources of knowledge. A handful of scholars have experimented with visual methods and outputs and co-production practices to this end. However, while this impetus continues to challenge and provoke interest in ideas, questions, and research, the methods and outputs we use curiously remain underdeveloped and unchanged in practice. This is a problem. It suggests that there is a will to change research practices and experiment with different outputs, but there is a blockage to that actually happening. A failure to change or develop can produce a stale research culture and discipline. This is at best boring and at worst can lead to specific research interests, voices, and issues going unseen and unexplored. As a discipline concerned with looking at and understanding change in the world, IR should work and communicate in ways that reflect such change. Thinking on what should be seen in IR has advanced, but the ways of seeing and being seen remain stagnant.

This book has explored one way of seeing politics differently and experimenting with new methods and outputs of research: the

co-production of a narrative feature film, *Pili*. *Pili* is the first narrative feature film to be used as a method and output of research in IR.
Seeing Politics is about the importance and potential of new methods
of seeing, how such methods can be used and can work in practice,
and the politics of what stops us from seeing – be it the informal politics of the relationships involved in co-production, petty corruption
masquerading as gatekeeping, or the hierarchies involved in global
film distribution. The disciplinary and practical challenges of doing
something new, the role of the researcher, and the putting into practice of the will to make the invisible visible cut across the main chapters of this book. The intent was not only to reveal the mechanisms
of using film as method and to demystify the process for those interested in employing film in research, but also to see the everyday politics within the research process of making the invisible seen. These
insights are immediately relevant to understanding transnational
or global feminism, co-produced and participatory action research,
decolonizing research methods, global governance, and the African
state. The insights have broader relevance to the ways in which we
understand research methods and outputs in IR.

This conclusion draws together the four contributions of *Seeing
Politics* to the understanding of politics and IR. First, film is a format
in which invisible power relations can be seen and in which agents
can explore, see, and express their own agency. Co-produced film as
method and output provides a new and important way of delivering
on the feminist project to make visible the invisible and hidden relations of power. Second, film demonstrates the importance of showing
rather than explaining politics. Film can show the shifting dynamics
of informal politics and the relationship between structure and agency
in ways the written word cannot. Politics and IR form a fluid and
changing space with multiple dimensions; such dimensions should
not be confined to written explanation. Third, the process of film
production itself offers new insight into how transnational relations
and state-based and global gatekeeping constrain and problematize
both what we see and how knowledge is produced. It is through the
practice of engaging in different forms of international relations that
we can see old and new expressions of formal and informal politics.
Finally, *Seeing Politics* is about confronting the disciplinary boundaries of what constitutes method, output, and audience, boundaries that
can curtail knowledge and stop us from seeing. *Seeing Politics* is about
the politics of seeing, being seen, and what stops us from seeing.

SEEING AND BEING SEEN

Film is both a method of conducting research and producing new knowledge and a method of disseminating this knowledge to diverse audiences. Film is thus a method of seeing and being seen. *Seeing* refers to who is seen, how agents see themselves and their own agency, and how film provides a new means of seeing old questions of structure, agency, and security. *Being seen* is about the relationship between the film and the audience, about the impact and the affect.

Seeing

In the first instance *Pili* is a method of seeing the lives of women living with HIV/AIDS in rural Tanzania. As the introduction and chapter 1 argued, the lives of women living with HIV/AIDS are conspicuously invisible in global health and invisible in film representations of HIV/AIDS. Women such as Pili are conspicuous in the communities in which they live, in the statistics of HIV/AIDS agencies, and in NGO fundraising, but their needs, wants, and characters and the everyday politics of their lives are invisible to national and international policy-makers, film audiences, and academic researchers interested in the international politics of HIV/AIDS. Policy-makers recognize the importance of gender as a key factor in both the prevalence and the spread of the HIV/AIDS epidemic; however, the nuance and informal practices that drive this relationship are hard to see or untangle and often easy to ignore. Critics of the relationship between HIV/AIDS and security or the securitization of HIV/AIDS have noted the problematic position of people living with HIV/AIDS being the referent object or threat. Only a few studies (Anderson 2015; Seckinelgin 2012) have addressed the gendered nature of this threat. There is a gulf between understanding global security risks and HIV/AIDS and the way in which this relationships manifests in the everyday lives of women living with the disease. Accounts of the international politics of HIV/AIDS are skewed to consider the global dimension of threat, security, risk, and response with no understanding or concern about the impact of such politics on the people most affected – women living with HIV/AIDS. Film is a method of seeing women living with HIV/AIDS.

Film offers an ontological focus away from those who are to be protected from health threats (Europeans, North Americans) to the needs of the perceived threat (African women) and, crucially, the threats and security risks these women encounter and navigate every day. At the beginning of the film, Pili is seen as the person to be protected against the multiple risks and threats she has to encounter. Over the course of the film the risk shifts, and it becomes apparent that Pili herself may be the risk or threat. As chapter 2 outlined, the film allows us to understand micro-levels of the securitization of disease from the perspective of those most affected, how threat manifests in different ways and is not linear, and how threats are challenged or embedded. Film as a method of seeing reverses the trend of international relations that sees politics from the top down, to see what and whose stories are missing, why they matter, and how they can explain political practice. As chapters 1 and 3 argued, film is feminist method.

Film is a method of exploring the ways in which agents see themselves and the political structures in which they operate. The co-productive and narrative element of the film manifested the invisible everyday politics of living with HIV/AIDS in a way that allowed the women living with or affected by HIV/AIDS to tell their own stories and explore their own agency. *Pili* depicts a specific form of agency. Agency is understood from the perspective of the women in the film with regard to their interests, needs, and wants and their navigation of life in pursuit of these. The women involved in the story of *Pili* recognize that their agency is limited by temporal factors – not having time in any day to think of their own needs after work, domestic labour, and care of their families – and material factors – living on less than US$2 a day, no job security, and dependents. As chapter 2 considered, these women describe life as being hard or a struggle, saying that their situation is common and that hardship is how life is. As in the film itself, agency to change was expressed as not about the need to be well and living positively with HIV but about being their own employer and in control of their own labour and profit. The women involved in the film were not confident about the possibility of change or their agency to make change happen; they just wanted life to be a bit easier and to have more money to help themselves and their wider families. Agency for the women involved in the film is therefore about their existing and maintaining their current quality of life rather than changing or having an instrumental will to challenge this existence. This is evident both in the story of *Pili* and in chapter 3.

Creating the story of *Pili* and producing the film provide a space in which the women involved in the film can explore their own agency. In contrast to their understanding of agency as limited and

constrained, *Pili* takes the ambition of the majority of these women'
and hopes to explore one version of what may happen if they use
their agency to get what they want. *Pili* is the realization of both their
hopes (financial independence, living positively, effective agency)
and their fears (risk, fear, isolation). *Pili* could be read as an instrumental story of a woman pulling herself out of poverty through her
own will and agency in tight corners. However, it could also be read
as a cautionary tale of what happens when an individual risks everything – savings, children, friendships, and health – to get what they
want. This is less about instrumental agency than about the burden
of agency: you enact agency but potentially at a cost to you and
others. The co-productive part of the project, outlined in chapters 3
and 4, allowed this particular group of women to explore, explain,
and show their agency. It is through seeing agency in this way that
we can think about the moral and ethical dilemmas of agency and
its relationship to HIV/AIDS (the choices Pili makes), the temporal
framing of these dilemmas (small choices, big consequences), and
the drudgery and anger of agency as existence.

Film visualizes the relationship between structure and agency.
It is a format in which the shifting dynamics, rhythms, and everyday practices of agency in tight corners can be seen. It shows the
dynamics of individuals as they singularly and collectively address
structures of economic inequality, wealth ownership, gatekeeping,
and gender. As anyone who has explained the relationship between
structure and agency to undergraduate students knows, it is difficult
to depict the dynamics in this relationship. Agency is sometimes easier for students and researchers to grasp because agents are easy to
see. Structures are less easy to see, even though we can understand
how our agency is limited by specific dynamics in our own lives.
In addition, the relationship between structure and agency is often
subtle, nuanced, and fluid.

There are four central structures that the film explores: uneven
development, structural drivers of health and disease, gender, and
political patronage. The ways in which these structures shape or
restrict the lives of women living in poverty or of people living with
HIV/AIDS is well covered in academic literature. Uneven development
is a core interest of scholars of international politics and inequality.
The structural determinants of disease is a well-established field in
global public health. The gendered dynamics of disease and poverty drives aspects of feminist political economy, decolonial and

postcolonial feminism, and feminist approaches to international development. As chapter 4 explained, few studies on the African state begin without even a minor discussion on patronage politics. What is rare is an understanding of how these different structures intersect and reinforce one another. A common way of exploring these intersections has been to visualize them in diagrams or models. Such models and diagrams have been helpful in enriching our understanding of how structures overlap and the relationship between structure and agency. However, these models are static and formal and have no space for the blurred politics that happens within and outside of them. Film progresses from the use of models and diagrams in politics and IR and provides a multidimensional visualization of how structures intersect, shift, and become embedded in formal and informal ways. Structural dynamics permeates even minor levels of existence, and film provides a format in which the different permeations and levels of structural dynamics can be seen and understood. It does so through narrative and the audiovisual element: the viewer can see the individualized, human aspect of how different agents act and confront structures that they engage, ignore, and reproduce. Film shows the aspects of politics and IR that cannot be explained.

You can watch *Pili* and not pick up on all these issues. You can watch *Pili* and read different politics in it. Audiences have picked up different political aspects of the film that I had not thought about or intended. This is the purpose of film: to provoke reaction, emotion, understanding, and thinking about politics and IR across a range of audiences. Film is a way of showing and exploring classic issues in politics and IR; it is also a method of co-producing knowledge. Narrative feature film as method is unique in that it combines four sources of knowledge – co-produced research, narrative, audio techniques, and visual representation – to explore hidden politics, to show the fluid dynamics and rhythms of the relationship between structure and agency, and to reach and affect audiences. Politics and IR moves and shifts; film is a method and output that captures the multiple dimensions in which these moves and shifts occur.

Being Seen

In the second component of Seeing Politics, the invisible and hidden ways in which politics plays out within the film are being seen. As chapter 1 explored, one of the key reasons to make the film was one of audience, affect, and reach. Films reach diverse and broader audiences than academic outputs do. Narrative feature films reach more people than documentaries do. Film has the potential to engage academic audiences, policy-makers and practitioners, film critics and judges, and the general public. The audience is thus both global in reach and diversified in terms of the people who watch film.

Not only does film provide a format in which the invisible is seen, but, through seeing, impact and affect resonate with audiences. The most straightforward impact is one of information or education. Some audience members from a screening in collaboration with Stop AIDS in London expressed that they had not known how HIV/AIDS affected women or had assumed that it was mostly men who lived with the virus. For others the film confirmed what they already knew through research or their own lived experiences: for example, "I already had a good understanding, but the film was a true portrayal, the way I remember it when living in Kenya," or "I can picture it better," and "it brings alive the issues (read lots of research and done policy work) – never been to a village in Africa/Tanzania. Brings it to life." "Brings it to life" is a common audience response to the film; for some the impact of this response is encouragement to sustain or become involved in HIV/AIDS advocacy work. At a screening in Geneva, UN officials privately told me that it was important to screen the film because many people working in the specialized agencies at UN headquarters had little understanding of what happens "in the field."

Impact and affect can be revealed through immediate responses. For example, in the Miono screenings of the film, the majority of audience members laughed at tense moments and were vocal throughout the screening. In contrast, at the East End Film Festival screening, the audience was quiet and reflective at the end of the film. At an early private screening to crew members, key film industry invitees, selected academic colleagues, and a small group of friends and family, some audience members were in tears at the end of the film and stayed in their seats as others left the screening room. Following the Geneva screening in collaboration with Ciné-ONU and UNAIDS, an audience member wrote in an email, "I have been talking about your film ever since I saw it." It is one thing to be told about the risks to poor, rural women of living with HIV/AIDS or about the number of women living with HIV; it is another to see how this affects their lives and to give a name to the women. Seeing their lives and issues play out over a three-day narrative gives an intensity and intimacy to global issues.

When combined with audiovisual skills that build tension and are designed to amplify affect among audiences, film has the power to resonate and connect with individuals in lasting ways. Affect can be immediate (showing emotion in response to key scenes) and long term as people think about issues involved in the film (single parenthood, harassment, making ends meet) as part of their everyday lives. It is by using visual methods to see Pili and bringing the politics she encounters to life through film that generate an emotional reaction and resonate with audiences. The impact on audiences can be physical (crying, laughing, physically recoiling), emotional (sadness, anger), informative and educational, self-reflective, inspirational (to do something), or inquisitive. Watching *Pili*, the audience cannot hide from the difficult choices she faces and the structures she has to navigate. Film is not only a method of seeing; it is a way for women such as Pili and the character "Pili" to be seen.

WHAT STOPS US FROM SEEING

"Oh, all academics want to make a film" was the response of a senior colleague when I first suggested the use of film as method and academic output. This throwaway comment was quite revealing: it was dismissive, and it suggested that film was not only a common desire of academics but also a desire that rarely translated into an output. A straightforward reason that more academics in IR do not make film involves expense and expertise. Although the cost of filmmaking is becoming cheaper with new personalized technologies, recording devices, and editing software accessible to beginners, quality filmmaking remains expensive. Filmmaking thus requires research funding and time to make the film. It also requires new skills and expertise from directing to editing to producing. As chapter 3 explored, the main skills I developed were in film production and story development. These processes were significant and new to me. I did not undergo any formal training but engaged in practice-based learning – or, more accurately, made it up as I went along. To make a film you need to learn new skills through formal training or practice or to collaborate with people who have the skills you need. Fundamentally, as with any large research project, filmmaking and seeing politics requires time. *Pili* would have not been possible without an external research grant, research leave from academic teaching and administration, a highly skilled crew, and a supportive academic department that understood what I wanted to achieve. The first barrier to seeing politics is thus a straightforward issue of resources: time, finance, and skill.

What is less straightforward is the political gatekeeping to what we see. As chapters 4 and 5 discussed, actors working within the state and the wider political economy of film governance operate as gates for the type of films that are made and of audiences that films are able to reach. Gatekeeping by the state and by the political economy of global film governance keeps the stories of women such as Pili in the periphery through gendered and racialized hierarchies. At the state level, gatekeeping is about controlling the stories that are told and the Tanzania that is seen on screen. At the global level, gatekeeping is about protecting profit and monopoly on audience time and spending, and about ensuring the commercial imperative behind what is seen. The only stories that are seen are those that turn a profit. There is profit potential for the investors or distributors of the film, as well as for the different individuals and government agencies who can claim from the production the everyday minor kickbacks, expenses, and fees. To be seen requires formal and informal navigation of gates. While the formal processes suggest an openness to visibility based on procedure, talent, and ability, the informal processes of gatekeeping suggest that being seen is more about networks and the profit potential. Whether it was Tanzanian government agencies changing the height of the gate to make the film, or the structures of film governance regulating the films that are seen, the higher the gate or formal structures, the more informal networks mattered. Navigating the symbiotic relationship between the formal and the informal involves knowledge of the ways in which bureaucracies function, money to open official and semi-official gates, and temporality with regard to the classical political imperative of turning up and knowing when to enact agency.

A more subtle form of gatekeeping can be seen in what constitutes knowledge, method, and research in IR. As the introduction and chapter 1 argued, film in politics and IR is uncommon to nonexistent. As the introduction set out, for some, research that considers the ontological subject of a poor woman living with HIV/AIDS in rural Tanzania (marginal gender, marginal state) and the epistemological way of knowing, ethnographic storytelling, does not constitute IR.

The knowledge produced in the film is therefore discredited as not being a subject for IR or a method of researching IR. *Pili* therefore contributes to wider questions of epistemology (co-production of knowledge, everyday knowledge), ontology (rural women living with HIV/AIDS as relevant ontological subjects of IR), and methodology in IR (film as method).

Where film does exist, it is read, used in teaching, or seen as a tool to translate research to wider audiences. Film in research practice is a vehicle for disseminating research; it is not seen as a method of creating research or an output of research. This is even more the case with regard to narrative feature films. Everyone assumes that, because I am an academic and the film was made with research funding, it must be a documentary. Documentary is an accepted method in visual anthropology, geography, and sociology, which has translated into the accepted wisdom that this is the type of film produced by academics. Gatekeeping about what constitutes method happens through research-funding agencies, peer review, and research-assessment exercises. It is no coincidence that *Pili* was financed through the research fund of a private company; I applied for funds to support a film component of different projects from two large philanthropic research bodies and a UK government research agency, and they all were rejected. Reviewers liked the idea of a film but saw it as a stretch or, at best, that "all academics want to make a film." In research seminars about the film I have been asked: "Is it research?" "Is it IR?" "Is it a method or an output?" "Could an early-career researcher do something similar?" Peer-review questions similarly concentrated on questions such as, "Is it research?" "Is it a documentary?" As chapter 5 reflected, in meetings about my career the film is not even mentioned as a research output.

In many respects these questions and concerns over funding do suggest gatekeeping about what constitutes IR and research method and outputs, and who can engage in these new ways of seeing. However, this belies the context in which these questions were asked. Academics who have watched *Pili* or listened as I have presented some of the findings of this book have been engaged and reflective of the possibilities of film as method and output and its potential for the discipline of IR. These difficult questions were not ones of keeping the gate but ones of exploring the parameters by which the discipline could be pushed and developed. Research is about pushing the parameters of a discipline, while keeping fundamental interests and theories at the core. As chapter 1 argued, this has been one of the core contributions of the aesthetic turn in IR. *Pili* and the process of making the film reveal new insights into old questions of structure and agency, the state, transnationalism, and global governance – all core questions in IR. Film offers a new way of seeing old questions and pushes the boundaries of what stops us from seeing.

Research methods and practices need not stop us from seeing ourselves. Chapters 3, 4, and 5 addressed a range of issues that were uncomfortable, upsetting, or unpleasant. Research collaborators enacting agency over each other, assistants trying to extort research leads, and government agencies using research to leverage funds were the unseen politics of conducting research. Throughout the project I was engaged with the wider transnational politics of co-production and embedded within the gatekeeping practices of the Tanzanian state and global film governance. Aspects of these three chapters will be familiar to researchers involved in co-production or conducting research in a country where there are forms and permits that allow the research to take place. However, these issues are often missing from research findings. It is presumed that the researcher is somewhat neutral or separate from politics: the politics of what they are studying, the politics of knowledge creation, and the politics of the research encounter. Presumed neutrality and distinctions between the observer and the observed stop us from seeing politics. Although the introduction and chapter 1 noted a shift in how the distinction between research subject and researcher has been blurred and how feminists reject such a distinction, there still lacks an honesty or reflection on how the shift manifests in practice. The lack of honesty stems from concerns about our own research ethics: where our ethics have been compromised or we have to think through our own behaviour, there is a disincentive to disclose because of the criticism that would be generated. This is a mistake. Ethics are fluid and difficult. Research ethical standards and rigour remain a core component of the standards of academic research. They should be upheld; however, the rigour with which they are upheld depends on enriching our understanding of the ways in which ethical dilemmas play out in the context of new and different research methods and on being honest in how we think through ethical dilemmas in the research process. The lack of honesty also arises from embarrassment, admission of some type of failure, or the thought that the researcher is above politics, understands politics, and therefore knows how to navigate politics. Not all politics occurs at a critical distance for us to understand; often the most difficult politics to understand is that which we cannot immediately see.

To see politics in research we need to see ourselves and be honest about the difficulties and challenges involved in the research process and about our unintentional reproduction of the hierarchies we seek to challenge. As suggested in chapters 2 and 3, global or transnational feminism or work of this kind does involve some difficult conversations and Carty and Mohanty's "uncomfortable truths." The difficulty of having conversations over topics such as whiteness and white privilege, white lens, white fragility, global inequalities, and health and well-being that collaborative and co-produced projects of this kind entail often means that scholars avoid research methods leading to an engagement with such truths. It is easier to avoid these topics; however, in doing so, stories, politics, and truths remain unseen. Women such as Pili do not have the mixed resources needed to tell their stories or be seen around the world; I do have these resources. This distinction is based on a myriad of global inequalities and, as explored in chapters 2, 3, 4, and 5, also entails multiple ethical dilemmas about whether the ability to make visible is the same as *should* make visible. As argued throughout the book, this project draws on Desai's notion of "dual politics of possibilities" (2007, 801); it sits in the uncomfortable truth of the political hierarchies of film and knowledge production as a way of thinking about what could be possible. International politics is messy; the research methods we use that engage in international relations are no different. As this book has demonstrated, it is through sitting in this difficulty and working through it that we can generate new outputs of research, engage in co-production, and open up the black box of how transnational social relations work. If scholars and researchers are honest in their commitment to decolonize knowledge; to develop global south and global north, high- and low-income country relationships; and to draw on the power of visual methods, we have to practise this commitment and acknowledge that aspects will be difficult, uncomfortable, and imbued with politics. The way to navigate this dilemma is to see and be open about both the difficulty and the position of researchers in potentially reproducing such difficulty. Future possibilities here are film as a method and output of co-produced research in politics and IR, greater production and distribution of African film, and recognition of women such as Pili and of their stories as central rather than peripheral to IR.

Research funding, conference calls for papers, and job advertisements often state an interest in the new or the innovative, particularly with regard to innovative methods or new ways of seeing old problems. However, in practice such calls do not take into account the institutional and disciplinary gates that act as barriers to this. As this section has shown, to do something new requires resources, knowledge of informal and formal practices, and confidence or security in academic employment or research funding in order to take a risk. IR is a risk-adverse discipline. This narrows the scope for interesting research, for researchers who are able to take risks and do research differently, and for the politics that is seen. As chapter 5 argued, if we are to understand the potential of visual method and the importance of seeing politics, we have to understand the context in which the visual is consumed. What we see is limited by resources, gatekeeping politics, and disciplinary boundaries to what constitutes method, research, and knowledge. To see politics therefore requires a mobilization and collaboration of different resources and of the ability to push open different gates.

CONCLUSION

"Will you make another film?" This is the most common question I am asked in response to *Pili* by academics, students, audiences, and film professionals. This is a common question in filmmaking because everyone is interested in the next project and opportunities for investment or work, with the sense that busy or in-demand people have greater value. It is a twist on the common academic question of "What are you working on?" – a question that is similarly about who is doing what, what cutting-edge research looks like, investment opportunity for publishers, with the sense that one is only as good as the next project. In both academia and the film industry it is a polite way of making small talk. My answer is always no.

Given that this is a book about film as method as a way of pushing methodological and epistemological boundaries in IR, my answer may be read as odd or contradictory. There are minor reasons for my response that would be familiar to anyone at the end of a large project: fatigue over the negative aspects, concerns over repeating success, and the need to do something new. As chapters 3 to 5 in particular have highlighted, making *Pili* was challenging and at times unpleasant. I am still unsure that it was the right thing to do. Doing new research should be challenging, and new ideas and ways of thinking about politics should make us uncomfortable. As outlined earlier, what stops us from seeing politics is the need to be secure in the methods we use and in the audiences we engage, and the uncomfortable politics in which we as researchers find ourselves. It is the discomfort and challenge that advances knowledge. The unpleasant aspect of film as a method of co-production may be avoidable should I produce another film; it is also not uncommon for large research projects to have negative aspects. Such negative aspects can come at a personal and a professional cost. It is important to see this as part of the politics of the research process but also to see that this is a consequence of doing something new.

A similar, small issue common to the end of a research project is whether you have the ability to repeat success. To produce *Pili* I was able to use my lack of knowledge and my first-time experience to my advantage in contract negotiations, the running of the production, and the distribution and promotion of the film. I was able to negotiate from a position of ignorance in how things worked and the lack of a track record in turning a profit from a film. For my first film, *Pili* met several measures of success in the film world: a film festival premiere, awards, and a sales and distribution agreement. To produce another film I would start from the position of Sophie the producer rather than Sophie the academic; there would be heightened expectations of the film being as good, if not better, than *Pili*. This would bring another political dimension to both the process and the distribution of another film.

Film provides a new way of showing how power works to broad audiences and is a new method of research that challenges established ways of thinking about knowledge creation in politics and IR. However, this does not mean that film as method, or film as output, should trump or replace all other ways of knowing and seeing. The intent of this book is to open up ways of seeing, not to close down more established methods. IR should engage more in the production of film as a method and output within a plurality of ways in which research is conducted, but not to the exclusion of other methods and ways of working. As advocates of aesthetics and plural methods such as Bleiker (2009a, 2009b) and Shapiro (2013) have long argued, visual methods such as film are emphasized to draw on whatever we can to make sense of the world. Film as method and output is about inclusion, not exclusion, and about thinking of different ways to explore questions of power in the international. I am now interested in exploring the next way of doing this. I cannot go back to standard methods of conducting research, and I do not want to repeat what I have done.

Substantively, I do not intend to make another film, because *Pili* is the story I wanted to tell and the politics I wanted people to see. For over a decade I had seen the everyday politics of HIV/AIDS and how it connected to the international, and this was the hidden story I wanted to make visible. My previous research interests in conspicuously invisible women (Harman 2011a, 2012b, 2016), the lives of people living with HIV/AIDS in Miono, the structural dynamics of HIV/AIDS and the Tanzanian state (Harman 2009), African agency (Brown and Harman 2013b; Harman and Brown 2013), and the hierarchies of global governance (Harman 2012a) all combined to make this film. I had access to communities affected by HIV/AIDS and a drive to do something different to communicate how the everyday risk of HIV/AIDS affected people's lives. This is what makes *Pili* unique.

The story of *Pili* is also not over. The film will have an impact on my career, the careers of the filmmakers, the lives of the women in the film, and the community of Miono. The co-productive element of the project will continue as the film is seen, revenue is generated, and the women and community of Miono decide how the revenue will be spent. In keeping with the findings of this book, this film will affect the women, the community, the filmmakers, and me in seen and unseen ways. My intention for the film is that it will continue to have an impact on how people see Pili and women like her in responding to the HIV/AIDS epidemic and on how women like Pili see themselves. As cast member Sesilia stated when we discussed the story outline of the film, "Pili is everywhere."

Seeing Politics demonstrates the importance of exploring new methods and the need to think differently about how we produce knowledge and conduct and disseminate research. Film allowed people living the everyday risk of HIV/AIDS, and a rural community in Tanzania, to represent themselves in their own words and actions and to reach a global audience. Co-production between academic research, a specific community, and filmmakers showed the potential of film as a source of African agency and feminist method that would have educational, professional, and material impact. Film as co-produced method is a powerful way of shedding new light on old issues and reaching a range of audiences. Aesthetics and visual politics do have the potential to change how we conduct research; we need to be bolder in our use of such methods and work in the visual and aesthetic form. We need new methods of understanding IR that are reflexive and see the formal and informal ways in which power works both in the subject of interest and in the researching of it. This book is a call for others to use new methods such as film to see international politics differently and to reach and engage different audiences and sources of knowledge. *Seeing Politics* has shown the possibility, frustration, and messiness of doing research in IR differently. It is now up to others to also tell their stories and change how we see politics.

Kit List

CAMERA
Canon EOS C300 PL camera

CAMERA ACCESSORIES
19 mm rod bridge
15 mm rod bridge
Short 30-degree offset arm (two)
Long 30-degree offset arm (two)
Handle (two)
Arri locking knobs (two)
Laminates
Carry case
Canon C300 handle
Canon C300 hand grip
 and strap
On board 4-inch monitor
 and mic bracket
Battery cover plate
Rubber eyepiece
Camera front cap
Viewfinder cap
Camera strap
Canon C300 camera manual
Vocas riser for Canon C300 rig
Vocas shoulder page for Canon
 C300 rig200 mm black bar (two)
400 mm black bar (two)
Zacuto moose bar attachment

Zacuto moose bar handle (two)
Brass 15 mm bar joiner (two)
Laminated diagram
Zacuto Matrix cheese plate
Hawk-Woods Vl-C300 DF-Tap
 power block
Hoodman C300/ XF305 (HD450)
XF305/C300 software disc October
 2015
Canon C300 Camrade rain
 jacket
Portabrace black C300 bag and
 large pouch
Ball head shoe mount
Standard noga arm DGI108

CAMERA POWER
Canon CA-930 charger/
 XF ONLY mains adapter
Canon BP955 XF battery (two)
Sony NPF charger and mains cable
Sony NPF 970 battery (two)
IEC-C7
Senheiser

CAMERA AUDIO
Sennheiser ME64 & K6
 microphones

Rycote short fluffy
  (for ME64 & 62)
AKG K450/1 headphones
Case for AKG headphones
Short XLR

CARDS AND READERS
64 GB CF card (two)
USB3 Multi-card reader
USB 3 A – Micro B cable
  (blue end)

MATTE BOXES AND FOLLOW FOCUS KITS
Raven matte box
Raven 114 mm ring for Red/Ang/
  Zeiss CP
Raven 87 mm ring for Cooke lenses
Raven 110 mm ring for 18 mm
  Cooke S5
PV/ 5 x 5 filter tray (two)
200 mm x 15 mm bars
170 mm x 15 mm bars
PV Grad filter 0.3 ND S/E
PV Grad filter 0.6 ND S/E
PV Grad filter 0.9 ND S/E
ND Straight 0.3
ND Straight 0.6
ND Straight 0.9
Arri FF5 follow focus and 15 mm
  bar support
Long right focus knob
Short left focus knob
19 mm bar adaptor bracket
Whip wheel (handle)
Long whip shaft wheel (handle)
Focus gear (78 tooth) 6 mm
  (Canon ENG lenses)

Focus gear large (64 tooth) 6 mm
  (FF5)
Toffee hammer handle
Marking disc
Short flexi whip
Long flexi whip
FF4/FF5 overview sheet

MONITORS
TV Logic LVM-095W/091W 9-inch
  LCD monitor
Plastic screen guard (for TV Logic
  095W monitor)
Petrol bag for 091/95W (PM803)
Mains unit for LVM-091/95W
TV Logic VFM-056W monitor
TV Logic VFM-056W mains unit
Plastic screen guard
Battery adaptor for NPF
Plastic hood for 056
Mini XLR to D-Tap DC lead
  (LA-58A)
IEC lead (two)
Instruction manual for monitor
BNC lead 75 ohm
Short BNC lead 75 ohm
Medium BNC lead 75 ohm
BNC barrel 75 ohm
HDMI lead (five)
Mini HDMI–HDMI lead, 0.5 m
Mini HDMI–HDMI lead

CHARGERS AND BATTERIES
Hawk-Woods VL-2x2p charger
  (dual)
Hawk-Woods VL-90HP V-Lok
  battery (three)
IEC–C13 (13 amp)

LENSES
Mini Panchro 18 mm T2.8 lens
Mini Panchro 25 mm T2.8 lens
Mini Panchro 32 mm T2.8 lens
Mini Panchro 50 mm T2.8 lens
Mini Panchro 75 mm T2.8 lens
Mini Panchro 100 mm T2.8 lens
Rear lens cap (six)
Front lens cap (six)

CASES
Small Peli 1400 (34 x 30 x 15 cm)
Medium Peli 1520 (49 x 39 x 19
   cm) (two)
Large Peli 1620 (63 x 49 x 35 cm)

CONSUMABLES
(PURCHASED, NOT HIRED)
Sharpie pens
Masking tape
Camera cleaner
Cleaning cloths
AA batteries

Notes

CHAPTER ONE

1 For example, *The Last King of Scotland* won forty-seven film awards, including an Oscar, Golden Globe, BAFTA, and SAG for Forrest Whitaker's performance as Idi Amin, and a BAFTA for Best Screenplay; *Tsotsi* won seventeen film awards, including the Oscar for Best Foreign Language Film; *Hotel Rwanda* won sixteen film awards and was nominated for Oscars, BAFTAS, and Golden Globes; *Blood Diamond* won eight film awards and was nominated for Oscars, SAGS, and Golden Globes. For further information see www.imdb.com.

2 See for example Visual Anthropology, Visual Studies; the International Festival of Ethnographic Film; and UK research and teaching hubs in visual methods such as Visual Sociology Goldsmiths and the Granada Centre for Visual Anthropology, University of Manchester.

3 "Claire" was introduced to me by participants at the workshop Impact of Global Health Film led by BRITDOC Foundation at the Global Health Film Festival in 2015.

CHAPTER TWO

1 Estimates of film budgets are sourced from IMDB, Variety, and Rotten Tomatoes and from film specialists' and writers' websites (e.g., Stephen Follows, No Film School) as of 2017. These estimates roughly translate as follows: big budget, US$200 million (for films such as the James Bond franchise) to US$100 million; mid-budget, US$40 million to US$60 million; low budget, US$500,000 to US$5 million. To note the increase in budgets, twenty years prior, in 1998, the average studio film budget was

US$40 million (the film *Titanic* at US$200 million at the time was seen to be one of the most expensive films ever made and required financing from two studios). *Independent Feature Film Production: A Complete Guide from Concept through Distribution* (New York: St Martin's Griffin, 1998).

2 Real name changed on account of events explored in chapter 5.
3 Real name changed on account of events explored in chapter 5.
4 Real name changed on account of events explored in chapter 5.
5 Name changed on account of political affiliation.

References

Achebe, Chinua. 1977. "An Image of Africa: Racism in Conrad's *Heart of Darkness*." *Massachusetts Review* 18: 251–61.

Adorno, Theodor, Walter Benjamin, Ernst Block, Bertolt Brecht, and Georg Lukács. 1977. *Aesthetics and Politics*. London: Verso Books.

Agathangelou, Anna M., and Heather M. Turcotte. 2010. "Postcolonial Theories and Challenges to 'First World-ism.'" In *Gender Matters in Global Politics: A Feminist Introduction to International Relations*, edited by Laura J. Shepherd, 44–58. Abingdon, UK: Routledge.

Ahmed, Sara. 2004. *The Cultural Politics of Emotion*. Edinburgh: Edinburgh University Press.

Akram-Lodhi, A. Haroon. 2018. "'Old Wine in New Bottles': Enclosure, Neoliberal Capitalism and Post-colonial Politics." In *Routledge Handbook of Postcolonial Politics*, edited by Robbie Shilliam and Olivia Rutazibwa, 272–86. Abingdon, UK: Routledge.

Alcoff, Linda Martin. 2017. "Decolonizing Feminist Philosophy." In *Decolonizing Feminism: Transnational Feminism and Globalisation*, edited by Margaret A. McLaren, 19–36. London: Rowman & Littlefield.

Alexander, M. Jacqui, and Chandra Talpade Mohanty. 1997. "Introduction: Genealogies, Legacies, Movements." In *Feminist Genealogies, Colonial Legacies, Democratic Futures*, edited by M. Jacqui Alexander and Chandra Talpade Mohanty, xii–xlii. London: Routledge.

Almukhtar, Sarah, Michael Gold, and Larry Buchanan. 2018. "After Weinstein: 71 Men Accused of Sexual Misconduct and Their Fall from Power." *New York Times*, 8 February 2018. Accessed March 2018. https://www.nytimes.com/interactive/2017/11/10/us/men-accused-sexual-misconduct-weinstein.html.

Amoore, Louise. 2007. "Vigilant Visualities: The Watchful Politics of the War on Terror." *Security Dialogue* 38 (2): 215–32.

Amoore, Louise, and Alexandra Hall. 2010. "Border Theatre: On the Arts of Security and Resistance." *Cultural Geographies* 17 (3): 299–319.

Anderson, Emma-Louise. 2015. *Gender, HIV and Risk: Navigating Structural Violence.* Basingstoke, UK: Palgrave.

Anderson, Emma-Louise, and Alexander Beresford. 2016. "Infectious Injustice: The Political Foundations of the Ebola Crisis in Sierra Leone." *Third World Quarterly* 37 (3): 468–86.

Aradau, Claudia, and Jef Huysmans. 2014. "Critical Methods in International Relations: The Politics of Techniques, Devices and Acts." *European Journal of International Relations* 20 (3): 596–619.

Artis, Anthony Q. 2008. *Shut Up and Shoot: Documentary Guide.* London: Elsevier.

Baker, Catherine. 2016. "'Ancient Volscian Border Dispute Flares': Representations of Militarism, Masculinity and the Balkans in Ralph Fiennes' *Coriolanus.*" *International Feminist Journal of Politics* 18 (3): 429–48.

Baksh, Rawwida, and Wendy Harcourt. 2015. "Introduction: Rethinking Knowledge, Power, and Social Change." In *The Oxford Handbook of Transnational Feminist Movements*, edited by Rawwida Baksh and Wendy Harcourt, 1–50. Oxford: Oxford University Press.

Balio, Tino. 1998. "A Major Presence in All of the World's Important Markets: The Globalization of Hollywood in the 1990s." In *The Oxford Guide to Film Studies*, edited by John Hill and Pamela Church, 58–73. Oxford: Oxford University Press.

– 2013. *Hollywood in the New Millennium.* London: BFI/Palgrave.

Barabantseva, Elena, and Andy Lawrence. 2015. "Encountering Vulnerabilities through 'Filmmaking for Fieldwork.'" *Millennium: Journal of International Studies* 43 (3): 911–30.

Barry, Michele, Zohray Talib, Ashley Jowell, Kelly Thompson, Cheryl Moyer, Heidi Larson, Katherine Burke, and the Steering Committee of the Women Leaders in Global Health Conference. 2017. "A New Vision for Global Health Leadership." *The Lancet* 390 (10112): 2536–7.

Bayart, Jean-Francois. 2012. *The State in Africa: The Politics of the Belly.* 2nd ed. Cambridge: Polity Press.

BBC. 2015. "Tanzania's Magufuli Scraps Independence Day Celebration." *BBC News*, 24 November 2015. Accessed January 2016. http://www.bbc.co.uk/news/world-africa-34909111.

– 2017. "Harvey Weinstein: Did Everyone Really Know?" *BBC News*, 12

October 2017. Accessed March 2018. http://www.bbc.co.uk/news/entertainment-arts-41593384.

– 2018. "Harvey Weinstein Timeline: How the Scandal Unfolded." *BBC News*, 12 February 2018. Accessed March 2018. http://www.bbc.co.uk/news/entertainment-arts-41594672.

Beaupre, Lee. 1986. "How to Distribute a Film." In *The Hollywood film industry,* edited by Paul Kerr, 185–203. London: Routledge.

Benton, Adia. 2015. *HIV Exceptionalism: Development through Disease in Sierra Leone.* Minneapolis: University of Minnesota Press.

Beresford, Alexander. 2015. "Power, Patronage, and Gatekeeper Politics in South Africa." *African Affairs* 114 (455): 226–48.

BFI. 2018. "Diversity: Our Commitment to Diversity." *BFI.* Accessed April 2018. http://www.bfi.org.uk/about-bfi/policy-strategy/diversity.

Blackwell, Maylei, Laura Briggs, and Mignonette Chiu. 2015. "Transnational Feminisms Roundtable." *Frontiers: A Journal of Women Studies* 36 (3): 1–24.

Bleiker, Roland. 2006. "Art after 9/11." *Alternatives: Global, Local, Political* 31 (1): 77-99.

– 2009a. *Aesthetics and World Politics.* London: Palgrave Macmillan.

– 2009b. "The Aesthetic Turn in International Political Theory." *Millennium: Journal of International Studies* 30 (3): 509–33.

– 2015. "Pluralist Methods for Visual Global Politics." *Millennium: Journal of International Studies* 43 (3): 872–90.

Bleiker, Roland, David Campbell, and Emma Hutchison. 2014. "Visual Cultures of Inhospitality." *Peace Review* 26 (2): 192–200.

Bleiker, Roland, and Emma Hutchison. 2008. "Fear No More: Emotions and World Politics." *Review of International Studies* 34 (1): 115–35.

Bleiker, Roland, and Amy Kay. 2007. "Representing HIV/AIDS in Africa: Pluralist Photography and Local Empowerment." *International Studies Quarterly* 51 (1): 139–63.

Brigg, Morgan, and Roland Bleiker. 2010. "Autoethnographic International Relations: Exploring the Self as a Source of Knowledge." *Review of International Studies* 36 (3): 779–98.

Britt, Brett Remkus. 2015. "Pinkwashed: Gay Rights, Colonial Cartographies and Racial Categories in the Pornographic Film *Men of Israel.*" *International Feminist Journal of Politics* 17 (3): 398–415.

Brockington, Dan. 2008. "Corruption, Taxation and Natural Resource Management in Tanzania." *Journal of Development Studies* 44 (1): 103–26.

Brown, William, and Sophie Harman. 2013a. "African Agency in International Politics." In *African Agency in International Politics,* edited by William Brown and Sophie Harman, 1–15. Abingdon, UK: Routledge.

– eds. 2013b. *African Agency in International Politics*. Abingdon, UK: Routledge.

Callahan, William A. 2015. "The Visual Turn in IR: Documentary Filmmaking as a Critical Method." *Millennium: Journal of International Studies* 43 (3): 891–910.

Cameron, Edwin. 2005. *Witness to AIDS*. London: I.B. Tauris.

Carty, Linda E., and Chandra Talpade Mohanty. 2015. "Mapping Transnational Feminist Engagements: Neoliberalism and the Politics of Solidarity." In *The Oxford Handbook of Transnational Feminist Movements*, edited by Rawwida Baksh and Wendy Harcourt, 82–115. Oxford: Oxford University Press.

Chabal, Patrick, and Jean-Pascal Daloz. 1999. *Africa Works: Disorder as Political Instrument*. Oxford: James Currey.

Cham, Mbye. 2004. "Film and History in Africa: A Critical Survey of Current Trends and Tendencies." In *Focus on African Films*, edited by Francoise Pfaff, 48–68. Bloomington and Indianapolis: Indiana University Press.

Chamarette, Jenny. 2015. "Embodied Worlds and Situated Bodies: Feminism, Phenomenology, Film Theory." *Signs* 40 (2): 289–95.

Chant, Sylvia. 2006. "Rethinking the 'Feminisation of Poverty' in Relation to Gender Aggregate Indices." *Journal of International Development* 7 (2): 201–20.

Chowdhry, Geeta, and Sheila Nair. 2002. "Introduction: Power in a Postcolonial World; Race, Gender and Class in International Relations." In *Power, Postcolonialism and International Relations: Reading Race, Gender and Class*, edited by Geeta Chowdhry and Sheila Nair, 1–32. London: Routledge.

Chowdhury, Elora Halim. 2002. "Research, Representation and Responsibility: Unraveling the Sixteen Decisions Perspective on 'Impoverished Bangladeshi Women.'" *International Feminist Journal of Politics* 4 (3): 408–14.

– 2006. "Global Feminism: Feminist Theory's Cul-de-sac." *Human Architecture* 4 (3): 291–302.

Clapham, Christopher. 1996. *Africa and the International System*. Cambridge: Cambridge University Press.

– 1998. "Degrees of Statehood." *Review of International Studies* 24 (2): 143–57.

Cohan, Steven, and Ina Rae Hark. 1993. *Screening the Male: Exploring Masculinities in Hollywood Cinema*. London: Routledge.

Cooke, Bill, and Uma Kothari. 2001. "The Case for Participation as Tyranny." In *Participation: The New Tyranny*, edited by Bill Cook and Uma Kothari, 1–15. London: Zed Books.

Cooper, Frederick. 2012. *Africa since 1940: The Past of the Present*. Cambridge: Cambridge University Press.

Crawford, Neta. 2000. "The Passion of World Politics: Propositions on Emotions and Emotional Relationships." *International Security* 24 (4): 116–36.

Dalby, Simon. 2008. "Warrior Geopolitics: *Gladiator, Black Hawk Down* and the *Kingdom of Heaven*." *Political Geography* 27 (4): 439–55.

Danchev, Alex. 2012. *On Art and War and Terror*. Cambridge: Cambridge University Press.

Danchev, Alex, and Debbie Lisle. 2009. "Introduction: Art, Politics, Purpose." *Review of International Studies* 35 (4): 775–9.

Dauphinee, Elizabeth. 2013a. "Critical Methodological and Narrative Developments in IR: A Forum." *The Disorder of Things*. Accessed August 2018. https://thedisorderofthings.com/2013/03/12/critical-methodological-and-narrative-developments-in-ir-a-forum/.

– 2013b. "Writing as Hope: Reflections on *The Politics of Exile*." *Security Dialogue* 44 (4): 347–61.

Davies, Sara E., and Belinda Bennett. 2016. "A Gendered Human Rights Analysis of Ebola and Zika: Locating Gender in Global Health Emergencies." *International Affairs* 92 (5): 1041–60.

Death, Carl. 2015. "Naming the Beast: Gate-Keeping and African State-Natures." Paper presented at BISA@40 Workshop, Beyond the Gatekeeper State: IR Perspectives on African States in the 21st Century, London, June 2015.

Debrix, Francois. 2006. "The Sublime Spectatorship of War: The Erasure of the Event in America's Politics of Terror and Aesthetics of Violence." *Millennium: Journal of International Studies* 34 (3): 767–91.

Der Derian, James. 2009. *Virtuous War: Mapping the Military-Industrial-Media-Entertainment Network*. New York: Routledge.

– 2010. "Now We Are All Avatars." *Millennium: Journal of International Studies* 29 (1): 181–6.

– 2015. *Project Z*. Accessed August 2018. http://www.projectzmovie.com/#!bio.

Desai, Manisha. 2007. "The Messy Relationship between Feminisms and Globalizations." *Gender and Society* 21 (6): 797–803.

– 2009. *Gender and the Politics of Possibilities: Rethinking Globalization.* Plymouth, UK: Rowman & Littlefield.

Devetak, Richard. 2009. "After the Event: Don DeLillo's *White Noise* and September 11 Narratives." *Review of International Studies* 35 (4): 795–815.

Dhatt, Roopa, Ilona Kickbusch, and Kelly Thompson. 2017. "Act Now: A Call to Action for Gender Equality in Global Health." *The Lancet* 389 (10069): 602.

Diawara, Manthia. 1992. *African Cinema: Politics and Culture.* Bloomington and Indianapolis: Indiana University Press.

Dingli, Sophia. 2015. "We Need to Talk about Silence: Re-examining Silence in International Relations Theory." *European Journal of International Relations* 21(4): 721–42.

Doane, Mary Ann. 2004. "Aesthetics and Politics." *Signs* 30 (1): 1229–35.

Doty, Roxanne Lynn. 2004. "Maladies of Our Souls: Identity and Voice in the Writing of Academic International Relations." *Cambridge Review of International Affairs* 17 (2): 377–92.

Dunlop, Jo. 2016. *Freetown Fashpack.* Accessed March 2017. http://freetownfashpack.com/.

Dunn, Kevin C. 2009. "Contested State Spaces: African National Parks and the State." *European Journal of International Relations* 15 (3): 423–46.

Dunne, Tim, Lene Hansen, and Colin Wight. 2013. "The End of International Relations Theory?" *European Journal of International Relations* 19 (3): 405–25.

Durose, Catherine, Yasminah Beebeejaun, James Rees, Jo Richardson, and Liz Richardson. 2012. *Connected Communities: Towards Co-production in Research with Communities.* Bristol, UK: Connected Communities. Accessed August 2017. http://www.ahrc.ac.uk/documents/project-reports-and-reviews/connected-communities/towards-co-production-in-research-with-communities/.

Elias, Juanita, and Lucy Ferguson. 2010. "Production, Employment and Consumption." In *Gender Matters in Global Politics: A Feminist Introduction to International Relations*, edited by Laura J. Shepherd, 234–47. Abingdon, UK: Routledge.

Elias, Juanita, and Stephanie Kuttner. 2001. "2000 BISA Gender and International Relations Working Group Workshop: Methodologies in Feminist Research." *International Journal of Feminist Politics* 3 (2): 284–7.

Enloe, Cynthia. 1996. "Margins, Silences and Bottom Rungs: How to Overcome the Underestimation of Power in the Study of International

Relations." In *International Theory: Positivism and Beyond*, edited by Steve Smith, Ken Booth, and Marysia Zalewski, 186–202. Cambridge: Cambridge University Press.

– 2004. *The Curious Feminist: Searching for Women in a New Age of Empire*. Berkeley: University of California Press.

Epstein, Helen. 2007. *The Invisible Cure: Africa, the West and the Fight against AIDS*. London: Penguin.

Farrow, Ronan. 2017a. "From Aggressive Overtures to Sexual Assault: Harvey Weinstein's Accusers Tell Their Stories." *New Yorker*, 10 October 2017. Accessed March 2018. https://www.newyorker.com/news/news-desk/from-aggressive-overtures-to-sexual-assault-harvey-weinsteins-accusers-tell-their-stories.

– 2017b. "Harvey Weinstein's Army of Spies." *New Yorker*, 6 November 2017. Accessed March 2018. https://www.newyorker.com/news/news-desk/harvey-weinsteins-army-of-spies.

Ferguson, Lucy, and Sophie Harman. 2015. "Gender and Infrastructure in the World Bank." *Development Policy Review* 33 (5): 653–71.

Fierke, Karin M. 2012. *Political Self-Sacrifice: Agency, Body and Emotion in International Relations*. Cambridge: Cambridge University Press.

Fonow, Mary Margaret, and Judith A. Cook. 2005. "Feminist Methodology: New Applications in the Academy and Public Policy." *Signs* 30 (4): 2211–36.

Gallagher, Julia. 2009. "Healing the Scar? Idealizing Britain in Africa, 1997–2007." *African Affairs* 108 (432): 435–51.

Garrett, Laurie. 2017. "The Next AIDS Pandemic." *Foreign Policy*, 26 July 2017. Accessed January 2018. http://foreignpolicy.com/2017/07/26/the-next-AIDS-pandemic/.

Gaventa, John, and Andrea Cornwall. 2008. "Power and Knowledge." In *The SAGE Handbook of Action Research: Participative Inquiry and Practice*, 2nd ed., edited by Peter Reason and Hilary Bradbury, 172–89. London: SAGE Publications.

Geffen, Nathan. 2010. *Debunking Delusions: The Inside Story of the Treatment Action Campaign*. Johannesburg: Jacana.

Germano, Roy. 2014. "Analytic Filmmaking: A New Approach to Research and Publication in the Social Sciences." *Perspectives on Politics* 12 (3): 663–76.

Gomery, Douglas. 1998a. "Hollywood as Industry." In *The Oxford Guide to Film Studies*, edited by John Hill and Pamela Church, 245–54. Oxford: Oxford University Press.

– 1998b. "Hollywood Corporate Business Practice and Periodizing Contemporary Film History." In *Contemporary Hollywood Cinema*, edited by Steve Neale and Murray Smith, 47–57. London: Routledge.

Goodell, Gregory. 1998. *Independent Feature Film Production: A Complete Guide from Concept through Distribution*. New York: St Martin's Griffin.

Grant, Jill, Geoff Nelson, and Terry Mitchell. 2008. "Negotiating the Challenges of Participatory Action Research: Relationships, Power, Participation, Change and Credibility." In *The SAGE Handbook of Action Research: Participative Inquiry and Practice*, 2nd ed., edited by Peter Reason and Hilary Bradbury, 589–601. London: SAGE Publications.

Gray, Hazel S. 2013. "Industrial Policy and the Political Settlement in Tanzania: Aspects of Continuity and Change since Independence." *Review of African Political Economy* 40 (136): 185–201.

– 2015. "The Political Economy of Grand Corruption in Tanzania." *African Affairs* 114 (456): 1–22.

Gray, Hazel S., and Mushtaq Hussain Khan. 2010. "Good Governance and Growth in Africa: What Can We Learn from Tanzania?" In *The Political Economy of Africa*, edited by Vishnu Padayaachee, 339–56. London: Routledge.

Griffin, Penny. 2006. "The World Bank." *New Political Economy* 11 (4): 571–81.

Grimshaw, Anna, and Amanda Ravetz. 2009. "Rethinking Observational Cinema." *Journal of the Royal Anthropological Institute* 15 (3): 538–56.

Grosfoguel, Ramón. 2007. "The Epistemic Decolonial Turn: Beyond Political-Economy Paradigms." *Cultural Studies* 21 (2–3): 211–23.

Guback, Thomas. 1982. Foreword to *Movies and Money: Financing the American Film Industry*, by Janet Wasko, xi–xv. Norwood, NJ: ABLEX Publishing.

Gugler, Josef. 2003. *African Film: Re-imagining a Continent*. Oxford: James Currey.

Guillaume, Xavier. 2011. "Resistance and the International: The Challenge of the Everyday." *International Political Sociology* 5 (4): 459–62.

Gupta, Geeta Rao. 2002. "How Men's Power over Women Fuels the HIV Epidemic." *British Medical Journal* 324 (7331): 184–5.

Hall, Stuart, and Paddy Whannel. 1964. *The Popular Arts*. London: Hutchinson Educational.

Hall, Todd H., and Andrew A.G. Ross. 2015. "Affective Politics after 9/11." *International Organization* 69 (4): 847–79.

Hamblin, Julie, and Elizabeth Reid. 1991. "Women, the HIV Epidemic and Human Rights: A Tragic Imperative." United Nations Development Program Issues Paper no. 8. Accessed November 2009. http://www.undp.org/HIV/publications/issues/english/issue08e.htm.

Hammonds, Evelynn M. 1997. "Toward a Genealogy of Black Female Sexuality: The Problematic of Silence." In *Feminist Genealogies, Colonial Legacies, Democratic Futures*, edited by M. Jacqui Alexander and Chandra Talpade Mohanty, 170–83. London: Routledge.

Hansen, Lene. 2011. "Theorizing the Image for Security Studies: Visual Securitization and the Muhammad Cartoon Crisis." *European Journal of International Relations* 17 (1): 51–74.

Harcourt, Wendy, L.H.M. Ling, Marysia Zalewski, and Swiss International Relations Collective (Elisabeth Prügl, Rahel Kunz, Jonas Hagmann, Xavier Guillaume, and Jean-Christophe Graz). 2015. "Assessing, Engaging, and Enacting Worlds: Tensions in Feminist Method/ologies." *International Feminist Journal of Politics* 17 (1): 158–72.

Harding, Sandra, and Kathryn Norberg. 2005. "New Feminist Approaches to Social Science Methodologies: An Introduction." *Signs* 30 (4): 2009–15.

Harman, Sophie. 2009. "Fighting HIV/AIDS: Reconfiguring the State." *Review of African Political Economy* 36 (121): 353–67.

– 2010. *The World Bank and HIV/AIDS: Setting a Global Agenda*. Abingdon, UK: Routledge.

– 2011a. "The Dual Feminisation of HIV/AIDS." *Globalizations* 8 (2): 213–28.

– 2011b. "Governing Health Risk by Buying Behaviour." *Political Studies* 59 (4): 867–83.

– 2012a. *Global Health Governance*. London: Routledge.

– 2012b. "Women and the Millennium Development Goals: Too Little Too Late Too Gendered." In *The Millennium Development Goals and Beyond: Global Development after 2015*, edited by Rorden Wilkinson and David Hulme, 84–101. London and New York: Routledge.

– 2016. "Ebola, Gender and Conspicuously Invisible Women in Global Health Governance." *Third World Quarterly* 37 (3): 524–41.

Harman, Sophie, and William Brown. 2013. "In from the Margins? The Changing Place of Africa in International Relations." *International Affairs* 89 (1): 69–87.

Harrison, Graham. 2004. *The World Bank and Africa: The Construction of Governance States*. London: Routledge.

– 2010. "The Africanization of Poverty: A Retrospective on 'Make Poverty History.'" *African Affairs* 109 (436): 391–408.

#whatwouldmagufulido. Twitter. Accessed on January 2016. https://twitter.com/hashtag/whatwouldmagufulido.

Hillbom, Ellen. 2011. "Botswana: A Development-Oriented Gate-Keeping State." *African Affairs* 111 (442): 67–89.

– 2012. "Botswana: A Development-Oriented Gate-Keeping State – A Reply to Ian Taylor." *African Affairs* 111 (444): 477–82.

hooks, bell. 1992. *Black Looks: Race and Representation.* Boston: South End Press.

Hulme, David, and Thankom Arun. 2009. *Microfinance: A Reader.* Abingdon, UK: Routledge.

Hutchings, Kimberly. 2000. "Towards a Feminist International Ethics." *Review of International Studies* 26: 111–30.

Hutchison, Emma. 2016. *Affective Communities in World Politics: Collective Emotions after Trauma.* Cambridge: Cambridge University Press.

Hyden, Goran. 1980. *Beyond Ujamaa in Tanzania.* London: Heinemann.

– 1983. *No Shortcuts to Progress.* Berkeley: University of California Press.

Ingram, Alan. 2011. "Making Geopolitics Otherwise: Artistic Interventions in Global Political Space." *Geographical Journal* 177 (3): 218–22.

Jabri, Vivienne. 2006. "Shock and Awe: Power and the Resistance of Art." *Millennium: Journal of International Studies* 34 (3): 819–39.

Jackson, Robert H. 1990. *Quasi-states: Sovereignty, International Relations and the Third World.* Cambridge: Cambridge University Press.

Jacobs, Jessica. 2015. "Visualizing the Visceral: Using Film to Research the Ineffable." *Area* 48 (4): 480–7.

Jessop, Bob. 1990. *State Theory: Putting the Capitalist State in Its Place.* Cambridge: Polity Press.

Johnson, Chalmers. 1982. MITI *and the Japanese Miracle: The Growth of Industrial Policy, 1925–1975.* Stanford, CA: Stanford University Press.

Johnson, Susan. 2005. "Gender Relations, Empowerment, and Microcredit: Moving On from a Lost Decade." *European Journal of Development Research* 17 (2): 224–8.

Kantor, Jodi, and Megan Twohey. 2017. "Harvey Weinstein Paid Off Sexual Harassment Accusers for Decades." *New York Times*, 5 October 2017. Accessed March 2018. https://www.nytimes.com/2017/10/05/us/harvey-weinstein-harassment-allegations.html.

Kaplan, E. Ann. 1997. *Looking for the Other: Feminism, Film and the Imperial Gaze*. London: Routledge.

Kaplan, Robert. 1994. "The Coming Anarchy: How Scarcity, Crime, Overpopulation, Tribalism, and Disease Are Rapidly Destroying the Social Fabric of Our Planet." *The Atlantic*, February 1994.

Kellner, Douglas. 1998. "Hollywood Film and Society." In *The Oxford Guide to Film Studies*, edited by John Hill and Pamela Church, 354–64. Oxford: Oxford University Press.

Kennedy, Liam. 2009. "Soldier Photography: Visualising the War in Iraq." *Review of International Studies* 35 (4): 817–33.

Krings, Matthias, and Onookame Okome. 2013. "Nollywood and Its Diaspora: An Introduction." In *Global Nollywood: The Transnational Dimensions of an African Video Film Industry*, edited by Matthias Krings and Onookame Okome, 1–22. Bloomington and Indianapolis: Indiana University Press.

Lauzen, Martha M. 2018. "The Celluloid Ceiling: Behind-the-Scenes Employment of Women on the Top 100, 250, and 500 Films of 2017." *Center for the Study of Women in Film and Television*. Accessed March 2018. https://womenintvfilm.sdsu.edu/wp-content/uploads/2018/01/2017_Celluloid_Ceiling_Report.pdf.

Lewis, David, Dennis Rodgers, and Michael Woolcock. 2014. "The Project of Development: Cinematic Representation as An(other)." In *Popular Representations of Development: Insights from Novels, Film, Television and Social Media*, edited by David Lewis, Dennis Rodger, and Michael Woolcock, 113–30. Abingdon, UK: Routledge.

Lidinsky, April. 2005. "The Gender of War: What Fahrenheit 9/11's Women (Don't) Say." *International Feminist Journal of Politics* 7 (1): 142–6.

Ling, L.H.M. 2007. "Said's Exile: Strategic Insights for Postcolonial Feminists." *Millennium: Journal of International Studies* 36 (1): 135–45.

Lisk, Franklyn. 2010. *Global Institutions and the HIV/AIDS Epidemic: Responding to an International Crisis*. London: Routledge.

Lisle, Debbie. 2007. "Benevolent Patriotism: Art, Dissent and the American Effect." *Security Dialogue* 38 (2): 233–50.

Lorde, Audre. 1984. "The Master's Tools Will Never Dismantle the Master's House." In *Sister Outsider*, 110–13. Berkeley, CA: Crossing Points Press.

MacDougall, David. 2003. "Beyond Observational Cinema." In *Principles of Visual Anthropology*, 3rd ed., edited by Paul Hockings, 115–32. Berlin: Mouton de Gruyter.

Magombe, P. Vincent. 1996. "The Cinemas of Sub-Saharan Africa." In *The Oxford History of World Cinema,* edited by Geoffrey Nowell-Smith, 667–72. Oxford: Oxford University Press.

Mbembe, Achille. 2001. *On the Postcolony.* Berkeley: University of California Press.

Mbilinyi, Marjorie, and International Labour Organisation (ILO). 1986. *Women's Employment Patterns: Discrimination and Promotion of Equality in Africa; The Case of Tanzania.* Addis Ababa: ILO.

McInnes, Colin. 2006. "HIV/AIDS and Security." *International Affairs* 82 (2): 315–26.

McInnes, Colin, and Simon Rushton. 2006. "HIV/AIDS and Security: Where Are We Now?" *International Affairs* 32 (1): 5–23.

– 2013. "HIV/AIDS and Securitization Theory." *European Journal of International Relations* 19 (1): 115–38.

McLaren, Margaret A. 2017. "Introduction: Decolonizing Feminism." In *Decolonizing Feminism: Transnational Feminism and Globalisation,* edited by Margaret A. McLaren, 1–18. London: Rowman & Littlefield.

McLeod, Laura. 2015. *Gender Politics and Security Discourse: Personal-Political Imaginations and Feminism in "Post-Conflict" Serbia.* Abingdon, UK: Routledge.

Mead, Margaret. 2003. "Visual Anthropology in a Discipline of Words." In *Principles of Visual Anthropology,* 3rd ed., edited by Paul Hockings, 3–10. Berlin: Mouton de Gruyter.

Meagher, Kate. 2012. "The Strength of Weak States? Non-state Security Forces and Hybrid Governance in Africa." *Development and Change* 43 (5): 1073–1101.

Meagher, Kate, Tom De Herdt, and Kristof Titeca. 2014. "Hybrid Governance in Africa: Buzzword or Paradigm Shift?" *African Arguments,* 25 April 2014. Accessed July 2017. http://africanarguments. org/2014/04/25/hybrid-governance-in-africa-buzzword-or-paradigm-shift-by-kristof-titeca-kate-meagher-and-tom-de-herdt/.

Mercer, Jonathan. 2010. "Emotional Beliefs." *International Organization* 64 (1): 1–31.

Miller, Toby, Nitin Govil, John McMurria, Richard Maxwell, and Tina Wang. 2005. *Global Hollywood 2.* London: BFI Publishing.

Mohanty, Chandra Talpade. 1998. "Crafting Feminist Genealogies: On the Geography and Politics of Home, Nation, and Community." In *Talking Visions: Multicultural Feminism in a Transnational Age,* edited by Ella Shohat, 485–500. New York: MIT Press.

– 2003. *Feminism without Borders: Decolonizing Theory, Practicing Solidarity*. Durham, NC, and London: Duke University Press.

Moniuszko, Sara M., and Cara Kelly. 2017. "Harvey Weinstein Scandal: A Complete List of the 85 Accusers." *USA Today*, 27 October 2017, updated 22 March 2018. Accessed March 2018. https://www.usatoday.com/story/life/people/2017/10/27/weinstein-scandal-complete-list-accusers/804663001/.

Monks, Kieron. 2016. "John Magufuli, the No-Frills President Who Declared War on Waste." *CNN*, 14 January 2016. Accessed January 2016. http://edition.cnn.com/2016/01/14/africa/tanzania-president-john-magufuli/.

Moudio, Rebecca. 2013. "Nigeria's Film Industry: A Potential Gold Mine?" *AfricaRenewal Online*, May 2013. Accessed June 2016. http://www.un.org/africarenewal/magazine/may-2013/nigeria%E2%80%99s-film-industry-potential-gold-mine.

Mwenda, Andrew M. 2016. "Behind Magufuli's Political Stunts." *AllAfrica*, 18 January 2016. Accessed January 2016. http://allafrica.com/stories/201601190736.html.

Nguyen, Vinh-Kim. 2010. *The Republic of Therapy: Triage and Sovereignty in West Africa's Time of AIDS*. Durham, NC: Duke University Press.

Nkhoma, Alice N., Assemy Muro, and Ruth Meena. 1993. *The Impact of Structural Adjustment Programs on Rural Women in Tanzania (Case Study): Mwanza, Mbinga, and Arumeru*. Research Report no. 22. Dar es Salaam, Tanzania: Women's Research and Documentation Project.

Nothias, Toussaint. 2014. "'Rising,' 'Hopeful,' 'New': Visualizing Africa in the Age of Globalization." *Visual Communication* 13 (3): 323–39.

Nussbaum, Martha. 2003. *Upheavals of Thought: The Intelligence of Emotions*. Cambridge: Cambridge University Press.

Ogola, George. 2015. "Constructing Images of Africa: From Troubled Pan-African Media to Sprawling Nollywood." In *Images of Africa: Creation, Negotiation and Subversion*, edited by Julia Gallagher, 21–41. Manchester, UK: Manchester University Press.

O'Manique, Colleen. 2005. "The Securitisation of HIV/AIDS in Sub-Saharan Africa: A Critical Feminist Lens." *Policy and Society* 24 (1): 24–47.

Omanufeme, Steve. 2016. "Runaway Success." *Finance and Development* 53 (2): 30–32. Accessed June, 2016. http://www.imf.org/external/pubs/ft/fandd/2016/06/omanufeme.htm.

Parmar, Aradhana. 2003. "Micro-credit, Empowerment and Agency: Re-evaluating the Discourse." *Canadian Journal of Development Studies* 24 (3): 461–76.

Parpart, Jane L. 2010. "Choosing Silence: Rethinking Voice, Agency and Women's Empowerment." In *Secrecy and Silence in the Research Process: Feminist Reflections*, edited by Róisín Ryan-Flood and Rosalind Gill, 15–29. London: Routledge.

PEPFAR (United States President's Emergency Plan for AIDS Relief). 2017. "PEPFAR Funding." Accessed November 2017. https://www.pepfar.gov/documents/organization/252516.pdf.

Pfaff, Francoise. 2004a. *Focus on African Films*. Bloomington and Indianapolis: Indiana University Press.

– 2004b. Introduction to *Focus on African Films*, edited by Francoise Pfaff, 1–14. Bloomington and Indianapolis: Indiana University Press.

Pink, Sarah. 2007. *Doing Visual Ethnography*. 2nd ed. London: SAGE Publications.

Piot, Peter. 2012. *No Time to Lose: A Life in Pursuit of Deadly Viruses*. London: I.B. Tauris.

Polhaus, Gaile, Jr. 2017. "Knowing without Borders and the Work of Epistemic Gathering." In *Decolonizing Feminism: Transnational Feminism and Globalisation*, edited by Margaret A. McLaren, 37–53. London: Rowman & Littlefield.

Prins, Gwyn. 2004. "AIDS and Global Security." *International Affairs* 80 (5): 931–52.

Prügl, Elizabeth. 2004. "International Institutions and Feminist Politics." *Brown Journal of World Affairs* 2: 69–84.

Quijano, Aníbal. 1993. "Modernity, Identity, and Utopia in Latin America." *Boundary 2* 20 (3): 140–55.

– 2000. "Coloniality of Power, Ethrocentrism, and Latin America." *International Sociology* 15 (2): 215–32.

Rancière, Jacques. 2004. *The Politics of Aesthetics*. Translated by Gabriel Rockhill. London: Bloomsbury.

Rasmusson, Sarah L. 2005. "Masculinity and Fahrenheit 9/11: The Temperature at Which My Feminist Temper Burns." *International Feminist Journal of Politics* 7 (1): 137–41.

Razavi, Shahra. 2012. "World Development Report 2012: Gender Equality and Development – A Commentary." *Development and Change* 43 (1): 423–37.

Reason, Peter, and Hilary Bradbury. 2008. Introduction to *The SAGE Handbook of Action Research: Participative Inquiry and Practice*, 2nd ed., edited by Peter Reason and Hilary Bradbury, 1–13. London: SAGE Publications.

Reid, Colleen, and Wendy Frisby. 2008. "Continuing the Journey: Articulating Dimensions of Feminist Participatory Action Research (FPAR)." In *The SAGE Handbook of Action Research: Participative Inquiry and Practice*, 2nd ed., edited by Peter Reason and Hilary Bradbury, 93–105. London: SAGE Publications.

Rice, Xan. 2006. "Tanzania Sees Malice in Darwin's Nightmare." *The Guardian*, 17 August 2006. Accessed January 2016. http://www. theguardian.com/world/2006/aug/17/film.filmnews.

Rotberg, Robert I. 2004. *When States Fail: Causes and Consequences*. Princeton, NJ: Princeton University Press.

Rushton, Simon. 2011. "Global Health Security: Security for Whom? Security for What?" *Political Studies* 59 (4): 779–96.

Ryan, Holly Eva. 2017. *Political Street Art: Communication, Culture and Resistance in Latin America*. London: Routledge.

Ryan, Lisa. 2017. "Weinstein Company and Miramax Hit with Class-Action Lawsuit over Harassment and Assault." *The Cut*, 15 November 2017. Accessed March 2018. https://www.thecut.com/2017/11/ weinstein-class-action-harassment-assault.html.

Saul, John S. 2012. "Tanzania Fifty Years On (1961–2011): Rethinking Ujamaa, Nyerere and Socialism in Africa." *Review of African Political Economy* 39 (131): 117–25.

Schamus, James. 1998. "To the Rear of the Back End: The Economics of Independent Cinema." In *The Oxford Guide to Film Studies*, edited by John Hill and Pamela Church, 91–105. Oxford: Oxford University Press.

Scott, James C. 1998. *Seeing Like a State: How Certain Schemes to Improve the Human Condition Have Failed*. New Haven, CT, and London: Yale University Press.

Scott, Joan W. 1991. "The Evidence of Experience." *Critical Inquiry* 17 (4): 773–97.

Seckinelgin, Hakan. 2012. *International Security, Conflict and Gender: "HIV Is Another War."* London: Routledge.

Shapiro, Michael. 2009. *Cinematic Politics*. London: Routledge.

– 2013. *Studies in Trans-disciplinary Method: After the Aesthetic Turn*. London: Routledge.

Shayo, Rose. 2005. *Women Participation in Party Politics during the Multiparty Era in Africa: The Case of Tanzania*. EISA (Electoral Institute for Southern Africa) Occasional Paper no. 34. Auckland Park, South Africa: EISA.

Shepherd, Laura J. 2017. *Gender, UN Peacebuilding, and the Politics of Space*. Oxford: Oxford University Press.

Shohat, Ella. 1998. Introduction to *Talking Visions: Multicultural Feminism in a Transnational Age*, edited by Ella Shohat, 1–63. New York: MIT Press.

Singer, P.W. 2002. "AIDS and International Security." *Survival* 44 (1): 145–58.

Sjoberg, Laura. 2013. *Gendering Global Conflict: Towards a Feminist Theory of War*. New York: Columbia University Press.

– 2014. *Gender, War and Conflict*. Cambridge: Polity Press.

Sklar, Richard L. 1975. *Corporate Power in an African State: The Political Impact of Multinational Mining Companies in Zambia*. Berkeley: University of California Press.

Smirl, Lisa. 2015. *Spaces of Aid: How Cars, Compounds, and Hotels Shape Humanitarianism*. London: Zed Books.

Smith, Steve. 1996. "Positivism and Beyond." In *International Theory: Positivism and Beyond*, edited by Steve Smith, Ken Booth, and Marysia Zalewski, 11–44. Cambridge: Cambridge University Press.

Smith, Valerie. 1997. Introduction to *Representing Blackness: Issues in Film and Video*, edited by Valerie Smith, 1–11. London: Athlone Press.

Soares de Oliveira, Ricardo. 2007. *Oil and Politics in the Gulf of Guinea*. London: Hurst & Co.

Stillwaggon, Eileen. 2003. "Racial Metaphors: Interpreting Sex and AIDS in Africa." *Development and Change* 34 (5): 809–32.

Sundet, Geir. 1994. "Beyond Developmentalism in Tanzania." *Review of African Political Economy* 21 (59): 39–49.

Sylvester, Christine. 1994. *Feminist Theory and International Relations in a Postmodern Era*. Cambridge: Cambridge University Press.

Talib, Zohray, Katherine States Burke, and Michele Barry. 2017. "Women Leaders in Global Health." *The Lancet Global Health* 5 (6): e565–e566.

Tan, Celine. 2011. *Governance through Development: Poverty Reduction Strategies, International Law and Disciplining of Third World States*. London: Routledge.

Taylor, Ian. 2012. "Botswana as a 'Development-Oriented Gate-Keeping State': A Response." *African Affairs* 111 (444): 466–76.

Thackway, Melissa. 2003. *Africa Shoots Back: Alternative Perspectives in Sub-Saharan Francophone African Film*. Oxford: James Currey.

Tickner, J. Ann. 1997. "You Just Don't Understand: Troubled Engagements between Feminists and IR Theorists." *International Studies Quarterly* 41 (4): 611–32.

– 2005. "What Is Your Research Program? Some Feminist Answers to
International Relations Methodological Questions." *International
Studies Quarterly* 49 (1): 1–21.

Tidy, Joanna. 2015. "Gender, Dissenting Subjectivity and the
Contemporary Military Peace Movement in *Body of War*."
International Feminist Journal of Politics 17 (3): 454–72.

Tilley, Lisa. 2017. "Resisting Piratic Method by Doing Research
Otherwise." *Sociology* 51 (1): 27–42.

Tordoff, William. 1997. *Government and Politics in Africa*. Bloomington
and Indianapolis: Indiana University Press.

Trans Tanz. n.d. "Welcome." *Trans Tanz*. Accessed June 2017. http://www.
transtanz.org/welcome/4521270847.

Treatment Action Campaign. 2010. *Fighting for Our Lives: The History
of the Treatment Action Campaign 1998–2010*. Cape Town: Treatment
Action Campaign. Accessed January 2017. http://www.tac.org.za/files/
10yearbook/files/tac%2010%20year%20draft5.pdf.

True, Jacqui. 2014. "The Global Governance of Gender." In *Handbook of
the International Political Economy of Governance*, edited by Anthony
Payne and Nicola Phillips, 329–43. Cheltenham, UK: Edward Elgar.

Turner, Graeme. 1998. "Cultural Studies and Film." In *The Oxford Guide
to Film Studies*, edited by John Hill and Pamela Church, 195–201.
Oxford: Oxford University Press.

UNAIDS. 2016. *Global AIDS Update 2016*. Geneva: UNAIDS. Accessed
January 2017. http://www.unAIDS.org/en/resources/documents/2016/
Global-AIDS-update-2016.

– 2017. *UNAIDS Data 2017*. Geneva: UNAIDS. Accessed January 2018.
http://www.unAIDS.org/sites/default/files/media_asset/2017_data-
book_en.pdf.

UNFPA, UNAIDS, and UNIFEM. 2004. *Women and HIV/AIDS: Confronting
the Crisis*. Geneva and New York: UNFPA.

United Nations. 2000. *Millennium Development Goals (MDGs)*. Accessed
November 2018. http://www.un.org/millenniumgoals/.

United Nations Security Council Resolution 1308. 2000. On the
Responsibility of the Security Council in the Maintenance of
International Peace and Security: HIV/AIDS and International Peace-
keeping Operations. Accessed January 2018. https://undocs.org/S/
RES/1308(2000).

UN Women. 2016. "Facts and Figures: HIV and AIDS." *UN Women*.
Accessed January 2018. http://www.unwomen.org/en/what-we-do/
HIV-and-AIDS/facts-and-figures.

Von Freyhold, Michaela. 1977. "The Post-Colonial State and Its Tanzanian Version." *Review of African Political Economy* 4 (8): 75–89.

Wade, Robert. 1992. *Governing the Market: Economic Theory and the Role of Government in East Asian Industrialization*. Princeton, NJ: Princeton University Press.

Wallerstein, Immanuel. 1974a. *The Modern World System: Capitalist Agriculture and the Origins of the European World Economy in the Sixteenth Century*. London: Academic Press.

– 1974b. "The Rise and Future Demise of the World Capitalist System: Concepts for Comparative Analysis." *Comparative Studies in Society and History* 16 (4): 387–415.

– 1979. *The Capitalist World-Economy*. Cambridge: Cambridge University Press.

– 2004. *World-Systems Analysis: An Introduction*. Durham, NC: Duke University Press.

Wasko, Janet. 1982. *Movies and Money: Financing the American Film Industry*. Norwood, NJ: ABLEX Publishing.

– 2003. *How Hollywood Works*. London: SAGE Publications.

Weber, Cynthia. 2006a. "An Aesthetics of Fear: The 7/7 London Bombings, the Sublime, and Werenotafraid.com." *Millennium: Journal of International Studies* 34 (3): 683–711.

– 2006b. *Imagining America at War: Morality, Politics and Film*. London: Routledge.

– 2010. *"I Am an American": Filming the Fear of Difference*. Chicago: University of Chicago Press.

Weldon, S. Laurel. 2006. "Inclusion and Understanding: A Collective Methodology for Feminist International Relations." In *Feminist Methodologies for International Relations*, edited by Brooke A. Ackerly, Maria Stern, and Jacqui True, 62–88. Cambridge: Cambridge University Press.

Wendt, Alexander. 1999. *Social Theory of International Politics*. Cambridge: Cambridge University Press.

Wheeler, Mark. 2006. *Hollywood Politics and Society*. London: BFI Publishing.

Women and Hollywood. 2017. "Statistics." *Women and Hollywood*. Accessed March 2018. https://womenandhollywood.com/resources/statistics/.

Women in Film and Television UK. 2017. "BFI Filmography Reveals Full Extent of Industry's Gender Imbalance over the Past Century." *Women in Film and Television* UK, 22 September 2017. Accessed March 2018. https://wftv.org.uk/resources/bfi-filmography-reveals-full-extent-industrys-gender-imbalance-past-century/.

World Bank, The. 2004. *Integrating Gender Issues into* HIV/AIDS *Programs: An Operational Guide.* Washington, DC: The World Bank.

– 2015. "Does Microfinance Still Hold Promise for Reaching the Poor?" *The World Bank,* 30 March 2015. Accessed March 2017. http://www.worldbank.org/en/news/feature/2015/03/30/does-microfinance-still-hold-promise-for-reaching-the-poor.

Youde, Jeremy. 2012. *Global Health Governance.* Cambridge: Polity Press.

Young, Colin. 2003. "Observational Cinema." In *Principles of Visual Anthropology,* 3rd ed., edited by Paul Hockings, 99–113. Berlin: Mouton de Gruyter.

Young, Crawford. 2012. *The Postcolonial State in Africa: Fifty Years of Independence, 1960–2010.* London: University of Wisconsin Press.

Index